MRS MILBURN'S
Diaries

AN ENGLISHWOMAN'S
DAY-TO-DAY REFLECTIONS
1939-1945

Edited by
PETER DONNELLY

An *Abacus* Book

First published in Great Britain by
George G Harrap & Co Ltd 1979
This edition published by Abacus 1995

A CIP catalogue record for this book
is available from the British Library.

ISBN 0 349 10623 1

Printed and bound in Great Britain by Clays Ltd, St Ives plc

Abacus
A Division of
Little, Brown and Company (UK)
Brettenham House
Lancaster Place
London WC2E 7EN

After Mrs Milburn's death in the spring of 1961, her Diaries, contained in fifteen exercise books and running to over half-a-million words, were stored away in an attic. There they remained, virtually undisturbed, until Christopher Morgan, now married to Mrs Milburn's granddaughter, re-discovered them one weekend in 1978. He became engrossed and approached Peter Donnelly, a journalist friend, for a second opinion. The second opinion was more than favourable, strengthening the belief that the Diaries should reach a wider audience.

Peter Donnelly, who has selected and edited the Diaries for publication, was born in Gateshead, County Durham in 1941. He began his career in journalism as a reporter on the local *Evening Chronicle*. From reporting he changed to sub-editorial work for both the *Daily Herald* and the *Daily Sketch*. Later, as a senior sub-editor for the *Daily Mail*, he had responsibility for the paper's Diary. Now he is a features writer on the *Daily Mirror*.

WHEN

How good 'twill be in days to come when peace is here again
To live in simple comfort free from worry, stress and strain,
When breakfast is a cheery meal with coffee rich and rare,
And cream a-floating on the top and lashings still to spare,
From *Times* or *Telegraph* we're roused, 'Please pass the marmalade',
To hand a jar of jellied gold – real, genuine homemade!
When 'butter' bends before it breaks in winter's icy grip,
When one may see without surprise the orange and its pip,
When blackout curtains disappear and all may show a light,
When shop assistants may be wrong – the customer be right,
When milkmen pour our milk in quarts, the butcher brings the joints,
And no one thinks of ration books, of coupons or of points.
When work has its allotted hours and there is time to play,
And no one needs to listen to the news but once a day;
When sugar's sweet and plentiful, and cakes are not a fluke,
When eggs are seldom mentioned, and Lord Woolton is a duke.
But oh, with hope and patience we are waiting for a day
When the tank is full of petrol and the dust sheet stowed away,
The engine's running smoothly and the M.G. free to roam,
When Oflag's gates have opened wide and Alan John is home.

CLARA MILBURN

CONTENTS

ILLUSTRATIONS

INTRODUCTIONS

By Peter Donnelly

IN the early uncertain days of 1940 Clara Milburn took time off from her loved (and sometimes loathed) garden and sat at her desk to begin a task she'd thought of starting for some time now. Opening a cheap soft-backed exercise book, she wrote 'Burleigh in Wartime' on the first thin blue line, underscored it, and set to work on a project without any forseeable end.

By the time she had finished, more than five years, many thousands of words and 15 exercise books later, she had written a vivid and very personal day-by-day account of how Britain, and her small part of the English countryside in particular, had faced the terrors and tragedies, the hardships and heartbreaks, of that time with hope and, often, humour.

Of course many millions of women throughout the world had shared that experience of war, and in many ways Clara Milburn was not very different from them. But she was of that breed of woman who have always to be busy, engaged, occupied. She had the good reporter's tidy and inquiring mind and a perceptive eye, which she used at the end of each day when she wrote of her doings and dealings, her meetings and conversations, and added her own very firm and forceful views on a world which, to her and countless others, seemed sadly to have taken leave of its sanity and its values.

She wrote mostly of the things that concerned her, and other women, in those fearful days: her constant worries and deep concern for a soldier son, the problems of food and rationing and—when a 1939 two-shilling piece, the current 10p, would buy 10 cigarettes, a ½lb bar of chocolate, a cinema ticket and a morning newspaper—the terrible, ever-rising price of what little there was in the shops. Being a woman, she also wrote of her clothes and her garden. Being an Englishwoman, she wrote a good

9

deal about the weather. Hers was not, and was never intended to be, a blow-by-blow and battle-by-battle account of the war—the generals, politicians and pundits could, and eventually would, take care of that. But she recorded, in neat and legible longhand, the progress of the war as it happened and as the people were told of it in their newspapers and on radio broadcasts. If her war reporting, or re-reporting, was at times not quite accurate or well-informed, there was good reason. The B.B.C. (as she records in her entry for 26th January 1945) could be 'a little previous in its statements sometimes'.

Alongside her daily Diary reports, Mrs Milburn glued treasured letters and telegrams and maps, news-items and pictures clipped from newspapers. Even as she wrote them, the Diaries became a fascinating work of reference for herself, her family and her friends as they looked back on the early events of a war through which they were living.

Years later they again became an invaluable guide for members of her family doing history homework and, towards the end of 1978 they were being studied once more when family friend Christopher Morgan, now married to Mrs Milburn's grand-daughter, read through one volume and very quickly became engrossed. His contagious enthusiasm led to Mrs Milburn's Diaries first being published in 1979—40 years after she began writing them—and happily reaching a far wider audience than she ever imagined.

You can be sure she would be thrilled by the critical acclaim which greeted that first publication: Arthur Marshall devoted a page of the *New Statesman* to singing her praises (and later told me how he'd been absorbed by her work); and that publishing doyen, the late Eric Hiscock, wrote in the *Bookseller*: 'Never has civilian life in wartime been chron-icled so effectively and so movingly before. I admit I wept many times before I reached the end. *Mrs Milburn's Diaries* is a classic of understate-ment, a restrained record of a household embroiled in a war it never made nor wanted. It should not be missed.'

High praise from such a critic, but Clara Milburn, you suspect, would be equally delighted by a letter from one of her 'ordinary' readers, Mrs Haill of Edgbaston, Birmingham, who wrote to me: 'If I were to be shipwrecked on a desert island, one book I would like with me would be *Mrs Milburn's Diaries*.' It is a sentiment which will now be under-stood and shared by many more as, to mark the 50th anniversary of the end of the Second World War, the Diaries are published again.

Mrs Milburn's 15 volumes have had to be edited to a manageable book length, but in doing so we have tried to keep them much as they were written. We have also taken the author's excellent advice on troublesome footnotes and done away with them completely. As she felt so strongly on the subject, as on other matters, this[1] is the only such irritant to mar these pages.

There are, however, certain introductions to be made:

Mrs Milburn herself was born Clara Emily Bagnall in Coventry on 24th June 1883, and lived there with her parents until her marriage to John Milburn, who worked with her brother Frank at Alfred Herbert Ltd, in Coventry

'Jack' Milburn, born in 1876 and a former pupil of Manchester Grammar School, had already seen the world by then. As a teenager he'd left England to find work in America, but by 1897 was thinking of home again and applying to Herberts for a job as a junior draughtsman. 'I am 21 years of age and of steady habits', he wrote. 'The salary I should like is £80 per annum, but this would depend upon location.' The location was firmly fixed when, in June 1905, he married Clara Bagnall and they set up their first home in Warwick Avenue, Coventry.

Caroline Kate Taylor, the redoubtable, unflagging Kate of the Diaries, joined them there three years later as their maid, and although it was not then remarkable for such a couple to have a servant, to have one as loyal and likeable as Kate must have seemed like something approaching a Godsend. With a break of only a few months in 1918, when she went to work in a canteen, the faithful Kate was with the Milburns for 47 years, and became a close and very valued friend.

Alan John Milburn was born at Warwick Avenue on 18th May 1914, but was soon at a new home—Canley Corner, the big detached house the Milburns had decided to have built by the main road between Coventry and Kenilworth. It was started the year their son was born and, despite a builders' strike, they were able to move in to it in September 1914. But the joy of a new home and a new baby were overshadowed by war and, writing in 1916, Mrs Milburn recorded: 'The foremost thing in my mind just now is the startling fact that German Zeppelins came inland and paid a most unwelcome visit. Alan was brought out of his warm cot into the cellar. . . .'

[1] See Mrs Milburn's entry for 4th November 1944.

Alan spent his childhood at Canley Corner (often referred to as just 'KK') looked after by adoring parents and a nanny, and looking after a succession of pet dogs called Tim, Tartar, Teddy, Turk and Tony. Twink of these Diaries was the last of the line. After school, Alan took a four-year engineering course at Birmingham University and, as his mother half-expected, did not do particularly well. He was far too interested in the university's motor club, she said, and spent all his time 'tearing off on trials'. So, with a good haul of trial trophies but few academic honours, he followed his father to Alfred Herbert with a job as a draughtsman.

By this time the family had moved again. Finding Canley Corner too big, they sold it in 1931 and moved to Burleigh, a spacious detached house some six miles from Coventry and three from the attractive village of Berkswell, where Mrs Milburn would spend much of her time. The ample garden of Burleigh— often her joy, sometimes her despair—took a great deal of time, and Jack, who'd retired early as he'd long intended, always found something to do in or around it. They were good times with good friends: Colin Bagnall, Mrs Milburn's nephew, who lost a leg in the London Blitz and his wife Peggy, who was killed in the same raid; Betty Law, and Joyce Healey from Hampshire; Florence—a second cousin of Jack's who was an Army nurse and later a hospital matron—and the Harry Spencers, whose nephew was John 'Cat's-eyes' Cunningham, who became a famous night-fighter pilot in the War that lay so close ahead. So close that Alan, who was a Territorial, would be called up. That is when Clara Milburn sat down to begin her Diaries.

South Harting, West Sussex, April, 1995.

VOLUME I

August 1939 – March 1940

AFTER five months of war, I feel I must write down what it has meant to us here at Burleigh—and although I write these first pages in February 1940, I want to start in the last week of August, when the grim shadow of war hanging over us and ready to engulf us all was as evil as the outbreak of war at the beginning of September.

Alan came home from Territorial Camp at Arundel in Sussex that week and told us the authorities were minded to keep the men in camp all ready 'in case of emergency' (how often we had heard that phrase by then!) but in the end decided to let them return home.

For a week we lived in a sort of evil dream and Alan, going to an outing of any kind, would say 'This might be the last for a bit', and we would shrug our shoulders and smile the kind of smile that feels a menace in the air and say 'Well, we hope not' or 'One never knows'.

During that time we also began to wonder why we lived at Balsall Common, and though war was expected almost any day, we felt we should like to make a change. So we went over to Leamington, put the matter before Locke and England's, the house agents, and got the key to a perfect little house at Barford. We spent two happy hours looking over it, decided to rent it if we were found acceptable tenants, planned the furniture positions, saw the owner and went home in an ecstacy of bliss—at least I did.

But on arrival home I found that the evacuation officer had been ringing me up. Evacuation was to take place soon—probably next day! This was grim news indeed, and the house dream began to fade. I sent a telegram to Mrs Gorton, the evacuation warden who had left me in charge, and asked her to come home.

Then one got busy and soon a meeting of all the billeting

officers, who had earlier in the year made a survey of the district, was arranged at Burleigh. It was during that meeting that I made a telephone call and was told: 'I suppose you know that hostilities have begun in Poland?' This news was conveyed to the people sitting around the table and our spirits sank.

However we were all ready to get on with our job and go round the billets again to see if all were still able and willing to take adults, women and children as previously arranged. All that day and evening the telephone rang incessantly, with questions to be asked and answered. Many people who months before were willing to take evacuees now found, through illness or death or one cause or another, that they could no longer give board and lodging. All these things had to be noted and the word passed on. Next morning, fortunately, Mrs Gorton came and took over the leadership again.

That same evening the telephone rang with 'a telegram for Second Lieutenant A. J. Milburn, Burleigh, Balsall Common: Please report at Drill Hall immediately'. The calling-up had come. I went upstairs and told Alan, who said: 'Ah well, I'd better get into uniform and go to Coventry'. He did so, but later came home to sleep and went off early next morning to be billeted in St John's Hall in Coventry.

The next day, Saturday, was full, with going round to billets early in the morning and then driving into Coventry, meeting Alan at the solicitors for him to make his will, and doing a little hasty shopping with the thought of two evacuee teachers being billeted upon us next day. Jack was busy all day making the dining-room gas-proof, and he did it in his usual thorough and effective manner. The blackout was already done—we'd gone to Leamington the week before to buy the blackout curtain material, and when they said 'How much do you want? There are 26 yards in this roll', I said I'd take the roll. But two large bay windows and two smaller windows in the living and dining-room ate a huge piece of the black Italian cloth, and by the time all the windows in little Burleigh had been draped, curtains made and re-made till I was nearly weeping with sewing black seams, undoing and re-stitching, the roll was entirely finished and a few more yards were needed. Then came a careful shading of lights, for the broadcast message was insistent as to the extent of the blackout required.

Sunday 3rd September

It was bright and sunny and a really hot day by 10 a.m., when all billeting wardens were to be in their appointed places in the school playground to receive the teachers and children arriving from Coventry by bus. Before that time one room in Burleigh had to be entirely re-arranged—Alan's room had to be put ready for the two teachers we had promised to accommodate.

A second bed was set up, drawers emptied, and Alan's own intimate things stuffed hurriedly away for two strange women to take possession. It was too much! Out went his desk into the spare room, his numberless ties taken out of their special drawer, the wardrobe cleared, tankards won in many motor trials parked away for the duration, photographs removed, and at last the room was ready. It was not Alan's room now, and I brimmed over—and felt relieved.

But there was no time for moaning. There was work to be done and I got off to the school. The sun worked wonders, and with an effort the tears were forced back and the business in hand took all one's attention. At last the buses came and queue after queue of clean and tidy children filed into the playground accompanied by many teachers.

We allotted children to foster-parents as we consulted our survey books, took their names and went with them into a schoolroom where they were given a card to be handed to their foster-parent, who later signed it as having received them. 'Please Miss'(!) one voice said. 'Sydney wants to be with his sister—he's only seven and she looks after him and puts him to bed'. What was to be done? Nobody in small cottage homes could put up a boy *and* a girl. But at last one of the billeting wardens said she would take Sydney—two boys instead of one—and Gwen, his sister, could be next door, where another billeting warden wanted 'a nice clean little girl to be with mine—and I *must* take one home today or my little girl will be *so* disappointed'.

In the meantime my eyes were open for teachers, and suddenly lighted on two *men* making towards me across the asphalt. Of course, men! That would be better in our household than two women. Kate and I are used to men, and they would be company for Jack. Full of the idea, I stopped work, dashed over to the officer for my district and said: 'I'd like to have these two men instead of two women teachers'.

So soon it was all fixed up. For the umpteenth time one wiped a heated brow. The children were all dispersed, everybody was getting ready to go home and I was able to start up the car, packing Mr Davis and Mr Bealt, our new 'lodgers', in the back with their rations for 48 hours—two tins of Ideal milk, two tins of Nestles, two tins of Fray Bentos corned beef, Woolworth's sweet biscuits and two cakes of chocolate!

Back at Burleigh, Jack and Kate were very surprised to see two male teachers, but we soon sat down to good old Sunday roast beef and Yorkshire pudding and an extra good apple tart—that most excellent meal belittled and reviled in every modern novel but which, when the quality is tip-top, cannot be beaten by little dishes with French names handed round by the most efficient parlour-maid.

The afternoon was glorious, and the garden delightful. Our new guests made themselves scarce for a few hours and I was able to get a little rest after a strenuous morning. Alan came home at suppertime to stay the night, which was a very pleasant surprise just as we had begun the meal. Mr Davis and Mr Bealt immediately took over the washing-up, and were always very wishful to help in any way.

That morning, at 11 a.m., the ultimatum to the Germans expired, and England was once again at war with 'the bad neighbour' of Europe.

Monday 4th September

Saw Kate and me up very early, as Alan had to be at the Drill Hall by 7.30 or 8 a.m. and, after the daily jobs, evacuation work had to be attended to again at the school. Mothers and children and other adults arrived by bus—not as many as we had expected, but enough to keep us very busy during the morning. Few people could accommodate them, but one whom I knew practically gave up the whole of her little house to two mothers and three children—one a babe in arms—only to have them 'flit' a week later while she had gone to church. They left a note behind them, but no payment for light, coal, etc., etc. Quite unsuitable people for the country, but I suppose that after a week without the expected air raids they felt the proper place for them was with their husbands. A problem indeed, the evacuation matter!

The builder came along and quickly made a dugout in the orchard.

Thursday 7th September

The day Alan arrived and told us he was going next day to Hythe, where he was to take a course at the Small Arms School, after which he 'would proceed to the concentration area', later found to be Swindon. I felt he was really leaving us then, and had to drop a tear when I waved him off next morning in his little green M.G. But at 10 a.m. came anti-climax when I heard his voice in the hall and found he had come for a few extra clothes, as the course was to cover a month instead of a fortnight.

Sleep was rather fitful that first week, as one expected German air raids. One night our guests came in rather late, and as we had not provided them with a latchkey, Jack went down to let them in and they said they thought they had heard the wail of the air raid warning. But when Jack listened with them, the sound proved to be the greyhounds at the kennels in Needler's End Lane!

During the week we were called up by the air raid warden, who found our blackout insufficient, and still more curtains had to be made. By now the price of the material had gone up from 2s. 6d. to 3s. 11d. a yard, and the quality was decidedly inferior. But a very definite blackout was obtained at the bay windows by covering the whole bay, from the top of the pelmet to a foot from the floor, with a great black pall reminiscent of a first-class French funeral! These had to be hung every evening at blackout time and not removed before a specified time in the morning. The lack of ventilation was stifling in hot weather, but it is wonderful how one can conform to an order when it is absolutely necessary to do so.

After a Month

It was found that many children had returned to Coventry, and Mr Bealt's work was not wanted in Balsall Common, and we were left with only Mr Davis as our guest. In another three weeks Mr Davis also left for the same reason, and we were alone once more.

The paralysing effect of the first few weeks of war began to wear off. Trains were more frequent and everything flowed more easily. Until then, everything seemed to be held up—trains were used for war traffic and the main road was crowded with convoy after convoy of trucks, vans, aeroplane carriers, ambulances and, from time to time, lorries full of troops. The convoys have continued ever since, and at night one hears the rumble and squeal of brakes as they slow up for the island at the end of this road.

Thursday 14th December

News came of the battle of the River Plate, and great was our thrill at the thought of such a gallant action on the part of the *Exeter*, *Ajax* and *Achilles*. The excitement grew with the news of the *Graf Spee*'s withdrawal from the fight and her retirement, badly battered, into Montevideo harbour. Then, after four days of expectancy, came the inglorious end when she was scuttled in the mouth of the River Plate—one of many German ships scuttled to prevent capture.

The Commander of the *Graf Spee* was evidently out of sympathy with Hitler's order to scuttle the pocket battleship and on 20th December shot himself in his room at Buenos Aires.

About this time a Russian attack was made on Finland, and a 'puppet' Government—which no-one acknowledges—was set up soon after fighting began. The Finns are wonderful, and in spite of continuous air raids, manage to hold out against fearful odds.

And so the days went by, with always the news of the marvellous doings of the Finns, and dreadful air raids by the Russians over Finland.

By Christmas

The expected air raids had not occurred. Threats from Hitler about a 'secret weapon' put the wind up a few people and the word 'jitters' came into vogue. But the great bulk of the people refused to be 'jittery' and got to work: air raid precaution exercises took definite shape, knitting got well under way, Red Cross sewing meetings flourished, plots of new land were turned over, and people prepared for the coming year. During this period we found ourselves getting a lot of pleasure from our fortnightly trip to Fillongley to take the laundry. With petrol so scarce, the laundry could no longer send to collect, and as the day of our journey came round we found we were greatly looking forward to the little trip into the country. Petrol had to be carefully saved for this run, and we often took an invalid, Mrs Pearson, along with us to give her a run.

Shortly before Christmas we drove to Warwick and Leamington, where I had the pleasure of being a proud mamma, with my soldier son walking through the Stores and going to the different counters with me. Christmas shopping was in full swing and we meant to have a good one this year, and so I bought the last little luxuries and presents.

Friday 29th December

This was the day of Alan's return to Swindon after our quiet, happy, Christmas together. Because there was a prospect of another day's leave before he went overseas, he decided to go by car instead of train, and was tremendously thrilled at the idea of taking the beloved M.G. once more. So about 8 p.m. he went out with all his belongings and, with a hasty kiss for me and a 'Goodbye' to Jack, off down the drive. I walked after the car and then watched the red tail light out of sight round the island on the main road. I came in thoughtfully, closed the gates, and wondered as I walked up the snow-covered path how long it would be before he came home again. Leave was not to be under six months, and I had no belief in another day's leave before the battalion left for 'overseas'. Next evening, Alan rang up to say he and his platoon were going off during the next week, but we spoke together on the telephone during the next few evenings.

Friday 5th January

The last time we'd hear Alan's voice for who knew how long. That day we went to see *The Corn Is Green*, which we did not care for, and when the theatre orchestra played 'Wish Me Luck As You Wave Me Goodbye', I found myself saying out loud: 'Oh no, not that' and wishing I could bury my head somewhere and weep. However such feelings had to be severely repressed, and we soon drove home to wait for the call from Alan. By 7.30 p.m. there was no word from him, so I rang up Swindon and was told by the orderly that 'Mr Milburn is out'. I wondered whether he had already gone, but I gave my name and a message asking him to ring.

All the evening went by and our spirits drooped lower and lower, till at last bedtime came and we went sadly upstairs. Then at 10.45 p.m. the telephone rang and, as I arrived breathless, a voice said: 'This is Alan'. He told us he was going early the next morning, and after the first six 'pips' we had a second call. Then I said: 'Well here's your father' and stood by wishing I could hear what he was saying, till Jack said: 'Well, goodbye old man—good luck!' And so I never really said my farewell, as he had rung off.

We toasted his health a few days later at a little sherry party which had its amusing side. We had invited our friends James and Edie to a chat and sherry at 11.30 a.m., because the blackout makes afternoons difficult. We all drank 'to Alan' . . . and then 'Oh my goodness! Cough! Splutter! Good heavens! We're drinking neat whisky!' And so we were—it was the wrong decanter! All I can say is that, after a sip of whisky, followed by a glass of sherry, I felt very warm and quite *pleasant*.

Saturday 27th January

We had The Great Snow—a thick fall which continued for about 24 hours with scarcely any intervals. The cold was intense, as it had been since about 14th January or even earlier, and we had hard work to keep the house reasonably warm.

The snow was piled high in places, in curious cornices and drifts in the lanes, and until the end of the week it was too deep to walk anywhere but in the middle of the road, where milk vans and the doctor's car had ploughed a little track. By the end of the week our car had been got out and I thought I would take it to visit two sick people, but the going was so bad—skidding and sliding along the tracks and with the number-plate catching in the snow between the ruts—that I felt unsafe and turned back home.

Walking was very difficult, too, but Twink and I managed to get out and found P.C. Thornborough and five men endeavouring to get a car out of deep snow in a gutter where it had skidded and stuck. They stopped a few moments to give a good push to the milk van, and sent it gaily along the slope, steering a zigzag course as its wheels slipped and stuck, but eventually getting hold and driving away.

That day—5th February—was the most difficult for walking, with soft, slushy snow on top and frozen snow below. Next day the slush was much worse and the thaw well on. But I packed two cakes and other things to send to Alan and drove to the village and got them posted. At bedtime, alas, I got an attack of gastric trouble, followed by a night of pain and restlessness.

Tuesday 6th February

The day I distinguished myself by fainting for the first time in my life, to the dismay of Jack and Kate. And very surprised I was to find myself sitting on the bathroom floor with Jack supporting me and Kate stroking my face. That meant the doctor, who prescribed sips of water and a little very weak tea. Next day, after a back-aching night, the lordly menu of a few water biscuits was allowed. And so, dozing and waking, the day went on till evening, when I read a good thriller and listened to the wireless. No longer, said the news, were children to run wild, but education would be compulsory. The Government was to take over the railways. The wonderful Finns were still holding their own in spite of violent battles on the front, where the Russians were doing their utmost to break the Mannerheim Line. The atrocities in Poland continued, with heartrending stories of German cruelty and wickedness.

Thursday 8th February

I have now caught up and can write my Diary on the proper day. At 2.30 p.m., as I write, the lordly diet continues. Three water biscuits and a cup of tea—that is nine water biscuits, four cups of tea and sips of water since Monday night! Five pounds down in weight. Good! Along the road I hear a pleasing sound—the clip-clop of horses' feet. After the dull quiet of the snow-stricken days it is good to feel that traffic is becoming rapidly normal again.

The butcher failed to arrive and we thanked our lucky stars for a piece of cold ham in the larder. Then a small boy appeared, bringing a small joint along. Such *little* joints, too, these days, conforming to the imposed rationing in a few weeks' time. It is a good thing to get down to hard facts, though, and make everyone come under the same rule and help to win the war.

Friday 9th February

Spent the day in bed, but a letter from Alan cheered things up, though he reported a few days in bed, too, with a temperature. In the morning we sent a telegram asking Florence if she could come back for a time and the reply soon came that she would. Then at 8.30 there was a great commotion in the hall and Kate, peering through the door into the black outside, was asked if she could 'Give a poor soul a lodging for the night'. Florence had arrived. Hurrah! Twink was so pleased he leapt and barked and brought offerings of ball and bone and continually bounded on to my bed and off again when he heard her voice. Wartime journeys are not easy and I think travelling had been very trying. Coming from Stoke-on-Trent had taken Florence four or five hours, with the blackout at the end of it.

Saturday 10th February

A frosty, clear sunny morning! And a lazy person is enjoying the luxurious care of one who knows how to look after the sick. Reading, writing, wireless, a real lunch of chicken, bread and butter and then a snuggle down to listen to Sir Kingsley Wood speaking for an hour. Unlike Nazi (and the speaker pronounced it as spelt, like Winston Churchill) speeches and propaganda, it was wholly truth, pleasant and unpleasant, palatable and unpalatable, and so worthy of a good hearing. At the very end an interruptor cried (I think) 'We want peace', but was quickly silenced. So do we, but we shall not get it by declaiming during public speeches. We have a wicked enemy to encounter and there is only one way of dealing with so ruthless a foe, and that is to fight him until he is beaten.

Monday 12th February

A very cold day and flakes of snow float around from time to time. We do not want another fall yet, as the remains of the last great fall are still much in evidence.

Canada, as well as the whole Empire, is mourning Lord

Tweedsmuir, its Governor-General, and the world in general has lost a brilliant author who wrote under the name of John Buchan.

In memory I see myself leaning against a haycock on a rough lawn one August afternoon some twenty of more years ago with the hot sun tempered by a delicate breeze. I was lost to everything but the story of *The Thirty-nine Steps*, that first thriller written by John Buchan when recovering from an illness, and written, he said, as 'a shilling shocker'. After that one always asked for the new John Buchans as they came out, eager to read anything written by his clever pen. Even now I remember glancing up from the haycock wondering whether it would *really* be possible for an aeroplane to seek out a fugitive who in desperation had taken to the heather, so that the hunted one felt there was no possible escape from the all-seeing eye overhead.

Tuesday 13th February

Last night I read John Bearder's book of his 17 days' tour in a Morris Minor with his two friends, and was thoroughly entertained by his diary of the trip through Belgium, Luxembourg, Germany, Austria, Italy, etc., all for the cost of under £14 per head. This was in 1936 and he writes of the anxiety of the Germans to give pleasure to the Englishmen everywhere they went. Alas that they should choose the wrong leader, and the worst elements in the German make-up should now be on top.

Downstairs for two hours today and no undue fatigue.

Friday 16th February

Up today at 11.30 and it was cold but not freezing. Florence and Jack went out to deliver packets of seeds—my duty as Secretary of the Women's Institute—all round this district. Every kind of small house and cottage had to be visited and the wonderfully comprehensive packet of Sutton's seeds delivered. They are only 2s. 6d.—a special price—though containing every ordinary vegetable seed, perfectly packed and labelled.

The news of the Finns is not good. They are worn out with this giant remorseless power of Russia against them. Who can help them? The Swedes have decided not to help by sending soldiers to fight, though volunteers are already there. It is so difficult to get to them, though we have sent aeroplanes, medical supplies, ambulances, clothes and money, and still they cry in their agony: 'If help does not come soon. . . .'

Saturday 17th February

A letter from Alan came with the morning tea. He is well again, but has had the final burst with 'Madame' where they are billeted, and so they hope to take an empty house and begin again, with English cooking by their own batman. I wonder how this will work out.

Good news of the Navy today. A German ship, the *Altmark*, containing between 300 and 400 sailors from the ships sunk by the *Graf Spee* some time ago managed to get into Norwegian waters, protected by Norwegian gunboats. It was protested that she had been inspected at Bergen. Orders were sent from the Admiralty that she should be boarded and inspected by one of our destroyers, while three others were on hand in case of need. Some hand-to-hand fighting ensued in which one of our men and four Germans were killed. Though the German ship was grounded, we were able to get our men safely away. The end of the story was that time-bombs were on hand and our men were to be blown up if things went adversely for the *Altmark*. They were later landed at Leith amid great excitement. The enemy fumes and splutters, as might be expected. But what does Norway mean by this?

Sunday 18th February

The world has received the news of the *Altmark's* discomfiture with mixed feelings. But by the news tonight they are mostly giving the British version of the affair. God bless our Navy, I say—and the men who live up to the old traditions.

Germany is fuming and bellowing like a mad bull, and we are asking Norway what she means by not examining the *Altmark* in a proper manner at Bergen. To *examine* a ship without finding 300 or more men battened down in the holds is curious indeed.

Monday 19th February

Some rain today and a slow thaw. The 1 p.m. news was full of the reactions of the world to the *Altmark* affair, with Germany calling it piratical and Norway furious too. Our position was lucidly and fully explained in *The Times* editorial, and we are full of rejoicing that the release of the prisoners of war from such a fate was requested by the Admiralty and so ably carried out by Captain Vian and H.M.S. *Cossack*.

Wednesday 21st February

Today has been comparatively warm and, though women are still going about in fur coats and the sloppy footgear known as 'Glastonbury's', neither were really necessary. The roads are mostly clear, but here and there are humps of frozen snow, gradually disappearing but still dangerous to come across unexpectedly.

Though the Russians have made 'dents' in the Mannerheim Line, the Finns still resist their onslaughts and wipe out whole divisions of the enemy. Tonight we hear there is a blizzard in Finland likely to last a fortnight. Mannerheim calls it 'Finland's ally'. Volunteers for Finland are on their way from England, Italy and Hungary, and supplies of arms have been sent from England and France, too. *Surely* there is great hope. The greatest hope comes from the continual intercession, which must also be rising to Heaven like a great flame.

Alan's letter today is very cheerful. The change of billet has been made and a house-warming sherry party held. So the biscuits sent in the last parcel were very welcome. He is now living quite comfortably with a bedroom next to the mess and is sleeping happily in a bed with sheets and other comforts! Tomorrow we must send another parcel—he seems greatly to appreciate them.

Thursday 22nd February

A warm day. Patches of snow linger still in the shady spots, and where it has been heaped up to make clearings, but I walked round the garden without a coat after lunch and the sun was really warm.

We went to Coventry this morning and I spent 20 minutes in the Food Controller's Office getting a permit for butter and sugar for the Women's Institute teas.

Later we heard a cheering talk on the wireless, being told that we have a good stock of petroleum products and a large quantity of whale oil, which is used for margarine, and was bought in April 1939 from under the very noses of the Germans. While they were haggling over the price, we paid it and secured two years' crops. Excellent.

Saturday 24th February

Not quite so warm today, but there have been glorious patches of sunshine from time to time, birds chirping and the grass looking rather less black and more green, and a general hopeful feeling of a stir in the earth.

In the morning Florence and I went out in the car, paid one or two small accounts and delivered packets of seeds here and there. We also called at the anti-aircraft detachment's quarters at Meer End and I went up a long ash path to the field beyond the road and found a whistling soldier and told him two men could come for hot baths each week. He thought they would like to come today.

At 3 p.m. we sat down to listen to the last of the Cabinet Saturday speeches by the Prime Minister at Birmingham Town Hall. He spoke very firmly and confidently and his speech had a vigorous, biting quality such as we have lately associated with Winston Churchill, but without his clever phrases. It was a trenchant speech, setting forth our deep feelings about the enemy, but not without hope of a future peace when a change of heart has set in and the bad neighbour becomes a friendly nation.

The two soldiers turned up about 3.45 p.m. and one was soon upstairs and splashing in the bath, coming down later with his fair hair standing on end. He asked to speak to me and soon began to thank us for 'saving his life'. Kate gave him tea while the other man whistled as he took his tub.

After they had gone, Florence and I cleaned up the bathroom and then had a quiet evening, with bed for me directly after supper. Alan's M.G. was delivered back here today.

Mrs Winser asked if we would like to run over and talk to Phil, who is at home from France taking the small arms course at Hythe as Alan has done. We now know where Alan is, but on the whole we did not learn a great deal, for really there is very little to ask: they just continue to train in much the same way as in England.

Tuesday 27th February
Still warmer, with all that heartening feeling of Spring. Lots of lambs are in the fields, new grass is springing up through the old drab tufts *and*—new hats are in the shops! All so lovely if there were no war!

Two Heinkels were brought down today off the east coast and there has been a review of Naval affairs given by Mr Churchill in the House, with news of the destruction of one or two U-boats. A heartening speech as usual, with lots of good news of ship-building to substantiate it. The Finns are retiring in one or two places, but still standing out marvellously against terrific Russian onslaughts, while the Russians are devastated in hundreds.

Thursday 29th February
We shall not write '29th February' for four more years! A great deal can happen in four years. One dare not speculate—only, God

be with us, for they may be very difficult.

Edward Ward spoke on the wireless tonight of the awful horrors of hordes of dead and frozen Russians where he had visited the Finnish battleground with one of its generals. The frightful losses the Russians get when the Finns retire was shown, too. And still fresh masses of them appear, division after division. If only one could deal with them and set them retreating!

I have been struck today by a picture of the King and Queen at Clydeside, just walking freely among the working men—the Queen all smiles and the men waving their cloth caps and cheering, and the King delighted to have her with him.

Friday 1st March

'Onlooker' (Norman Birkett, K.C.) gave his wireless talk tonight, answering some of the letters he had received from listeners. It was a reply, in effect, to the phrase we have heard so often: 'We have no quarrel with the German people.' He dwelt on the crime perpetrated on the 'Hitler Youth', compelled to join this body, having their adolescent minds moulded to the hard and brutal German Nazi pattern, disciplined, ruthless, owing no allegiance to their parents and families, only to the State of whom the head, the Leader, is Adolf Hitler. Hilter is their God. He reminded us that there must be millions who hate this regime, but who are coerced, or forced, to obey or be put into the horrors of a concentration camp. What a terrible thing it must be to have no freedom of mind or body!

Sunday 10th March

To church at 8.15, once more hearing the soft-toned bell bidding the worshippers. Alas that so lovely a service should be spoilt by one coughing man, and every service is the same. We all enjoy our simple services, except for that one blight. Friends at church inquire for Alan and send him their kind wishes. It is sweet how they remember him. And then home for the last unrationed meat dinner—and very good, too.

Wednesday 13th March

We are all sad today to think of Finland having to give in to a godless nation like the Russians. It is a real calamity! An armistice now waits on a cruel 'peace' treaty. For the moment one feels a real setback, for we learn that the Allies could have gone with 50,000 men and equipment if Finland had called for men, *and if Norway and Sweden had co-operated* against these brutal Russians.

Thursday 14th March

Kate, coming up with early tea, whispered in my ear: 'Snow—and it's still falling!' Amazed, I woke up and looked across at the bit of visible window and saw the trees laden with their white burden once more. 'Is there a letter?' I asked, meaning *the letter* from Alan. 'Postman hasn't been yet,' she said. But in two minutes a knock at the door and *the letter*. So we both woke up quickly and read it.

Our one thought today is of poor Finland. The whole world is sorry and some go so far as to blame us! Why one cannot think. It is very, very sad.

The butter ration is to be doubled next week.

Monday 18th March

Much milder today with some rain early and late, and half an inch of rain in the gauge this morning. Work in the house occupied the whole of the morning and Twink's walk was postponed till early afternoon. A fat parcel was then posted to Alan and we hope he will get it for Easter. The cake Mrs Deeley had made for him smelt so good I longed to taste it.

This evening I wrote to him a stiff sort of letter, not a bit what I wanted to write, but I put in an Easter card and hoped he would understand how I felt.

Hitler and Mussolini have met in the Brenner Pass. Poor dears, they have to travel in bullet-proof trains. A great contrast to our beloved King, who a few days ago suddenly took the place of a ticket-collector at 'a South Coast port', to the great surprise of a soldier on leave who found himself handing his ticket to His Majesty. He quickly drew himself to attention. But our King's life is safe with his people—there is love and not fear of him.

Friday 22nd March, Good Friday

No newspapers this morning, though we had a post, rather surprisingly. After breakfast the tank in the bathroom was found to be leaking and Mr Deeley came along to look at it. I think it looks like we will be having a new one after Easter.

Trawlers are being attacked and machine-gunned by German planes over the North Sea—they are ruthless and merciless. We sank a German ship in the Kattegat yesterday. It was carrying iron ore from Sweden and, having warned the captain and crew and given them time to get away, our submarine fired a torpedo and sank it.

Tuesday 26th March

A change in the wind today—north-east and decidedly cold. Real Easter weather! A W.I. Produce Meeting took me to Mrs Ford's at 10.45 a.m. to hear about sugar for jam and the arrangements to be made about getting it for W.I. members. We have to calculate the amount of fruit we are going to have in our gardens!

Later Florence and I went to Kenilworth to see Elizabeth and had tea with her. She is looking very fit for her 71 or 72 years and finds life and people very interesting. She was at variance (quite mildly) with her vicar for saying we must love Hitler—I don't wonder, though one knows what the vicar *really* means. We must hate, and do hate, the evil that is in Hitler and love what there is of good—if there is any! One remembers the Polish broadcast last Sunday and what Hitler is responsible for in that country and shudders.

VOLUME 2
March 1940 – June 1940

Thursday 28th March

Today has been fur-coat weather, with a strong cold wind. It was very unpleasant in Birmingham, where Florence and I spent the day. Jack took the car to the Rover Works to get the front wing put right after it had been damaged outside church last Sunday, and spent his day in Coventry, with lunch at the Draper's Club. Florence and I found Birmingham very dull and dirty. The shops look wretched, with strapping on the plate glass windows to save them from shattering should there be an air raid, and sandbags are piled in front of others right above the windows. Even the sparkle of the Ciro pearl shop was greatly diminished. It is generally a cheery shop window, but it seemed to have very few 'jewels' in it, and many of them were Regimental crest brooches. We walked to the Art Gallery, scarcely expecting to find it open, but the door yielded as we pushed it and we walked in to find the tapestries and large pictures on the staircase boarded up.

Saturday 30th March

It seemed chilly when we woke this morning, but soon the sun came out and the air was warm. By twelve o'clock we were doing our usual Saturday jaunt, Florence and I taking Twink to the shops, paying for the papers and then walking down Meetinghouse Lane. For the third or fourth time I called at a cottage, and this time said: 'I've come to collect the half-crown for the seeds.' No beating about the bush. The woman went and fetched the money and said she was sorry not to have let me have it before. So that is finished, and we got home.

A postscript to the news by Christopher Stone spoke of the German talks by 'Lord Haw Haw'. He seemed annoyed by them, and I think wondered whether some of the insidious poison of his broadcasts might penetrate the minds of a certain type of Englishman. Why sane people want to listen I can't think, but perhaps the ones who make a point of hearing 'Lord Haw Haw' are a bit queer!

Wednesday 3rd April

A showery day with more cloud than sunshine and a chilly spring wind. No walk in the fields today after so much rain in the night, so we went by Sunnyside Farm to Meetinghouse Lane. I noticed that the baker's on the corner has in the window rather fewer cakes than pre-war days, but still plenty of biscuits, sweets and tinned fruits, and Wednesday's pork pies as usual. Food supplies are excellent and we ought to be, and are, very thankful. Even with the meat ration of 1s. 10d. worth per person per week we do very well, for we can also buy fish, poultry and game, sausages and offal without coupons. Butter is also plentiful—the ration has been increased to ½ lb per head per week, and bacon is also ½ lb per head per week, which is as much as we require.

The 6 o'clock news reported that over 50 aeroplanes—one or two more today—have been brought down off our coast, but not one of our machines has been lost to the enemy in like circumstances. Goebbels has been haranguing the German youth, poor little wretches. They are to obey their leaders with blind devotion, and the State is to come before everything. Love of truth is at a discount in Germany. They must believe what they are told—mostly lies.

Friday 5th April

Florence left us today—we hope not for long—because she has things she must do at her rooms in London. So we set off with her 10 packages and her knitting-bag, and no room for anything else except us in the car. Then it was 'Goodbye Flossie' and at 5.15 Jack went off to meet Betty Law at the station. So now we have the spare room occupied again.

There is news tonight of an attempt to bomb a Norwegian passenger boat by German bombers which was frustrated by one of our destroyers.

Monday 8th April

What a day at this house! Bathroom cistern was being removed and replaced, so everybody had to be up bright and early. Then the sweep came to do the kitchen range at 2.30, so Kate was busy. At 3 p.m. visitors arrived—Tom and Doris Turner (Colonel and Mrs.

E. T. Turner!) and Peter—and Kate got tea for them and they stayed until 5 o'clock.

Betty and I were out of all this, as we left home at 10.30 a.m. to do the bi-weekly shopping, stayed on in Leamington to lunch, went to the pictures and saw Deanna Durbin in *First Love* at the Regal, had a vile Mondayish cafe tea and arrived home at 6 o'clock, having missed the worst of the upset and, sadly, the visitors.

British mine-laying in Norwegian territorial waters is a new effort on our part to tighten the blockade. A German troopship, apparently making for Norway, was torpedoed and sunk, and 150 of the 300 Germans were drowned. Much comment has been caused everywhere by our action in mining territorial waters— the next day or two may be very eventful.

Tuesday 9th April

A very eventful day! We heard on the news at 8 o'clock that Germany was reported to have invaded Denmark and Norway. Later this was confirmed. Like the other invasions, it was swiftly accomplished and is called 'protection', as the Russians called the invasion of Finland 'liberation'. Little resistance was met with in Denmark when the Germans crossed the frontier with tanks, etc., at 8 a.m.

In Norway they had prepared the way at some ports by sending marines disguised as merchant seamen with iron ore boats. Oslo is occupied, along with Bergen and Trondheim. The Germans say this invasion is because of our mines on Norway's coast, but that is nonsense, as it has all the signs of long and careful planning and began before we laid the mines.

And so a new phase of the war begins, and as I write a naval battle is in progress off the Norwegian coast in stormy weather. God be with us!

Wednesday 10th April

A still more eventful day, with a naval battle continuing off the Norwegian coast. Five of our ships—*Hunter, Hardy, Hostile, Hotspur* and *Havoc*—were in action. *Hunter* was sunk, *Hardy* went aground and *Hotspur* was damaged. The British sank six German merchant ships and blew up one loaded with ammunition. The cruisers *Blücher* and *Karlsruhe* were also sunk in this same battle, off Narvik. Norway is resisting the attack and is not disposed at present, as we at first feared, to make terms with Germany.

Denmark seems to be accepting the situation calmly. The

Germans arrived there without food, and soon began to requisition stores. King Christian calls upon the people to do nothing that will cause serious consequences for their country and to control themselves in the present situation.

Thursday 11th April

A blank day for me, laid low for a third time with a gastric 'do', supposed to be caused by tinned tongue. Poor old Kate is down with it, too, but as Jack and Betty are whole and sound one wonders about the cause.

Winston Churchill made a long speech in the Commons telling the story of the Navy's work since Monday, when the minefield was laid in Norwegian territorial waters. It was a vivid speech in Churchill's own direct, but unusual, language. 'This is the first crunch of the war,' he said. 'While I will not prophesy or boast about battles still to be fought, we feel ourselves ready to encounter the utmost malice of the enemy, and to devote all our life and strength to achieve victory for what is a world cause.'

Friday 12th April

Still in bed, and Kate too. Betty is doing all the housekeeping and nursing and Jack was up at seven to stoke the kitchen stove. We are lucky to have Betty here, and Mrs Poulton was able to come at 8 a.m. and do the housework.

Churchill's speech is well commented upon abroad and only the Italians express their dislike of us in their newspapers by belittling our Navy's work. I can do with the Italians as a nation, but now they are Mussolini-ed they have lost their courtesy and charm.

Saturday 13th April

A third day in bed for me and Kate. Mrs Poulton and Betty were busy all morning while Jack went off to Leamington to do the shopping and then to pick up Florence, coming at 1 p.m. from Paddington. Just after 1.30 they arrived here and we were all pleased to see Florence. She and Betty had not met since the latter was a little girl.

Our aeroplanes have bombed Stavanger aerodrome, where the enemy have gained a hold and where their machines were lined up. Two or three machines were destroyed and others damaged.

We waited from 10.15 p.m. till after 10.30, when the news came that seven German destroyers had been sunk in Narvik fiord. H.M.S. *Warspite*, the battleship, accompanied by our destroyers, had been in action with this splendid result. Three German destroyers a day or two ago, and now these—ten very recently. It is horrible to gloat, so one cannot do it, but everything that tends to shorten the war by crippling the enemy's fleet is good.

A letter came from Alan today, calling attention to the top right-hand corner, where these words were written:

> Lieut. A. J. Milburn,
> H.Q. C Coy,
> 1/7th Bn. Royal Warwickshire Regiment,
> B.E.F.

He said he had almost given up hope and evidently the extra cloth pips (which he took with him in readiness) had, too, for they had disappeared. However the Q.M. had others and so all was well.

Monday 15th April

A day of hailstorms and sunshine, with a cold wind. Primula is out with its mauve globular clusters, backed here and there by King Alfred daffodils, while golden forsythia bells hang above. Lovely spring colouring, so fresh and bright. Batchelor has set the W.I. 'Majestic' potatoes and cut laurels, with Jack keeping an eye on operations. Kate and I got up to lunch and managed to keep up with 'do a bit' and 'rest a bit' till after supper. Betty left us at 4 p.m. and then, after tea, the doctor came and 'crossed us off'.

British forces have landed in Norway at several points. Germans are pretty harrassing round Oslo, and King Haakon, the Crown Prince and the Government are fleeing from place to place, with the enemy bombing wherever they are thought to be. The Fleet Air Arm is busy bombing Stavanger with good results, sinking ships and setting a flying boat ablaze. Our air losses are comparatively few, we are very thankful to say.

Thursday 18th April

This morning Florence and I went to Leamington, myself feeling lots better, and did the necessary shopping before 1.15 p.m. We had lunch at the Stores and afterwards went to ask the Great Western Station about trains to Milford-on-Sea for my proposed journey on Friday week.

The prices of things generally are going up—a shilling more a yard on silk which I bought today. And three of Christy's linen towels, formerly 3s. and later 4s., are now 6s. 11d. each! They had only six, but I stopped at three. Also I bought a few more tinned goods, and tomorrow must look through my stock in the larder.

Saturday 20th April

Breakfast was excellent today—more especially as a letter arrived from Alan. It had been written as usual on Sunday, but this time it was censored and had on it 'Examined by Base Censor'. I thought he was very base to be so long about it!

The W.I. notice board was in place today in front of Mrs Turney's shop. It looked bright and neat, but the lettering is yellow instead of the white lettering ordered, for which I am sorry. White on apple green would have been excellent, and yellow just gives it a common look. However I put in the notices and locked it up, and decided it was too high and must be lowered to be right.

Much the same war news today.

Tuesday 23rd April

St George's Day and the men of England—the St Georges—are still at their old work of slaying the dragon, which is a particularly evil one.

Florence left this morning and later rang up and reported a good journey and very kindly gave me times of trains for my proposed journey to see Joyce in Milford-on-Sea on Friday. Nothing is too much trouble for her.

Our airmen continue bombing Stavanger, Oslo and Alborg in Denmark. Germany continues to bully Sweden and Switzerland, and any nation who opposes her in the slightest degree. She 'will not tolerate', her 'patience is exhausted', etc. All the old cries or lies—or both, I think.

Friday 26th April

This morning up betimes and then, after brekker, finished packing and got off to Leamington by 11.30, where Jack saw me off. A kind lady helped me to wind a hank of wool, but my hands were so tired I did no more. At Reading I had to change, and again at Basingstoke. Here was a very long train and at the last moment many troops, bag and baggage, got in. At last we came near to New Milton, and the guard came to inquire who was alighting there. I popped up and said 'Me, sir', or words to that effect.

He explained that the train was so long it would not reach the platform, so when we arrived I peered out of the window to find a steep drop to the line below. It was not possible to negotiate it so, gathering up my awkward packages, I bumped along the corridor towards the middle of the train. It then began to move and drew out of the station and went on to Christchurch! So I had to get out there and return by the next train, to find Joyce had gone, with her car.

Taking a taxi, I came along to Milford, and it was very nice to be at Redscar again.

The war news is of Norway—the Germans are very busy thrusting and pushing out from Oslo. We are quiet about our movements there and, anyway, one must allow time for an army to establish itself on strange territory. It is a great feat to get men, ammunition and supplies safely over the North Sea.

Monday 29th April

A soft, grey day and warm, with the nightingale singing at the corner of the garden. We saw him sitting on the topmost branch of the crab tree as we came back from shopping in the village this morning. We took with us little curly-headed David, an evacuee baby, whose voice is heard in this house—which is strange indeed to me. Then, after lunch, came one of those unforgettable times, those times we store in our memory as Wordsworth stored his picture of the jocund company of daffodils 'fluttering and dancing in the breeze'.

Joyce took the nice little wife of the doctor, and me, to a primrose wood not far away. With baskets and our tea, we set off in the car. Wellingtons on our feet ready for the boggy, sloshy patches we were to come across. The car was parked at the edge of the wood and off we went, first along a path, coming out into a clearing, next through brown, oily mud splashes, under branches, over brambles, with tufts of primroses here and there. But the best was yet to be, and soon we came to masses of huge primroses, and, setting down our baskets, began to pick. Chatting and picking, we tied up bunches from time to time with wool brought by Joyce.

The plovers were calling in a field close by, a chaffinch singing the old song, and the chiffchaff repeating his monotonous call. Tea was very welcome, and we sat and enjoyed every sip and every crumb. Then we picked more pale primroses, bunch after bunch. And then home to pack up the bunches for less fortunate people, and Joyce took them on her bicycle to the post.

Monday 6th May

Goodbye to Joyce and Redscar! She drove me to New Milton at 11.30 a.m. and I went off in good company with one Army and one Air Force man. They were deep in conversation about driving cars, lorries, etc., and then ended with dogs. When Air Force blue got out, battledress and I had a chat, so that when Basingstoke was reached he handed out my baggage. I wished him luck and a good leave, and he gave me good wishes and a friendly wave.

The next stage to Reading was in a full compartment, with a wailing child next to me eating a biscuit between wails. Then in came another battledress and kit. Such an unloading there was! The rifle was placed in the corner behind me and I had to lean against it till we reached Reading. But it did not matter in wartime. He had been travelling a long time and had had no food since 4 a.m., poor chap. The next change was good and Leamington was reached ten minutes later.

Friday 10th May

The most eventful day of the war! This morning Holland and Belgium were invaded by Germany, and very soon afterwards they both appealed to the Allies for help. The reply was given in the affirmative half an hour later, and now Holland and Belgium are our allies. Now we know where we stand.

We were up in good time and, on hearing the news via the postman and Kate, we had the wireless on at 8 a.m. All day at intervals we have been listening in—at 10.30 a.m., at 12, at 1 p.m., 4.15 p.m., 6 p.m. and lastly at 9 p.m. Air raids over Brussels and many other Dutch and Belgian towns, as well as towns in France. Nancy—of loved memory to us—has been raided and 16 civilians killed. There was a raid in south-east England and incendiary bombs were dropped at Canterbury. The last news spoke of the dash over the Belgian frontier of our mechanized forces after the call for help—an historic moment.

Mr. Chamberlain has resigned the Premiership and Mr Churchill takes his place. The former spoke before the 9 o'clock news, rather sadly, but putting his country's wish before himself, as one knew he would—a great man!

Saturday 11th May

Jack was downstairs to listen to the 8 a.m. news and, having had my bath, I hung over the banisters to hear. The loss of over 100 planes by Germany in Holland, as well as many others in various places, was one item. We also heard of the landing of German parachute-troops all over Holland and Belgium and air raids in many of their towns, as well as raids over France. Civilians have been killed in these raids—many of them women and children. We are wondering whether Alan was among the mechanical transport and its personnel that streamed over the Franco-Belgian frontier yesterday. Lots of air fights are reported and our men, often outnumbered, acquit themselves bravely and well. Brussels was badly raided yesterday and many lives were lost. Today bombs fell in Amsterdam, and Rotterdam seems mostly in German hands.

The Dutch have fought well and driven the Germans out of the aerodromes they had taken. Planes have battered transports of troops arriving on the coast—a train of troops was blown up and lots of other damage done to the enemy. British and French troops are proceeding into Belgium, as had already been planned should help be called for.

The new Cabinet under Winston Churchill has been formed, with Mr Chamberlain as Lord President of Council.

Sunday 12th May

Whit Sunday and up early for the 9.15 a.m. service. A whole leg of lamb (Canterbury, be it said) was our midday meal. We have not seen so large a joint just recently, though there is always more than enough of one kind or another for each meal as it comes.

My mind runs on parachute troops today—we are hearing so much of them in Holland and Belgium. Our baker is said to have asked the local policeman what he should do if he saw a parachutist (he gets up at 4.30 a.m. some days), and the grinning bobby replied: 'If you were to shoot him, you wouldn't be brought up for murder.'

The Dutch say all parachute troops have been wiped out or taken prisoner, but in the news since then the Germans still seem to be landing them.

There is so much one could write. Each day there is so much news that one is appalled at all the happenings and the terrible loss of life, given out so calmly on the wireless. Thousands of Germans in troop-ships, armoured trains, aeroplanes. Over a hundred enemy aeroplanes brought down by the Dutch in one day! And much nearer 200, counting their losses everywhere. All this for a few madmen out for world-domination!

Whitsuntide holidays have been cancelled and factories are to work, shops to be open and, as far as possible, everything to continue as an ordinary working day tomorrow.

Wednesday 15th May

The 8 a.m. news told us of the capitulation of the greater part of the Netherlands. Harassed and overwhelmed by air attacks, by the treachery of the people living in Holland with Nazi sympathies so that it was difficult to tell friend from foe, and also by the loss of a quarter of the Dutch Army, Holland was obliged to give in. So determined had she been to be neutral—and no-one *can* be neutral these days, even if they wish—her little country, so sane and peaceably-minded, was quite unable to withstand the onslaught of the terrific German forces.

In the morning I went shopping to Leamington and tried to remember everything so as not to go again for a week. Having done all I set out to do, called at Kenilworth Cemetery and looked at the grave. The green thyme cross needs clipping and, seeing the caretaker, I arranged with him to do it. It is six years since Father went and he was buried on his own birthday, just a year before Alan was 21.

Friday 17th May

Another glorious warm day, bright sun and lovely colouring eyerywhere. Out early in the garden to make it as it ought to be. The bird garden was sad-looking, the soil green-mouldy through lack of attention for months, and the tulips there devastated by a hailstorm the other day. So in an hour-and-a-half they were removed, along with the wallflowers, and the soil forked and freshened and given new life—redemption.

The war news is grave. The Germans have turned the salient into a bulge on the Western Front and great strength will be needed to flatten it again. The R.A.F. are doing magnificent work in preventing easy advance by bombing roads, railways, key points, etc. On the whole they are clever and, having done their work, the announcement says: 'All our aeroplanes returned safely.' Sometimes it is 'One of our aeroplanes failed to return'. In a tremendous effort on a key position today, 'Eleven of our aeroplanes failed to return'.

Last night, just as I was in the half-dreamy stage of dropping off to sleep, I suddenly saw a face, rather white, against the dark background of my closed lids, and tried to keep it long enough to see whose face it was. As it faded away, it seemed to be Alan, calmly asleep.

Saturday 18th May

Alan's 26th birthday and another lovely warm spring day. Out early on my bicycle into the village for shopping and to put up a poster for salvage in the W.I. board. Then back to work in the garden. All day long we were thinking and talking of Alan, recalling other birthdays when he was a little boy and invited the three dogs to tea in the nursery!

War news is still grave—neither desperate nor catastrophic, but serious. A withdrawal in Belgium by Allied troops is announced. The French are doing well and endeavouring to hold the enemy, while the R.A.F. bombs petrol dumps, railways, oil stores and columns moving to the Western Front from Germany.

Tuesday 21st May

A startling revelation in the French Cabinet meeting was made known today. The German thrust penetrated unexpectedly and blunders had been made. The Meuse bridges were not blown up as intended when the French withdrew. This is indeed bad news, and later in the day we learn that Amiens and Arras have fallen. The German tanks are enormous and their onslaught is covered by aeroplanes. They want to get to Calais, and so to us. America still dilly-dallies, thinking about her own skin. A black day indeed. No news of Alan yet.

Friday 24th May

Empire Day, and I was in a deep sleep at 7.40 a.m., but soon awakened when Kate, knocking at the door, cried: 'There's a letter!' Of course these days there is only *one* letter, so my hand went out for it and my glasses went on to see it. It was written on Whit Sunday, 12th May. The M.F. Course had stopped the day before the exam., which Alan felt was trying after all the note-writing and work, but still he thought what he had learned would be very useful. 'I have been feeling rather tired, but the weather is glorious,' he says. He ends: 'I think all my civilian clothes will need to be let out when I come on leave.'

At 9 p.m. the King broadcast, very gravely and with great expression—a most impressive speech, calling on us all to do our part with courage and endurance in these perilous times and to call on 'God most High' on our National Day of Prayer next Sunday and to 'commit our just cause to Him'. God save our King!

Tuesday 28th May

Up and round the household jobs so as to be ready to leave for Berkswell Rectory at 10 a.m., where we all worked hard making triangular bandages—nine dozen today—as well as an operation garment. We talk and work and the machines chatter too till at 12.45 we stopped for lunch (sandwiches), and then took a little breather outside. I bought a few toffees at the village shop, but on hearing the sad news of Belgium's capitulation through Leopold, their King, I forgot to eat them. This is indeed bad news and we were all rather overcome at first, but settled to work again, discussing parachutes and parashooters, etc., till 4 p.m.

The news at 9 p.m. was still very grave: the Belgian capitulation has increased the difficulties of the B.E.F. and the thought of Alan being with them in Belgium is almost more than one can bear tonight. It has been a hard day for us, though we do not say a great deal to each other, for one must keep up.

Wednesday 29th May

The Army is bitter about King Leopold's let-down and, though Parliament and the Press are restrained, there is no doubt of the feelings of this country. Our men of the B.E.F. are now exposed on another flank to the enemy through this treacherous act. 'Come over and help us,' cried the King of the Belgians, and then, without consultation with those who had befriended him, he surrendered. Many of his people are not with him and fight on.

The R.A.F. continue to pound and bomb and shatter and fight the enemy, fiercely covering as best they can the withdrawal of our brave forces to the coast. Dunkirk is a vast entrenchment and from its coast our men are embarked, in the shallow waters, to the warships, bombed and machine-gunned in boats and in the water. Oh, the horror and bitterness of war!

Friday 31st May

The longest day ever! Every time the telephone rang one expected news. Mrs Carter came in at 10 a.m. to say that she had heard through Major Cox that two days before our men of the 1/7th Battalion Royal Warwickshire Regiment were safe. We were so happy to hear this, but later, on ringing up one and another, we found each had heard something of the kind and no-one seemed to set great store by it. So our spirits went down and down and the day wore slowly on. We worked in the garden and, lest we should not hear the telephone, we gave our big bell to Mrs Biggs at the telephone exchange next to us to ring for us while Kate was out. After supper a walk with Twink in an endeavour to calm and compose oneself in the tranquil fields, so rich in their late spring growth.

Saturday 1st June

Still no news. The men are evacuated from Flanders via Dunkirk day by day and great are the deeds of the Navy and Air Force. Against fearful odds the men withdraw from their perilous position. Many more are able to get away than was at first thought possible. Grim stories are told. Their bravery is unexcelled. The land is flooded on either side of a wide passage to Dunkirk near the coast and, in spite of terrific bombardment, our men are coming through.

This morning we heard the evacuees are not coming here this weekend and I had to go round to my district and tell people. This afternoon Joan Spencer rang up. She gave me sad news—first that Guy Glover, one of 'ours', has been killed, and also Philip Winser, but the latter was not officially announced. These are the first of men we really know and my heart aches for the Winsers; Philip was so cheery and such a good fellow.

When I was out today I saw dozens of vehicles going along the main road, all camouflaged. Queer vehicles, too, as well as charabancs in khaki. The Army doesn't always march now, but the men in Flanders have had a long trek. Trains await them on the English coast and they are whisked away and fed further inland, so as not to congest the stations on the coast.

Wednesday 5th June

A glorious day with a strong cool breeze to temper the heat. We decided to spring-clean the hut in the garden and there came across the little car Alan made and the box of motor trial trophies put away at the beginning of the war. This, on top of a restless night, was too much altogether, and to cry a bit relieved the tension. Mrs Gorton came then, full of sympathy, and her embrace set us both weeping. But it was a case of pulling oneself together. One can't afford to break down often.

Thursday 6th June

Still perfect hot weather. I never remember such a lovely spell, and the mornings are just grand.

The telephone rings at intervals all day with rumours and snippets of news from one or another, but nothing definite about our boys. As we sat down to dinner tonight, very tired and thirsty after digging and hoeing, Mrs Cutler rang up. She is just an acquaintance in Balsall Common whom I knew through billeting. But she said: 'Mrs Milburn, I am going to Olton Monastery tomorrow and I am having candles lit and prayers said for the safe return of your son'. Surprised and touched, I could scarcely answer properly before the voice said 'Goodnight'. The kindness and sympathy everywhere is wonderful. After dinner a rest and then, as we were about to continue our gardening, Harry and Ethel Spencer came, and she and I talked of Nevill and Alan, both thinking of them as our 'little boys'—mothers always do—and wiping away a tear or two. How drawn together we all are these dark days. Tonight, as they left, we all kissed each other like brothers and sisters. It is good to have so many real friends.

Friday 7th June

A brilliant day again—hotter than ever, but a clear and glorious heat such as we seldom have in England.

When I was writing a few notes this afternoon I heard Twink bark and a voice called out 'Can I come in?' It was Mrs Winser. She soon told me that they felt they had real confirmation now that Philip is killed, and I felt how splendidly brave and calm she is. So we talked a little together about our boys and she has the feeling that the dreadful anxiety is over and that it is even comforting to know the worst.

Cooper from the garage reports that a man named Smith in Alan's platoon saw him near Dunkirk, but one wants to see the man and hear his story. The 1/7th seem to have held the line against great odds before the real evacuation took place. And so the days go by with hopes rising and falling, the telephone ringing and still no definite or genuine news.

Saturday 8th June

Tales of the gallantry of Dunkirk are still pouring in and the thought of the beach and the men on the open sand dunes waiting, waiting to embark, perhaps for 24 hours and then to be told they will have to wait another 24, is haunting to the imagination. The stories of bombing and machine-gunning are so terrible, with no cover for the troops.

Sunday 9th June

I was up early for church, but disturbed by the very kind questioning of one and another.

A message from Harry Spencer about a man of the 1/7th Bn. R.W.R. at Meriden sent us dashing over there just before supper to get news of Alan from him. The woman from a small shop brought him to talk to us in the car. He saw Alan a fortnight ago and was sure he was a prisoner. The man himself was in the evacuation, but said Alan was probably captured the day before King Leopold's capitulation—May 27th. We went back for supper and then Ethne Green rang up to say that Ivan Woodcock was home and reported that Alan was a prisoner of war and was surprised that we did not know this. Jack went round to see him and gleaned a little more of the same story. Though we dare not take this as authentic, somehow it seemed more hopeful and we went to bed and slept well, thankful for a quiet night.

Monday 10th June

Jack started his new job today—a Government job with the Ministry of Labour—so was up at 7.15 and away to Coventry soon after 8.30. It seemed queer to be without him all day.

Mussolini has decided to come into the war and so Italy is now definitely our enemy and we now know where we are with them. Blow after blow falls upon us. A telegram from the War Office arrived saying that Alan's unit reported him as believed missing. This may fit in with the story of the capture. Oh, what a long and weary business it seems. Still we ring up other parents and wives and we are all just hanging on.

Tuesday 11th June

A letter arrived today from Major Cox describing the action in which he thinks it likely Alan and his colleague Purchas (who was wounded) and 40 men were taken prisoner. A farmhouse where Major Cox and his men were taking up station could not be vacated for a moment because of 'murderous machine-gun fire'. Later, after a counter-attack, they went to look for Purchas and Alan and for men who were placed earlier in a house 200 yards away. But nothing was to be seen of them at all, and so it was concluded that they had been taken prisoner.

One's mind seems numbed, and the last day or two I go on, keeping on the surface of things as it were, lest I go down and be drowned. Every moment Alan is in my thoughts, every hour I send out my love to him—and wonder and wonder. This queer unreal world, carrying on in some ways here just as before, with this gorgeous weather and summer heat heartening us, and yet most other things so sombre and heartbreaking.

Monday 17th June

A cool morning, growing hotter as the day wore on. I gardened in the morning and received the 1 p.m. news quietly—for we felt that France was not going to hold out, and when the announcer said 'France has ceased hostilities' we were scarcely surprised. It seems bad news nevertheless—ourselves standing alone, and yet what could France do, with the enemy streaming over her territory and her capital in their hands? Mr Churchill spoke very briefly on the wireless at 6 p.m. 'This will make no difference, we fight on,' he said.

Friday 21st June

How curious this life is! A sort of deep stillness comes over everything from time to time. There is not much traffic on the roads during the week and the village seems empty in the evenings. One misses the young life everywhere, particularly Alan coming in in the early evening. It is strange indeed not to know where he is—or whether he *is*. And always one wants to write and tell him things and cannot.

This was our wedding-day, and the 35th anniversary. A real summer's day again which ended with a quiet walk in the fields with Twink.

How I wish Alan could have been with me. He loved a late walk.

VOLUME 3

June 1940 – September 1940

Saturday 22nd June

On this day, 26 years ago, Alan was christened at St Thomas's Church in Coventry, and it is awful to think that today we do not know where he is or what has happened to him. This waiting for news is the most wearing, trying time and we—or I—find it hard to be patient and courageous. An air raid last night killed two civilians and injured several. There is still no *definite* news of France's acceptance of Hitler's terms.

Monday 24th June

Midsummer Day and my birthday.

The morning sped away on swift wings, and in the afternoon the two soldiers came and I got their tea and sewed while they sat in the garden playing with Twink.

Everyone feels very bitterly the capitulation of the Bordeaux (French) Government. And so many of the French are amazed and ashamed, too. We cannot know how much they suffered, but we had been led to understand that they were ready to withstand the onslaught of the Germans when it should come. Instead of which the Meuse bridges were left unharmed for the enemy to pour over into France.

We sent a telegram to the Prime Minister! It said: 'Why not declare war on the treacherous Bordeaux Government, seize French ships and protect French colonies.' I signed it, as Jack is at the Ministry of Labour and a Government servant. So 'Mrs Milburn, Balsall Common, near Coventry' had the effrontery to telegraph to the Prime Minister of Great Britain!

Tuesday 25th June

And we might not have slept so well if we had heard the Coventry air raid sirens last night! Many of the Red Cross members told me they heard them and some got up and were surprised to find no-one about. But tonight, about 11.30, just as I had settled myself for sleep, an aeroplane came beating along. 'Oh, bother!' I said, 'these planes always come over just as one wants to drop off to sleep.' I raised my head from the pillow and thought of Joyce's words in a letter this morning: 'Their engines have an uneven beat—not like ours.' This one had an uneven beat, a queer ragged noise, so I was soon out of bed and saw the searchlights busy and heard the sirens, too. Jack and I both dressed quickly, picked up a few oddments, got into our gumboots and—leaving Kate in the house because she did not want to come—went to the dugout in the orchard. It was a coolish night, but, though the shelter is damp, it is warm, and we spread our rug and sat down. The biscuits were found nice and crisp in the airtight jars, and we talked a bit. Occasionally Jack went up to prospect at the top of the ladder, till at last, after three-quarters of an hour, we heard the plain blast of the 'All Clear' and came in to bed just after 12.30.

Monday 1st July

The raiders were over last night and I was glad we did not have them. A morning full of household jobs and oddments of tidying, washing and putting away—a typical Monday morning. Still longing to have some word of Alan. Everyone asks and still we say: 'No news.' Always is one thinking of him, wondering whether he still lives and, if so, whether he is well, where he is, what he does all day, what discomforts he is suffering. If ... if ... And so the days go by. Always one works and works and occupies oneself from morning till night, getting up at 7.30, breakfast at 8; seeing Jack off at the gates and closing them about 8.40, working in house and garden, going out into the village, walking Twink, once a week going to Leamington, sewing at Berkswell Rectory on Tuesdays, occasional W.I. and M.U. meetings, always something to do.

This afternoon I visited the schools—it seems a long time since I did my duty as a school manager—and after several other little jobs got home late for a cup of tea. About 6.30, just after Jack came home, we heard the sound of an enemy plane not very far away. Later I heard it was over Solihull. In the news at 9 p.m. they reported that two of the few who came over were shot down, but one had done damage on the east coast of Scotland. Three houses were demolished and several people killed. It is a few days since the Channel Islands were raided, although they were de-militarized, and today the Germans have made landings there. Hong Kong was being evacuated of women and children yesterday.

Saturday 6th July

Twink and I took our little walk in the peaceful fields after lunch. No-one to be seen there—just trees and hedges and the quiet, restful haystacks and the great blue arch of heaven. The tranquillity is marvellous. There is very little so far of the war to be seen in this place. No longer is the road crowded with pleasure cars, business vans and vehicles, but the long, empty road stretches for half a mile or so, often with nothing to be seen on it at all. In the evening the village is quiet, with scarcely a soul to be seen walking about. But it is not a happy tranquillity. It is unnatural and eerie, and tense at times. Behind it lies the unhappiness and anxiety of war and the not knowing what will happen to our dear, dear land in the next few months.

Mr and Mrs Gutteridge, the new curate-in-charge of St Peter's and his wife, came to tea. They decided they would like it in the garden, and so we sat and talked there till they had to go at 5.30. A nice young couple, very human.

We have had two or three bombers over today and we lost three—only ours accomplish hits on proper objectives.

Monday 8th July

Some thunder today and a sharp, three-minute shower this morning. The garden is greatly freshened. The peas have filled out their pods, the leeks are upstanding and the cabbages are too marvellous for words—they have grown enormously in two days. This morning I raked and raked 'to a fine tilth' and then sowed four short rows of carrots.

Lord Woolton, the forceful food controller, spoke on the wireless tonight. Without previous warning, tea is to be rationed—2 oz per head per week—and margarine and cooking fats are to come under the rationing scheme. Well, it is all to the good, and a very prudent move.

Sunday 14th July

It was so lovely out of doors this Sunday afternoon. We both sat in Birch Tree Corner with the light shade of the birch moderating the heat of the sun. I lay down on the seat and looked up at the beautiful blue of the sky and the full white roundness of the cumulus clouds sailing across in great stateliness, so perfect and so satisfying to the heart in their majestic beauty. And trees are so lovely when one has time to study them and the varieties of green, from bronze to yellow, in their foliage. Yes, even in this terrible wartime, I thanked God for the capacity for enjoyment of His everyday gifts—and they are many.

Tonight Churchill spoke with great eloquence. He is a marvellous speaker and uses uncommon rhetoric which is singularly apt and inspiring. He is a born leader. Five enemy planes were brought down over the Channel this afternoon as they tried to attack a convoy, and a wonderful record of it was given by Charles Gardner, really recorded on the spot. One felt actually there with him. J. B. Priestley gave a talk on a present-day visit to Margate—an empty shell of a place, complete with lidos and bandstands and all the paraphernalia of a popular watering place, with no people there. How queer it must be!

Tuesday 16th July

I looked in for a moment or two at the Institute, where the Produce Exhibition was being held, to see how the judges were getting on and found them in the thick of things, tasting and judging the merits of jams, jellies, chutneys, salad cream and bottled fruit. Mrs Ford was sipping each bottle of wine and looking flushed by the time she had got to the eleventh!

About 5.30 I sauntered rather heavily off through the field at the back to take Twink for his walk. When I was well away, I heard Jack calling and saw him waving to me from the hedge. 'It can't be a telegram about Alan!' I thought, so I crammed that thought back and we met in the middle of the field. 'Kate has just had a telegram over the phone for us from the War Office. Alan is a prisoner of war,' he said. There and then, saying 'Thank God', we embraced each other for sheer joy at the good news. Oh, how delighted we were to hear at last that he is alive—and apparently unwounded.

Well, Twink and I went through the fields and then I came home to telegraph and telephone messages round to all the very kind friends who had so often inquired, or even shown their sympathy by their one expression and then their silence. Everybody has been so sweet and kind, it was almost too much to bear. Even the garage proprietor, Mr Cooper, said: 'We thought a lot of him.' After a very busy evening it is 11.30 and, with a heart full of thankfulness, I hope to sleep.

My darling dear, you are alive!

Wednesday 17th July

How different was this morning's awakening! No dead weight of woe hanging over one, such as we have had the past six or eight weeks. The war? Yes, but not the war and the anxiety about Alan in the same way. Everybody just overwhelms us with warm-heartedness. 'God bless you both,' they say, and many of them seem quite overcome. People have been coming with tears in their eyes saying how glad they are. It is simply wonderful.

A half-bottle of champagne, left from Alan's 21st birthday party, went down very well by way of a celebration tonight, and we drank to him and his safe and early return.

Thursday 18th July

'Bert', the Austin, took us both to Leamington this morning and we did a good deal of shopping and stayed to lunch at the Stores, doing ourselves really well: chicken and sausage and sweets and coffee—oh, and grapefruit to begin with! *Some* lunch for wartime! Many were the kind words from shop assistants at the Stores and even in the post office at Kenilworth, where the man remembered my talking about Alan being missing a few weeks ago. It is all too marvellous for words.

The first one to ring me up today was Joan Spencer to say she had had a letter from Nevill! That was truly wonderful and she was so happy. He says he is 'in lovely country' and there are 200 others in the camp. I do wonder whether Alan is there, too.

R.A.F. raids continue over Germany, but news is thin just now. We are trying to soothe Japan, as we do not want more worries in the Far East just now!

Friday 19th July

Roosevelt is nominated for a third term as President of the U.S.A.—an unprecedented happening. Also he has said just the right things in his speech: How he will stand for freedom of the people, liberty of the individual and have no part or parcel with aggressive nations who overpower small peace-loving countries. Nothing could be plainer than that for Hitler, but he made a speech too, with the usual stuffing about Britain being the aggressor and having deep-laid schemes to invade and oppress the Low Countries, etc., etc. All the usual lies. We are unmoved by his protestations of how greatly he desired peace but Britain would not have it. How he sleeps at night I can't think—or why he does not choke himself with his 'terminological inexactitudes'!

Monday 22nd July

Off to London today! But not much sleep last night with aeroplanes floating round. Crowhurst's car was outside at 7.35 a.m. and we got to Coventry station well before 8 a.m. Joan was waiting and Ethel Spencer was there, too. From Euston we went to the Red Cross at St James's Palace. We passed through lovely, well-proportioned rooms with ladies at tables and desks and packages with tinned food lying about—all wrong in these magnificent surroundings. After going through enormous doors, which ought to have had a bewigged silk-stockinged footman to open them, we went down to the ground floor into a sort of large hall, with a door opening on to a courtyard. There, at each end, a lady sat at a table, and presently we went to one and the names of our men were entered on a form, with other particulars about them.

So then we took a taxi to the War Office and I sat outside in an armchair while Joan told them about Nevill's message.

Of course, I left my gas mask in the taxi and the next taxi took us to the lost property office over Lambeth Bridge, but, if found, it will not arrive for a day or two. Dear, dear, I knew I'd leave the thing somewhere! And so to Harvey Nichols for lunch, and a jolly good one too. Then the afternoon was spent shopping and back we went to H.N.'s for tea, and eventually to Euston and home.

Wednesday 24th July

A letter from the War Office Casualty Branch giving us Alan's address: 'Stalag XXA', Germany. That cheered us a bit, for now we can write to him. And, of course, it was not long before I wrote him a stilted little letter on a single sheet of notepaper, which is all one may do at a time. One can write as often as one likes—but how little one can really say! For one thing, news is scarce when one cuts out the war, and one may not say anything to give any information to the enemy. So things have to be carefully sifted till there is very little said. However one can send love and give facts in a veiled way, as I did today when I wrote: 'Little Bert Austin takes your father to his daily work', which meant 'Father has a Austin 7 to drive into Coventry, where he has taken a job at the Labour Exchange'. And then continued: 'and Maria stays with me at Burleigh. She is as good a girl as ever and behaves nicely, so I am glad to have her with me'. That meant: 'I have the Rover car for my use', because we call the Rover 'Maria'. He knows that and will put two and two together.

Friday 2nd August

Still hoping for a letter from Alan, but as now there is only one post we have no hope for the day after 8.30 a.m.

Our R.A.F. has been very active over Cherbourg and Germany. Hamburg is badly knocked about and we had names of several other badly damaged places. Last night's air raids on this country took the form of leaflet-dropping in the South-West. They gave parts of Hitler's speech a week or two ago suggesting a reasonable peace. As if we had not already heard it all, summed it up and dismissed it, knowing what we have to deal with! A woman picked up scores of the leaflets in a field and sold them as souvenirs for benefit of the Red Cross! She soon made £2 2s. 0d.

Tuesday 13th August

The Battle of Britain has begun in earnest. We hear on the news of airmen's experiences during these exciting fights, usually told very calmly, quickly and tersely. Tonight we hear that in fighting round our south-east and south coasts, as well as over Berkshire, Wiltshire and Hampshire, the Germans have lost 57 planes and our losses are nine here and 14 on the Continent. A scrap or two had also taken place between torpedo boats and E-boats, with no loss of men to us and only one damaged boat, which got home safely.

Wednesday 14th August

Yesterday's 'bag' of Nazi planes was 78 to 13 of ours. And everybody was tired today because we have all been up the best part of the night. The Nazi planes came over about 11.15 p.m., and so we dressed and went out to the dugout, taking two rugs and a few oddments in a suitcase. For hours we heard planes, bombs and gunfire, and in the lulls came up and got some fresh air. Once I came to see how Kate was getting on. She was quite cheerful by that time, and I went back until, at 3.15, we heard the 'All Clear'. As soon as we got back to bed we fell asleep, but I wakened at 6.30—after three hours' sleep. Tonight I was upstairs and in bed towards the end of the 9 o'clock news. Anthony Eden spoke afterwards and I heard practically all of his marvellous speech but the last few sentences, by which time I was asleep!

Sunday 18th August

At 11.30 last night over came the planes again and we dressed quickly and dashed out to the dugout, with another plane going by as we went. Soon afterwards we heard bombs, and if we had known then where they fell we should have had a shock! For we have just heard from Kate that the bombs fell down the lane at Canley Corner! Our old home! At 3 a.m. the 'All Clear' sounded and we were very thankful to get back to bed.

After Sunday service at St. Peter's, as I took Twink for a walk, an air battle was in progress on the south-east coast—and there had been an attempt to reach London. The raiders had eventually been driven off, but Hampshire had also been raided.

The 9 p.m. news says 86 enemy planes have been destroyed today and the R.A.F. have heavily bombed Boulogne and all returned safely. Tonight I shall sleep in my clothes, I think—if we are allowed to sleep—so that I have only to get up and slip on my coat, pick up the cushions, slip on the gumboots and carry out my little case full of oddments.

Monday 19th August

And a good thing one was ready! At 11 p.m. over came the enemy planes again, and I was dressed in record time! We three sat in the dugout—myself nodding off—till 1 a.m., when the 'All Clear' sounded. But it seemed early and we waited awhile and then Jack went in and rang up Biggs at the telephone exchange next door. He reported the 'A.C.' signal as correct, but added: 'I shouldn't trust 'em—it's early yet.' So we stayed down below until 2 a.m. and then came up and went to bed.

This afternoon we heard the good news that 140 aircraft had been destroyed in yesterday's attempt to bomb London—a quarter to one-fifth of the planes which came over.

Wednesday 21st August

We had a long, quiet night and I am thankful to say I did not wake until 8 a.m. There were a few things to do in the garden and at 12 I sat down to make up a scene for a W.I. charade. It is to represent National Savings, with Britannia, holding the baby called National Savings, talking to the various people who come to look at it. After lunch the drama members went through the charade and we had an amusing afternoon. When supper was over, I finished W.I. notices and took them out to the village, picking up 6 lb of greengages at the amazing price of 2d. a lb! Plums, damsons and greengages all are so very plentiful this year. Plums are a 1d. a lb, though best dessert ones fetch 6d. in the shops. Eggs are 2s. 6d. or 2s. 9d., butter is a controlled price of 1s. 7d. and milk 4d. per pint.

Eight raiders were brought down yesterday and seven today. There was little raiding last night, but today there have been single raiders operating all over the country. A speaker is saying on the wireless now that the Germans have so far lost 709 planes and we have lost 194. Nevertheless there is still the danger of invasion and we are likely to have many more and worse raids. So we must pull ourselves up and face whatever comes.

Saturday 24th August

For me no sleep last night! One of our planes went over just as I was settling down, and that woke me up so thoroughly that I dozed for part of an hour. Then, after hearing 2 a.m. strike, I heard the enemy 'zoom-a-zoom-a-zoom' plane. There seemed another following on, so we got up and I was dressed in wizard time and down in the dugout before the others. We settled down in our chairs, hearing planes over at intervals, until at 4.30 we heard the 'All Clear'. Almost immediately there was a German plane over and a few minutes later the sirens wailed again. Eventually, about 5 a.m., we were able to come up and turn in.

We slept till 9 a.m. and Kate told us the planes had been over Leamington and machine-gunned the streets and dropped a bomb. I'm glad I went there the day before yesterday!

Oh, dear, what madness all this is—parents separated from their children, husbands from wives, guns and bombs blowing houses and people to pieces—Insanity Fair in truth, but what could one do? Nothing can be severe enough punishment for the nation allowing itself to begin such dreadful deeds. God knows we tried hard not to make war, but it could not have been His will that we should allow ourselves to be trampled on and annihilated finally. There are times when one must fight, and Germany, having set out to dominate the world, had to be paid in her own coin.

Monday 26th August

They came over just as I had taken off my dress to go early to bed. So to ground we went and stayed till 5 a.m., with fitful sleep in our deckchairs, eating biscuits, having a chat and nodding off again. Fierce air battles rage by day and by night. The raiders are mostly operating singly, they say—though as we sit in our dugout there seem to be dozens going over. This week I had hoped to see *Gone With The Wind* at Coventry, but in last night's raid the cinema was demolished.

And so we go on living hour by hour, day by day, longing for word of Alan. But nothing comes.

Wednesday 28th August

Shortly after supper a terribly fast aeroplane came over and a queer light came in the sky. Parachute flares—horrible things! The whole place was as light as day, and the flares hung in the sky like colossal stars. I was soon in my gumboots and coat, Twink was exhorted to come in and, at long last, came, and I flew fearfully across the garden, looking up anxiously as two flares hung just over us. Hugging the building as I went, I dashed down the steps into the 'hole'. Eventually a grunting pig—'a-grunt-a-grunt-a-grunt'—came over and then nothing much happened. So at 10 p.m. we came up and decided to go to bed.

However planes began to come over and we were down again. We both slept in our deckchairs till 3 a.m., ate some chocolate and, as nothing seemed about then, left one lid open and both slept again till daylight. At 5.15 a.m. we came in.

Thursday 29th August

This morning we heard that one of the parachute flare cases had landed across the road in the Longmore's garden—a canister of aluminium about 4' 6" long with L55 inscribed on it, and something in German. As the name is Longmore and Mr Longmore's age 55 this year, he said it was certainly intended for him! The thing fell between the garage and the greenhouse and it seems they saw it coming down as they sat under their verandah. If one hasn't a dugout, the thing is to sit under the stairs, and Mrs Longmore has made her little cupboard there into a tiny refuge. She has trailed a little electric wire into a lamp there, put in two upright folding chairs and a table and decorated it with Union Jacks! I tried on her 'siren suit' today and hope to make one.

Saturday 31st August

In the dugout for the night while plane after plane soared over. We finally emerged at daylight and stumbled out into the cool fresh air to the house, where we were soon asleep. But all this hot afternoon Jack has been back at the dugout arranging a ventilating pipe. As the pipe sticking out would look like a gun, he camouflaged it—and it now looks like a chicken coop. The arrangement both covers the pipe effectively, will prevent birds building in it and keep the rain out . . . if it ever rains again! Oh, how dry it is, with today's scorching on top of the recent long dry spell.

I must record that yesterday I brought a very small lemon for 5d., and in our local greengrocer's today they were 6d.! Lately—I mean a year or so ago—it was difficult to realize that in the Great War I once paid 22s. 6d. for a large fowl. Also I bought an evening frock in 1919 at sale price for £18 18s. 0d. and a jumper of black georgette for 12 guineas! There was money to buy these things then. I should also like to record that in 1913 we bought a 12 h.p. Rover, which we kept all through the war and in 1919 sold again. It was bought for £350 and sold for £568 six years later! I wonder what prices this war will see?

Monday 9th September

A proper night's sleep, but raids on London last night and the night before were severe. A good deal of damage has been done and about 350 people killed and 1,300 seriously injured. Dock warehouses were set on fire, and the fires, still smouldering, guided the raiders to their targets again. The R.A.F. go night by night and bomb Germany and France—aerodromes, oil depôts, concentration areas, dockyards, barges, convoys, etc. This has been going on for months, so that the bombing of London has been expected. Hitler threatens to 'erase all our towns'.

Mrs Longmore has kindly finished my 'siren suit' and I am now garbed in it, wishing I weighed a stone or two less, but feeling very cosy.

Wednesday 11th September

Four raids over London today, but last night's raid was not quite so disastrous as the others. A time bomb was dropped outside Buckingham Palace. No-one was hurt when it exploded, but some balustrading was blown up, a huge piece of masonry landed on the roof and the windows were blown out of the King's study and the Queen's private sitting-room. It fills me with cold rage. The King and Queen were not in residence. Their Majesties have visited the heavily-bombed areas today and, as an air raid warning was sounded, they went into a police station and had tea with A.R.P. workers and others in a room next to a court house which had suffered in yesterday's raids. Many people remarked that Hitler couldn't have gone out visiting like that—he would have needed an armed bodyguard. Pah!!

Well, we had 73 planes down yesterday for 17 of ours, and three pilots safe. Berlin has been terrifically bombed, as well as aerodromes, etc—all the usual things, and many barges in Ostend harbour and elsewhere. Mr Churchill broadcast at 6 p.m., still talking of possible invasion and the need for watchful care, though he felt we were ready to go for the enemy if he came. 'Grim and gay' were his words the other day—a motto and a slogan for us.

Friday 20th September

This was our Leamington day and with Florence, who is with us again, the three of us went early and did a marvellous amount of shopping and just got home for the news. It was a lovely day after the rain and everywhere looked charming in the fresh atmosphere. For supper we made sausages brown and crisp and enjoyed pears off our own tree, which were stewed, and had almost the last cream for a time—next week will be the end of it, according to law. Eggs are 3s. 6d. a dozen today—we think they went up to 6s. last war!

Monday 23rd September

The King broadcast tonight from Buckingham Palace—a very good speech and with much less hesitation. The Nazi crime we have heard of today is the torpedoing of an evacuee ship, without warning, 600 miles from land, and 83 evacuee children, as well as crew and helpers, are all drowned. A few children were saved, but in one case there were five of one family lost. The King expressed his sympathy with the parents, as well as with all those who had lost their homes and friends and relations in the bombing of London and elsewhere. There were raids over London again last night, mostly by lone raiders, and damage was done to houses, shops and other buildings, with some fatal casualties, alas! Also widespread raids elsewhere, with slight damage and few casualties.

Friday 27th September

A boatload of children and grown-ups have been found drifting in a lifeboat from the *City of Benares*, the evacuee ship which the Germans torpedoed without warning. A woman escort massaged the children (all boys) and kept them interested for eight days, on and off, with a long serial story which she made up more or less, beginning with John Buchan's *Thirty-nine Steps* and carrying on with anything she could remember or make up. On the eighth day a little boy who was a Scout suddenly called out: 'Oi—a Sunderland!' and there, overhead, was a flying boat. The Sunderland saw the lifeboat and a small boy waving a handkerchief. The pilot saw the child was signalling *City of Benares*. He soon understood, and went off to get help. When they dropped food by parachute, the boat load was near the end of its rations.

When, eventually, a warship arrived to pick them up, the children were too weak to climb the ladder and had to be carried aboard. A great story!

The days go by and no news of Alan. Today I have just heard of someone who has been waiting longer than we have and had news of her prisoner son yesterday. Hope is a great thing and patience a real virtue in these times, but difficult for me.

VOLUME 4

September 1940 – December 1940

Monday 30th September

Harry Spencer rang up early this morning to tell us he had had a letter from his Swiss friend, who promises to try and get in touch with Alan, as he has done with Nevill. He will send food parcels and clothes and has already sent food to Nevill, which he has acknowledged. He is very kind indeed to take so much trouble, but says it is nothing to what Britain is suffering.

Forty-five planes have been brought down today in four attacks on Britain.

Thursday 3rd October

On this day I hied me to the barber's and there did get my poll neatly trimmed! In other words, I have been bobbed! Florence and I set off about 10 a.m. for Coventry, where, to the hairdresser's surprise, I said I would have my hair cut and permanently waved. Months ago I thought I should not like to be having a permanent wave if the sirens sounded in the middle of it—and that is exactly what happened! Half-an-hour later the 'All Clear' went and I was happy to think the waving was yet to come, so settled down, glad it was all clear again. But a little later the wail began and another three-quarters of an hour went by till the A.C. sounded. We heard no planes and apparently the raiders went by Coventry.

Rain fell in the evening and continued gently most of the night.

Sunday 6th October

I wrote the 21st letter to Alan today, and just for a few moments this evening black depression flooded over me. This separation, for such a cause, and the prospect of a long war and consequent *long* separation, and not knowing where he is and what is happening to him, simply engulfed me. And the stifling, choking feeling of not being able to do anything. Oh, dear, it was dreadful! But 'Lift up your hearts' was said at church today and we replied: 'We lift them up unto the Lord'.

And then one's spirits just had to rise in the garden and one thought of the queer things one was thankful for personally—such varied things as the five tall cypresses on the lawn, so handsome; the bronze green of the yew hedge in the fading light, the *colour* of *colours*; a new thumbnail just grown to perfection after nearly a year; the feel of newly-cut hair and the blessing of a permanent wave; one's good bed; the rain and the sun; autumn colouring; good garden tools and a wickerwork barrow; the way Twink's ears fall and his easy action; and a thousand other things day by day. And then for one's good friends and most of all for the nearest and dearest—and home.

Saturday 12th October

A quiet night with no planes over, as far as we know. A sharp frost left a delicate silvery white coating over the lawn and roof, but after all the daily duties and many others were done I was able to get out into the garden, where Batchelor had placed a good load of manure. I dug and trenched and manured for an hour-and-a-half and put in some divided bits of plants. I wish I were 20 years younger when I do these things, though heartily thankful that at 57 I can still dig and garden generally and enjoy it.

Florence walked with a very good dog, and as I worked and she walked, the siren wailed. The sky seemed quite empty, but by and by a yellow trainer—a biplane—droned over and soon after the 'Raiders Passed' blew bravely from Knowle. This is the right way to describe the signal and not 'All Clear', which is really the signal after a gas attack when the air is clear again. But now that 'A.C.' has passed into common use it will be difficult to change.

Tonight the siren wailed before the 9 p.m. news and we were all four down below ground, with aircraft surging around overhead. There were bombs and gunfire and then a screaming bomb, but no explosion. Scarcely had the guns ceased when, just after 11 p.m., the 'Raiders Passed' rang out. After a discreet pause we came up and went to bed, expecting every minute to be roused with another alert. But soon we slept.

Sunday 13th October

No early church this Sunday as I was tired, but we three went to 11 a.m. and arrived just as Mr Whitaker was arranging his books. As he came down the nave past our pew he stopped and told us that a delayed-action bomb was just beyond High Cross on the Kenilworth Road and that Coventry had suffered quite a lot. Later I rang up the Bradley's, who live beyond High Cross, and found that the unexploded bomb was in front of their house. One had made a hole 'big enough to hold a wagon and horses', an incendiary had pierced their roof, another had set fire to a shed and some hay in the field behind, and 32 incendiaries had landed in the field next to them. The plaster in the house was cracked, but otherwise 'no damage'. The road was closed and traffic diverted.

Harry and Ethel Spencer came to tea and told us of the damage in Coventry. The Swift Works were demolished, the back of the Fire Station, a cinema, a public house and some other places. A bad raid indeed!

Princess Elizabeth made a very charming first broadcast at 5.15 p.m. Her voice is like her mother's, very pleasant and clear and womanly. She made no mistakes and evidently was not nervous—or we did not perceive it. The speech for Empire children was a truly royal one, just as her 'Come on, Margaret' was wholly natural and childlike when she called upon Princess Margaret to say 'Goodnight' to her listeners.

America speaks with no uncertain voice of her intentions of helping Britain and resisting the dictators.

Monday 14th October

The last alarm we heard last night came about 10 p.m., but nevertheless we went to bed and slept, though there were other 'alerts' and 'Raiders Passed' during the night. After lunch I went out delivering salvage papers along this road. I found myself tremendously interested in my neighbours, both well-to-do and otherwise, and the great thing one learns is how very much nicer everybody is than one thought. Everybody's house is interesting and I got a smile and kindly words everywhere, and many inquiries about Alan and much sympathy. And now I shall be able to nod much more understandingly to my neighbours.

Tea and telling all about it followed, and then there were little things to do with blackout and supper. Just as we sat down the sirens sounded, but we decided to get our supper over before thinking of going down below. As soon as the washing-up was done and we had begun to enjoy the living-room fire, over came a posse of planes and we got all our belongings and went down below. Soon bombs fell and guns fired and there we stayed, with planes over, bombs and gunfire at intervals. Then the 'R.P.' sounded and we went thankfully to bed about 2 a.m.

Tuesday 15th October

Poor Coventry! The lovely old almshouses, Ford's Hospital, has gone. A side aisle of the Cathedral has been damaged. Owen Owen's, the large drapery store, had a direct hit. We also heard that a brave A.R.P. warden who had just safely shepherded 200 people to a shelter was killed immediately afterwards the other night. Two policemen and another A.R.P. warden lost their lives, as well as 15 or 16 other people.

Friday 18th October

A little more digging, manuring and planting today on the pear tree border, with Jack doing most of the digging. About 4.30 p.m. I heard a terrific d-um-p and thought the Bradley's bomb had exploded at last. But later I learned, very sadly, from Kate that a bomb removed from Coventry to Whitley Common had just been placed in the crater made for it when it burst, killing five men—probably the engineers who had dug it up and moved it there. Very, very sad.

Tuesday 22nd October

A thousand mothers and children are to come from London to the Meriden Rural Area, and Balsall Common has to take 50. So we have to look up our billets again and find homes, if we can, for them. Last night's raid on Coventry was very trying and the people are pouring out of the city, by car, train and bicycle as well as on foot. I rang up Norah just before the siren sounded tonight about 7.45 and she asked if I knew of anyone who would give a man a bed for two or three nights. I said we would, and she is ringing up to let me know about it tomorrow.

Once more we are down in the shelter and the pigs are grunting overhead, going Coventrywards and dropping bombs and incendiaries.

Wednesday 23rd October

And a queer place to be writing one's diary! For here I am at Leamington at the hairdresser's with my hair washed and 'in the drier'. Just as it was being set, the nearby sirens sounded and Florence and I, with two armchairs and attendants, were taken downstairs into the passage, while the hairdressing was continued for five minutes. Later I took little 'Bert' to Balsall Street and went through my billets again, asking for room for women and children from London. I found only two houses which had any room at all. Jack reported at teatime that a mother and daughter were coming out to sleep and he had arranged to meet them at the station. However, just as we were having an early meal, the front door bell rang and our two guests had arrived. So we fed them, showed them their room and later they came and talked to us and knitted until they went early to bed. Fortunately no sirens sounded and we all had a quiet night.

Our new air raid shelter was begun today.

Thursday 24th October

Our two guests, having slept in one single bed to save trouble, rose about 7.30 a.m. and, after a cup of tea, went into Coventry. They did not arrive back, but the Germans did! Sirens sounded at 7.45 p.m. and down we went till 10 p.m. Birmingham had the raid and we saw a red glow of fires quite soon after the first planes went over.

Hitler is doing his best to persuade Spain to join him; Turkey says she will hold out against any aggression; the Russian bear is silently watching; Rumania is swamped; and eyes are turned to the Middle East. London was raided and so was Berlin last night.

News of Alan is long-delayed and, though the name 'Lieut. A. J. Milburn' appears in the War Office casualty list with Captain H. N. Spencer as 'Prisoners of War', it means no more than we already have heard. It is time to send another parcel, but we have to wait for instructions from the Red Cross. Poor old dear, he must be badly needing things. A notice in the newspaper said that money up to £2 0s. 0d. per month could be sent to prisoners of war and Jack has inquired at Barclays. They say they will send it, if it is possible, on instructions from us. Yesterday I sent the 23rd letter, finding it is very difficult to know what to say, unable to tell the things that really concern us and having to be content with twitterings about Twink or any little thing I can about our friends and their doings.

Saturday 26th October

Just as breakfast was finished Nephew Colin rang up from the War Office—news of Alan at last! 'Not very good news,' he said. Evidently, though we had applied to the War Office for further news, Colin got busy himself and finds that Alan was wounded and that on 1st July he was at No. 7 Place Conscience, Antwerp, and apparently has never been at Stalag XXA at all!

He was furious with the sheer incompetence of the people concerned, and says he will now get something done through Geneva. Oh, the time wasted through somebody's incompetence!

1st July! Nearly four months, and yet on 16th July came the first 'prisoner of war' telegram, and a week later the address 'Stalag XXA'. Oh, my dearest dear, where can you be now? How badly were you wounded and how are they treating you? All day you are in my thoughts, close and deep, and we are both praying for you.

Florence and I made our usual trip into the village, where we met several people who asked about Alan, and so the tale was told again and again. It was Red Cross flag day, and if this muddle about Alan is part of the Red Cross's work, then I do not feel pleased with it.

Just before darkness fell we took the chairs down to the dugout, and as we came back our two guests arrived, very thankful to come out again for a night's sleep. We left them to chat to Kate while we had supper, and when Kate came in with a khaki rice pudding (made from condensed milk, and queer!) and damsons she said sirens had sounded a quarter of an hour before. We had not heard them, but we listened and heard the first plane—or perhaps second or third—over and decided to finish our meal and wait awhile before descending. Soon we heard the first big guns pounding 'pom-pom', so got into our warm things and came down, while Kate decided to stay with our guests and get under the stairs if necessary.

Monday 28th October

Events were very trying last night, with planes and heavy gunfire on and off from 7.45 till after 2 a.m. We were all terribly weary. The news reports that Greece received an ultimatum from Germany at 3 o'clock this morning, asking for a reply by 6 o'clock, and then started fighting at 5.30.

Greece calls upon Britain to help her, and so begin the operations in the Middle East. Coventry suffered a lot of damage last night, we are told, as Birmingham did the night before. America is in the throes of her pre-election skirmishes and fights, and until she gets that over isn't much use.

After supper tonight a brief sit and then the sirens sounded. So the shelter it is at 8.30. We have been here three-quarters of an hour and planes and gunfire sound intermittently. Our guests have not turned up tonight. They took all their belongings this morning, which looked as if they did not intend to return.

Saturday 2nd November

We were off to Leamington at 10 o'clock this morning. The Rover was our chariot and we greatly enjoyed driving her, as the

Austin is a bit cramped. But shopping is difficult, post offices are crowded and so many people have come into the heart of England from the coasts and danger spots. In Balsall Common there is very little in the bakers late in the morning. It is only right that the extra people in the village should be catered for, but the wife of the baker said they were rationed with their goods and really had not enough for the number of people here now.

We got the basic ration papers for the cars—six gallons for the Rover and five for the Austin. I got my hat, which had been altered to fit my new-cut hair, and fell deeply in love with a brown tricorne which suited me exactly, and about which I will ponder. The purchase tax came into force this week or last and will operate on the brown hat if I have it. One wears winter hats so long it is nice to have a change with one's dark clothes—they begin in November and carry on till April very often. Also I brought my new coat home, and am very pleased with it. (Pepys loved to tell of his new clothes.)

Sunday 3rd November

A long, quiet night, Sunday service and then a quiet afternoon, which was very restful and pleasing. Later I wrote to the Red Cross, telling them I had no correct address to write to Alan at present, unless he is still in the same place at Antwerp. We also had a talk to Colin on the telephone and heard how the mistake in the address occurred. A long list of names was sent from Geneva headed 'The following are prisoners of war in Stalag XXA'. Further down the same page was a second heading 'The following are wounded and at No. 7 Place Conscience, Antwerp'. Then came Alan's name, and three others. Evidently the second heading had been missed and the name added to those in Stalag XXA.

It makes one furious to think of four wasted months when we might have been writing and sending parcels.

Tuesday 5th November

Nine years today since we came to Burleigh, and what a wet day it was, and what a wretched few weeks those first ones were! Packing oneselves into a smaller house, bad weather, workmen everywhere, oh, it was a business! And it was not till a year or two later that I remember hearing Adolf Hitler mentioned when I went to a bridge drive and competitions for Missions to Seamen. My recollection is that he was thought to be a coming man(!) raising the status of Germany and a contributor to the well-being of the world. How sadly we were all mistaken! 'This wicked man,' as Churchill calls him, has plunged the whole world into disorder and ruined thousands of homes in Germany and elsewhere. That one man and his satellites should have this power seems monstrous. And he calls this misery the 'New Order'! God help us to annihilate all such wretchedness and bring the world to real peace.

Churchill had another 'say' in the Commons today, but my heart fails me when he talks of the campaign carrying on in 1943 and 1944. Oh, my darling Alan—four years! It is enough to make one quail. I can't look forward to that. One hopes the enemy will be sick of it before that and that something will happen to end it before then.

Work on our air-raid shelter has continued today. But it was so wet yesterday that one of the men went to Henley-in-Arden, where it was market day, and an enemy plane swooped down out of low cloud and machine-gunned the people in the streets. Near him they dropped a bomb and today he brought with him a jagged piece of metal which fell close by.

Sunday 10th November

Florence knocked at the door at 7.15 a.m. and, after a very quiet night, one was *almost* ready to get up. The Sunday service without that man's cough was very pleasant indeed. Nor was he at the next Service of Remembrance, thanks be, for we had 'Onward Christian Soldiers' and 'Fight the Good Fight', both of which he ruins.

Neville Chamberlain died last night and the nation will mourn him, 'steel-true and blade-straight', and our hearts go out to Mrs Chamberlain in her loss. The King and Queen went to see him a few weeks ago, we hear now, and stayed an hour.

Wednesday 13th November

A peaceful night, an uneventful morning and then I went to Stoneleigh Vicarage to lunch, arriving just in time for the good news of the R.A.F.'s smashing blow at the Italian Navy. Five of her big ships are out of action. They were attacked in the harbour of Taranto and have suffered severely. Molotov has lunched with Hitler!

On the way home I saw a road lined with oil containers and chimneys—for the provision of a smoke-screen for Coventry tonight, methinks, as it is nearing full moon. Darkness falls soon after tea now and we were not long before we drew the curtains. Ethel Spencer rang up then and says Harry has heard that Alan was in a Belgian Red Cross hospital in Antwerp on 15th June and was wounded in the leg. It is comforting to have that confirmation and to know something of the nature, if not the extent, of his wound. We are certainly very grateful and rather relieved, though we long to know still more.

Thursday 14th November

Shopping in Solihull with Florence this afternoon. I bought some cherry-coloured wool for a jumper. Then we came home to tea and afterwards I hastily wrote to Alan and elsewhere and Jack just got to the post by 5.50.

While we had supper, though we had not heard the sirens, we heard planes grunting overhead, and soon the guns began to sound. That was 7.30, and now it is nearly 10 o'clock and never have we had such a pounding of guns, almost without cessation for over two hours. I only hope we have brought some of them down. Heavens! What a bang! The house shook then. I think we could do without any more of this. We certainly have expended some ammunition on these Nazis tonight. Here comes another! Jack has been out to look a few times and has been up and downstairs looking out of the bedroom window at the lightning flashes and the bursting shells above the oak tree.

Friday 15th November

We had a terrible night—not so much for ourselves personally as for the people of Coventry. Jack and I stayed in the house till 11.15, then he said: 'Well, of all air raids, this is the one when we ought to be in the shelter.' So he went down and later came back for me, as Florence and Kate elected to stay in the house. When we went out the searchlights were probing the clear sky, the stars looked very near, the air was so clear and the moonlight was brilliant. I have never seen such a glorious night. Wave after wave of aircraft came over and heavy gunfire followed. Scarcely once was there a lull the whole night. I should have said they came over sometimes at one per minute.

Once or twice we came up the dugout steps and looked out at the lovely moon and sky, saw the flash of the shells as they burst high over the oak tree and the sudden glare as the big gun held forth away to the east. Always there was the sound of enemy aircraft, and as the near guns fired down we went and closed the lids above us. We read at first, then tried to sleep, but I had the only chair down there and Jack sat on the bench, which was very uncomfortable. He went up once and came back with a cushion for my head, which improved matters for me.

The planes ceased going over for a few minutes now and then towards 4 a.m. and at 4.20 we came up tired out, finding that Florence had gone to bed and Kate was still sitting in a chair in the kitchen with her toes tucked up nice and warm. I then lay down on the living-room sofa, still clad in my fur coat, for it was very cold and the frost was white on the grass and the roofs as we came in. We slept a bit and about 5.30, after ten hours, the sound of planes ceased and the guns fell silent, so at 5.45 we stumbled upstairs and tumbled into bed.

Poor, poor Coventry! The attack is described on the wireless as 'a vicious attack against an open town comparable to one of the worst raids on London, and the damage very considerable'. The casualties are in the neighbourhood of a thousand, and the beautiful fourteenth-century cathedral is destroyed. I feel numb with the pain of it all. We hear from here and there of this and that place demolished, damaged or burnt. The Curtises say their Works is burnt down and we hear of fires spreading because of the lack of water, as the water main is damaged. One cannot judge the reports as there is no telephonic communication with Leamington, Coventry and several places round. Often reports are grossly exaggerated and one dare not accept them.

But Coventry must look a sorry mess, and the loss of life and the injuries make one's heart ache. No-one was allowed to go into Coventry today and Leamington was full of those people who could not go into their work, and so were either walking about or shopping instead.

After blackout a woman called to ask if I could give a few nights' rest and shelter to a Coventry couple who were worn and tired, so I said 'Yes' at once, but she did not want the room tonight. Later, finding Mrs Gorton had nine people in her house, I offered to have two of them tonight, and before we could tidy the room she had brought them along. Their one idea was bed, and after a little chat we left them to go to bed and we had our dinner. Afterwards I went over to the Institute billiard-room and found many people sitting on hard chairs, babies and children rolled in rugs lying head to head on the billiard table, and a few young men playing darts—a pathetic crowd. My deckchair and rug was soon snapped up, and the husband of the woman who took it was delighted to have a pack of cards, too. Tomorrow we must see what we can do to make them a bit less uncomfortable, but it is too dark to go into the hut to look out things tonight.

We slept last night—in our clothes albeit—and except for being wakened by a loud burst of something, either bomb or gunfire, nothing further occurred. No newspapers for two days—we are cut off from Coventry by rail, and policemen stop your car at different points leading to the dear old city and inquire what your business is. Only people with genuine business can go into it apparently, and yesterday people who thought of going in, to works that were no longer there, were prevented by police. Fires are still burning and the difficulties of getting water are great. The main from Birmingham has been damaged and the other supply ran dry.

Alderman Moseley, Mayor of Coventry, living in a small house in one of Coventry's lesser streets, had a distinguished visitor. His wife heard a knock and, as the bombing had upset the front door and it could not be opened, she called out: 'Come round to the back!' The visitor came round. It was the King, who is going round bombed places!

The crowd who filled the Institute last night trailed off this morning in threes and fours, rather wearily. Our two guests left about 8 a.m. and Florence and I tidied up the bedroom and re-made the beds for the two others (Mr and Mrs Cope) who were coming this evening. Then we took Twink down to the grocer's and everyone we met talked of the bombing of Coventry. This afternoon we took laundry to Fillongley, calling at the Council Schools in which a room was being prepared for 150 people who were supposed to be trekking from Coventry. I took two deckchairs, a long cushion, rug and trays for their use, only to find that a Ministry of Health official had just arrived to say no-one would be coming today. People did not want to come to the extent they had provided for them. Evacuation of children over again! English folk cling to their homes. Those who are bombed out are the ones who *have* to leave. Others who are frightened (as they have every cause to be) go to friends or find their own lodgings, but those who still have their houses seem to feel they *must* stay in them.

So we came home just before dark and soon Mr and Mrs Cope came along and we put them in Alan's bedroom, with the biggest and best radiator and an armchair and deckchair, so that they could have a bedsitting-room. We had occasional sirens sounding the alert and the 'Raiders Passed' at intervals, but scarcely heard a plane and slept soundly.

Monday 18th November

These are dark mornings and we woke to find it raining again. Our visitors left before we were up and during the morning we again put the room ready for the next consignment, this time the Goss family, and soon they were settled in. Afterwards we took 'Bert' to Kenilworth. We tried the cake shop, but it was entirely cleared out of both bread and cakes. The greengrocer's opposite had some bananas, no oranges and excellent carrots at 3d. a pound, so I filled my basket with these two things and got a few tomatoes at 2s. 0d. a pound! The latter are *not* worth the money.

We called at the Council Schools, where a hundred or so people had poured in from Coventry. Poor wretched-looking things, unwashed and hungry, many with their homes bombed, some entirely demolished, and glad of a night's shelter. A pathetic company indeed. Later, feeling I ought to do more than look on and pity them, I went again to see if I could do anything and arranged to go at 10 a.m. tomorrow.

Tuesday 19th November
A burst of bombs woke me in the night, but I soon slept again, waking up about a quarter to eight, and managed to skim through my bath in time to hear the 8 a.m. news. Once more I write this in an air raid shelter. It is nearly midnight and we have been in our new shelter since 8.15 p.m. Planes came over just after siren sound at 7.30 and so we left our nice fire and soon were all seated round. The little boy staying with us was brought down wrapped in a blanket. The little girl was soon put on the floor on a waterproof rug on our garden seat cushion and immediately fell asleep. Then we brought down a Lilo bed and put the little boy next to her and they both look *very* comfortable. The shelter is barely finished, but just enough for us to sit in. The barrage has been terrific and dozens of planes have zoomed and grunted over. We do wonder what has happened—it sounded at first even worse than Thursday's raid on Coventry.

Wednesday 20th November
We finally got into bed at 4.30 a.m., having gone up earlier and found the planes coming again and the gunfire beginning once more. This morning I went to the schools to pick up passengers to take to fresh billets—it is necessary to clear the school as soon as possible, as we want the crowd dispersed and the children getting their daily discipline, instead of roaming the roads. Nearly all have been billeted, or are going back to Coventry, even if they have only part of a home. One woman, Eton-cropped and green-trousered, was determined to go back to the one room that was left of her house. She had a pram, a little girl who also had her doll's

pram, and a piano-accordion! The girl with her had a tin case painted scarlet, and the whole outfit looked like music-hall artistes. They walked away, but many others had to be carried to their new homes in the half-dozen cars that were waiting. The women had mostly washed their faces and combed their hair, but the old people looked as if an infirmary would have suited them better than billets.

Presently my party came along—a woman and two children, and then two more boys, all eating sandwiches!—and we set off to Bickenhill, a few miles distant. I had instructions to take them to the First Aid Point, but the baker of whom I asked the way said it had a time bomb there, dropped last night. I went on and soon a policeman stopped me, told me to get away at once and directed me to the other side of the village—scarcely a village, a mere hamlet. There was a lovely old church and farm close together, and beyond them the vicarage, which was the First Aid Point which harboured the time bomb.

I met the billeting officer along the road, picked her up and drove to the farm, where a kindly soul clad in a tin hat received us. They were a little upset there because everything was all arranged for their visitors—the stage set, so to speak—and then it could not be used. However she soon took them off and we all waved goodbye to each other, myself having enjoyed the warmheartedness of the lady in the unbecoming tin lid! And so back to the schools to find no more transport was needed. But oh the filth, which the energetic teachers were clearing up! They were all wonderful and getting on with the job in an amazing fashion.

Thursday 21st November

Florence and I went to Leamington as soon as we heard the 'All Clear' after a short alert at 10 a.m. We did our shopping as quickly as we could, but even then did not leave until after 1 p.m. Little news has come through about Coventry and we still do not know very much. A mass funeral of some of the victims of the air raid has taken place today. The Coventry paper is full of advertisements telling people where to go now that their shops have disappeared. They say: 'Accounts may be paid at . . .' and give a private address. One which has all its windows out says: 'Shopping will be chilly, but you will receive a warm welcome.' Already talk of re-building the city is in the air.

Saturday 25th November

It was a very bad night, with bursts of gunfire at intervals and the grunt of German planes until 5.30 a.m., when we slipped off to sleep. All woke up at 6 a.m. and went to bed. What a long night it seemed, and how one wondered what poor Birmingham was suffering.

This afternoon a letter arrived from the War Office confirming a telegram saying that Alan was in hospital with a wound in the right knee. The new bunks and mattresses for the shelter also arrived, and we are going to try them out tonight.

Tuesday 26th November

Once more a quiet night, awaking to a dark morning. No Florence, though—she returned to London yesterday. I saw her off, in the morning blackout, and was very sorry to say goodbye to a good companion.

One still feels the pain of Coventry's raid. I cannot really imagine what it looks like there, nor do I want to see it, but the loss of life must be much greater than at first thought. One hears of streets that have no whole house in them. This does not mean that all the people living there perished. Some would be in shelters and some out in their own, if they had them. Across at the Institute dozens of people come night after night, bringing their supper and their mattresses, hoping for peace and quiet, though some of them still have their homes—or part of them.

Monday 2nd December

After a peaceful night my mind was set on gardening and I planted a new lilac in the border next to the orchard and did the front of the bed, while Batchelor forked the back. Some bulbs were put in, old plants dug out and carted away and some divided and re-planted. The soil was just right for turning over today. The gate opened about a quarter to four and, looking up, I saw Mr and Mrs Whitaker. I went down to meet them and Mr Whitaker said: 'We have got some bad news—Peter's ship is missing.' He showed me the letter from Alfred Holts (Blue Funnel Line) which said that the ship was overdue at the port and must be presumed lost.

We feel very sorry indeed, but hope the Whitakers will not give up hope that he is still alive, though they did not sound very hopeful, even when bearing up bravely. They have to go through the suspense and anxiety that we have had for many months.

Southampton was raided severely last night. The 9 p.m. news says 'the casualties were not as heavy as might have been expected, considering the scale of the attack'.

Monday 9th December

It is so dreadfully dark in the mornings that it seems hopeless to get up early and barge about unable to see to do anything properly. However we soon had breakfast and began to move furniture about and get Alan's room ready for our new guests, Mr and Mrs Dickenson. It seemed to take the whole morning, and then immediately lunch was finished I had to be at the Institute opposite for an entertainment meeting for the W.I. Christmas Party. Then I took 'Bert' to the Wesleyan Chapel(!) where a dozen or so people were packing parcels for the local soldiers. Home again by 4.30 p.m. and Twink looked disconsolate and pressed the matter of a walk very strongly, so that we just had to go down the lane before blackout.

London had a very heavy raid last night after a free day and night from raiders. The Greeks continued their push yesterday and are rejoicing over their successes, with bells ringing and flags flying in Athens. Generals and admirals in Italy are falling out like ninepins. In Libya we are attacking on a wide front—real action has begun there, and we have captured 500 Italians.

Tuesday 10th December

A quiet night all over England last night, and how very thankful we are. But Mrs Whitaker has had official news that Peter went down with his ship on 11th November in the Indian Ocean. How sad we all felt! I felt choked, for I had not really thought that Peter was lost. Somehow there was the hope that he was a prisoner of war—and, anyway, one who was so alive as Peter *couldn't* be dead. Even now it is difficult to believe—only that the news has come to the Whitakers through survivors from the ship. Oh, dear, it just turns one over. Their only one—and so very precious. It is indeed hard for them, and for Margaret, the girl to whom he was engaged a few months ago. We feel we must go and see the Whitakers tomorrow.

'Bert' is sold to Harry Spencer and went today.

Thursday 12th December

After lunch I went to visit the schools, as a good schoolmanager should. I signed the registers and went to the classrooms. This interests me much more now that I begin to know the teachers better, and a very nice crowd they are! After the Coventry people had used the school in the great emergency, the staff worked very hard to get the place clear and fit for the children they are so fond of, and for whom they love to work.

Tea then and a little rest, blackout and news—and very good news, too. There are now 20,000 Italian prisoners taken in Africa and we are carrying on the encircling movement and mopping up the pockets as we go. It is now 9.45 p.m. and the alert sounded just as we sat down to supper. We got through it as swiftly as we could and here we are in the Bunkhole with guests, Kate and Twink, while planes go over and guns bang.

Friday 13th December

At midnight we said goodnight to our guests, as we were all very tired, and got undressed and went to sleep in the Bunkhole. Planes still went backwards and forwards and guns said things at intervals, but we slept snug and warm. The morning was dark, frosty and very cold. At 10 a.m. I went for a few hours' shopping in Leamington—such as it was. There was only one kind of sweet on sale at the sweet counter, at 4s. a pound. The counters, usually so attractive, were empty—and although the cardboard box and carton make a brave show, they are dummies! There are apples—at a price! Cox's Orange are 1s. 3d. a pound, Blenheims 11d. and 1s. and brazil nuts 1s. 3d. Biscuits are almost nil.

I bought under-woolies at the old price—without purchase tax—and each garment would have had 4s. 0d. added if it had been ordered from the manufacturers now. My fur coat, bought last year at £37, would be worth £90 today, the buyer told me. So I am very, very lucky and grateful for my good clothes.

VOLUME 5

December 1940 – March 1941

Sunday 15th December

It is typical of this period of the war that I should be sitting in the air raid shelter with our two evacuees while German aircraft go over at intervals and guns bang and putter-putter-put and boo-oo-oom according to their size and kind. In the darkness this Sunday morning I roused myself with great effort and soon was out starting the car. As I drove down the road to Lavender Hill the full moon was setting on my left while the sun was rising on my right, as much as to say 'It is my turn now'. It was darkish in church, with only the altar candles lighted, and one could not have seen a book at first. But in ten minutes Hitchcock, the verger, switched on the lights, probably five minutes before time, and all was bright. Mr Whitaker took the service much as usual, except for two pauses—one in speaking of 'the fallen' and a similar phrase elsewhere. One does feel so sad when one thinks of dear Peter. One feels the loss of him in church, where he was always seen when he was on leave and where he read the lessons so often.

Wednesday 18th December

Just after supper there was a telephone call from London. I have given up expecting news of Alan lately, so was really surprised when I found it was Peggy with good news of him. Colin had been trying all day to get us on the 'phone, but had not managed it. She said Alan's address is Oflag 9A, Germany, that he went there on 7th December and that his wound is healed. That was simply grand and we are so grateful to Colin. So now we can write to the dear, and it wasn't long before I was doing so.

The Greeks are still getting on and our African successes are enlarged upon. Talk of invasion again. This time the 23rd is the date specified—next Monday.

Sunday 22nd December

After a night in the Bunkhole, where we three slept soundly, I got up in time for church at 8.45. It is a real business getting up these extra dark mornings (British Summer Time is continued throughout the winter now) and there was no light in the church as I passed along the churchyard. But by the time I had shut the 700-year-old door behind me and walked up the nave to the third seat on the right, which I always choose, Hitchcock, the 82-year-old verger, was lighting the tall altar candles. 'Send out Thy light and Thy truth to lead the nations to peace' and 'Let Thy light illumine all', I thought. No-one could have seen a book if they had needed one and I expected any moment that the electric light would be switched on, as blackout was ended. But I learnt later that electricity was 'off'. It was certainly strange to see Mr Whitaker reading the Gospel by the light of a torch, which waved backwards and forwards across the page.

The 11 a.m. Sunday service was rather poorly attended, but nevertheless it was worship and, few as we were, we did our best with psalm and hymn and prayer. I thought of Coventry Cathedral in the day of Walter Hoyle, the organist. It was a wonderful organ and under his clever fingers it sang, shivered, thundered and wept, spoke and rang out triumphantly, all its music stirring the deepest and innermost feelings of one's heart And now he has gone, and the organ, too.

Monday 23rd December

Another good sleep in the Bunkhole, waking for a cup of tea at 7.30. We got off to Leamington about 10.30 a.m. and at 1 p.m., at Haseley, picked up a woman and two little pixie-like children in green overall garments, complete with pixie hoods. They were glad of a lift as buses are late and crowded. We took Alan's tunic to be mended at Brett's and gave them the news of him, got to the Stores about 12.30 and made a bee-line for the restaurant while Jack put the car away. Many Poles and Czechs are in the town and Jack met one in the ironmonger's who asked him what a piece of piping was called. Jack told him and they talked awhile, the foreigner speaking very good English and seeming a thoroughly nice man. We called on Elizabeth on the way through Kenilworth, and I took a holly wreath to my parents' grave.

Wednesday 25th December, Christmas Day

In the dark and cold of this morning I went to the service at 9 a.m., picking up two M.U. members from nearby cottages and taking them down to Berkswell. The church was brilliantly lit by the time we arrived and, though there was little decoration, a lovely variegated holly cross hung on the pulpit and the white altar flowers shone in the light of the candles. It was after ten when I got home to breakfast, and then I was busy the whole morning doing the daily round and preparing for our guests. Ethel and Harry Spencer came first, leaving Paddy, the black spaniel, in the Austin BUE 966, which once was ours. Then John and Peggy arrived and before long we were eating a very good turkey and accompanying sausages (instead of the usual ham) and filling in corners with celery and home-grown potatoes, bread sauce and gravy. There were twin plum puddings and mince pies, which Ethel brought, and then some little glasses of trifley peaches.

We all paid proper attention to everything—even the dessert— and it is marvellous to think of such a feast in these war days. The puddings, be it said, were last year's, as was a box of crystallized fruit. However, as this last was untouched, it may keep till next year. 'Next year'—one wonders! After lunch we talked and had the wireless, listened to our beloved King's speech to the Commonwealth of Nations—how bravely he overcomes the difficulties of public speaking—and then teatime came and our guests left soon after.

The great joy of the day is the telegram which came with the day's post. It came via the British Legion and said Alan is well, but had not heard from us since 13th May. We wired to the British Legion, Geneva: 'Please inform Lieut. A. J. Milburn, Oflag 1XA, No. 3604, glad to hear he is well, all well at home. Have written. Hoping to hear from him soon. Milburn.'

Evidently Alan soon began to think about getting in touch with us when he got to a prison camp, and that makes us feel he has really recovered and that his spirits are good. We do thank God this is so. A happy Christmas Day indeed!

Friday 27th December

The mornings seem darker than ever! We did not wake until 8 a.m., but it did not matter very much today. At 11 a.m. we both went off to Leamington via Warwick, where we picked up Alan's neatly mended tunic at the tailor's. Brett's window was untidy, with hat stands fallen over and field-service caps lying upside down. This disturbed me and I very nearly walked in and set them straight, which would really have been impertinence on my part. Shopping is rather troublesome as Leamington has 10,000 Coventry evacuees and, of course, supplies are soon used up. No razor blades, no shaving soap today and much less choice of most things, but thank God enough of the essentials. Fish is very dear. A smallish—or perhaps I should say a medium-sized—haddock (dried) costs 3s. 3d. and plaice was 3s. a pound.

This morning's post brought a letter from the Red Cross, from Lady Ampthill, and gives Alan's prison camp address as Stalag 1XB, so I had to write after lunch and point this out to her ladyship. I feel that Oflag 1XA must be correct, from the telegram which reached us on Christmas Day and which evidently came through Alan himself.

Monday 30th December

Alas, the first thing we heard in the morning was of a heavy raid on London. The City received the worst of its fire-raising raids and great fires were started all around St Paul's. Six churches have been destroyed and the Guildhall gutted. A few incendiaries fell on St Paul's, but they were quickly put out. It was a short attack, but serious damage was done. This morning I heard from Miss Brown (whom I felt sure was lost, either by enemy action or illness) and she says: 'One no longer weeps, but one just goes steely.'

The wickedness of this enemy is beyond words and tears. One hopes that they will lose all they possess and be made vassals of the other nations—not vindictively, but with a cold, hard feeling such as one feels for the destroyers of human life and sacred, holy things.

Mr Roosevelt's 'fireside talk' to the American people is most favourable to us and it looks as if America has at last woken up to the great need of this country for her whole-hearted help to shorten the war and keep the enemy from her own shores.

Lady Ampthill replies to my letter, saying we may take it that the correct address for Alan is Oflag 1XA.

Tuesday 31st December

The air raid on London has hit many of our oldest treasures in architecture—Johnson's house, Trinity House, St Bride's, the Guildhall, among others.

Lord Woolton asks us to 'go carefully with the tin opener' and to keep our tinned food as iron rations. Potatoes and oatmeal are plentiful, but we must eat less. Cheese he does not wish to ration, though he asks us to leave it for miners and vegetarians and those who need it to help them to do their daily work. Morrison, speaking of the fire-raising raid on London, says more 'spotters' are needed and employers of factories must see that their factories and premises are watched night by night. Householders must also arrange to look after the incendiaries falling in their streets, and so defeat the enemy in this newest of endeavours to destroy and terrify.

Wednesday 1st January

The new year dawns with hope and we look forward to progress towards peace. Alan's horoscope came today. It sounds very nice, but I do not know very much about horoscopes—nor am I sceptical entirely. According to this, he will be home in the autumn. God send him, say I.

At 10 a.m. I went down to the service at Berkswell and was home again, refreshed and renewed, by 10.40. Twink was walked for the day and then I did little jobs for the Institute party and arranged a fancy dress for myself. I made myself into Old Mother Hubbard, with an old green skirt, a dark-figured blouse, a mob cap, white stockings and a new pair of quilted bedroom slippers. Quite a comfortable rig, though the blouse was chilly. The party began at 2.30 p.m. and there was a prize for the most amusing and the prettiest costumes, and I was very pleased to win the latter.

Saturday 4th January

We spent a quiet night in the Bunkhole, having had an alert before bedtime, and then—and then—*when the post came there was a letter in the familiar handwriting, the long-looked for letter from Alan*. Kate made an extraordinary noise as she found it among the other letters and Jack came hastening downstairs to see it, too. It was simply grand to read it, written from Malines 'Caserne Baron Michel', saying he was well, that there would be nothing of his wound but 'a few scars' when he came home. Then there was talk of a football match, a humorous concert, and of himself reading the lesson at the Sunday service—'a difficult one from Timothy, but I did not slip up!' Then another assurance that he was quite well, a message to Kate and 'take care of the Midget'. The beloved M.G.!

Monday 6th January

Last night there was no alert here and we had a peaceful night upstairs. I was distraught with indigestion and Jack had suffered during the day, but managed to sleep peacefully. And when at last I slept, it was good sleep. I woke to hear the five-minutes' wireless talk proceeding downstairs, which is just before the 8 a.m. news. Then I heard the words: 'Bardia has fallen'.

We hear that 68,000 prisoners have fallen into our hands. What a nuisance they will be to guard and keep and feed! Nevertheless, it is a great haul. The Australians first penetrated the defences round Bardia and then, it seems, while their guns faced the potential enemy, we caught them from the rear—very fine strategy, with the compelling element of surprise. One wonders how long they will go on, with an estimated third of the Libyan Army in our hands.

Tuesday 7th January
A peaceful night as far as raids went, but alas for the Master of the House—a cold and chill through the night and then a great upheaval in the early morning. Very poorly indeed, poor dear, so we rang up the doctor-man and kept him in bed all day on a very light diet.

The Italians now acknowledge the fall of Bardia, the British continue to thrust forward and around Tobruk, and the Greeks still nibble their way forward in Albania. The shipping losses due to enemy action are lower than for some weeks, but a Naval spokesman says this may be due to a resting period for well-known enemy submarine commanders or the weather—maybe!

Lord Woolton says the meat ration of 1s. 6d. may have to be cut down to 1s. 3d. Eggs are 3s. 3d. a dozen—threepence down on last week.

Saturday 11th January
We had a quiet night in our beds, but Portsmouth received the enemy's attention in a heavy raid. The fires were quickly dealt with, though, as usual, churches and cinemas were badly bombed. From Red Cross correspondence this morning I find I can send Alan two parcels of 10 lb weight—a 'uniform' parcel and a 'personal' parcel—so I am busy getting the things together. At Brett's today we bought a forage cap at a staggering price—nearly £2—with the Warwick's badge.

Tobruk is being heavily shelled, and Benghazi raided, too. The U.S.A. is giving us increased aid. Three nights running we have bombed Brest.

Sunday 12th January
No raiders here last night, but London suffered further damage—incendiaries, quickly followed by bombs. Poor London! We did not go to church this Sunday—my cold was still unpleasant and Jack not fit enough either—and I spent the morning packing

up Alan's 'uniform parcel', writing forms and labels and studying the instructions till at last it was done. I had a further struggle about the small parcel of halibut oil capsules and Horlick's tablets to send through the Red Cross and finally decided I must go to Leamington and get the Stores to pack the parcel tomorrow, as the instruction says 'sealed and sent direct from the chemist'.

Evelyn Spencer's eldest boy, John Cunningham, has been in the news lately. He has been awarded the D.F.C. and is apparently the first R.A.F. man to intercept and bring down a night bomber. He is known to his friends as 'Cats-eyes'. She must be a proud mother.

Tuesday 14th January

Jack was going to pick up a new battery for the car at the Rover Company, and so I went with him to Coventry. It was not long after reaching the outskirts of the city that we saw evidence of the raiders' visit, and as we drew nearer the damage became greater. We went along Trinity Street and saw the devastated Rex Cinema, bombed twice over, and the other buildings near with all the windows blown out and boarded up. The old stone Grammar School had lost its windows, too, and was pitted and blackened, and the Hospital seemed much more damaged than we expected, with its windows all out. St Mark's Church opposite had suffered a good deal. Most decidedly *not* indiscriminate bombing, but deliberate bombing of non-military objectives guaranteed, as the German brutes think, to cow and terrify the ordinary citizen into fright and subjection.

So we drove on, past houses looking dead and dull, with broken windows and boarded windows and no shining panes and dainty curtains to brighten dull streets. Inside the Rover office were temporary arrangements, awkward and uncomfortable for those working there, but borne with exemplary cheerfulness. 'No privacy in here now,' said the girl washing her hands in the cloakroom. The door hung all out of place and was being held nearly closed by a hunk of metal. The walls and basin were cracked, but a smiling dumpling of a woman came in and hung up a clean towel and the girl made the best of things.

When the car was finished we parked in Trinity Street and walked round the shell of the Public Library to the ruined Cathedral. Its beautiful tower remains, but it is sad to think it was burnt because of lack of water that dreadful night. The temporary doors were locked, but a loose stone or two had been erected and a board placed there showing where the King stood when he visited the Cathedral after the great raid. It is said that a permanent memorial of his visit will be made by a brass plate placed on the floor of the new Cathedral of the future. That is looking rather far ahead, but is a fine example of faith and hope.

Saturday 18th January

Snow was falling at 8.30 a.m., so shopping in Leamington had to be abandoned for today and, after work was done, one could settle down to letters, letters, letters. Outside the snow fell ceaselessly and the poor birds, with feathers fluffed out, looked on from shrub and tree. From time to time I opened the window and put out a crushed biscuit or any little scraps, and how gladly they were received and devoured by sparrows, blackbirds, chaffinches, hedge-sparrows, robins, tits and the greedy gobbling starlings, who swoop down in flocks as soon as any food is thrown out.

One scarcely expected enemy activity over England today, but there has been some—a bomb on London and some on the east coast. Last night's raid was on Swansea, from dark almost to dawn, they say. The fires were well fought and put out by the early hours of the morning. Today compulsory fire-watching in air raids was announced for men between 16 and 60.

Thursday 23rd January

A letter came from Jan Johnson, with a page from *Country Life* of 30th November, which shows Oflag 1XA, Alan's camp now. It is a dignified-looking mansion—a schloss, one supposes—perched on top of a hill. Healthy but chilly, methinks. All very interesting, and I hope I may be allowed to keep the page and put it in this book.

The fall of Tobruk was announced today and thousands of Italians have been captured, with 200 guns and masses of equipment, food and stores. Again we have raided Catania heavily.

A patch of rheumatism developed in my left hip today.

Wednesday 29th January

Making an effort, we got off to our Leamington shopping at 10.45. It was very cold and damp, and I hastened back to put on my fur coat before getting into the car. Everybody we met that we knew rejoiced with us when they heard that this morning we received *a second letter from Alan*. It was written on 25th November from Stalag 1XB, so now we know why Lady Ampthill gave us this address in December. Evidently he left there soon afterwards to go to Oflag 1XA. He said he'd had a poisoned knee 'like a balloon, and immovable in June and part of July, but now completely cured'. This is wonderful news. Also they had then plenty of food. It was quite a happy letter.

General Metaxas died today—a blow for Greece and the Allied cause as he had pulled his country together and had a great following.

Saturday 8th February

A Christmas card came from Alan this morning, with the words 'Greetings! Better late than never. Alan.' This was a cheering thing to start the day, and the temperature was very different from the recent bitter days.

At 3 p.m. we went off in 'Maria' with the laundry to Fillongley, picking up the clothes all white and clean (not like they come from the town laundry) and drove back through Coventry. At Radford and the Bishop Street end of the town there has been great devastation. In one place the gable of a little house sat pathetically on the top of the rubble which it had once adorned, while the bath hung lengthwise from a beam, apparently undamaged. Across the road half a house was demolished, while the windows immediately next to it were whole and sound. Nearer Coventry the front of a house had gone, but the furniture was left as it was—a desk heaved up on one side, a chair with a leg sticking up out of the rubble, a picture askew on the wall, and a sleek, well-fed cat prowling in the ruins.

Sunday 9th February

As I took Twink for his walk today, an enormous dark grey bomber went over me. I thought of Belcher's drawing of the last war and the old charlady in her bonnet gazing up at the aeroplane, like a dragon-fly in the sky, and saying: 'I shouldn't like one o' them things to settle on me.' I shouldn't like even an egg from *that* dragon-fly to fall within 500 yards!

Afterwards I wrote to Alan, putting in snapshots of ourselves and Twink. The 6 p.m. news was very Benghazian and satisfactory. Petain and Vichy and Admiral Darlan are much in the news. No-one knows what Petain is going to do in reply to Hitler's suggestions—they will next become demands, if they are not practically that now.

Genoa has been well and truly bombed by us, with our Fleet, at dawn today. The Prime Minister gave a truly Churchillian speech in a broadcast at 9 p.m., praising the leaders of our Forces in the East for victories in Africa and saying that the Decline and Fall of the Italian Empire would not take Gibbon so long to write!

Thursday 13th February

Off to Leamington today and, walking into Malin's shop, which was empty of customers, I asked: 'Any oranges?'

'What a thing to ask, madam, after seeing the notice on the door.'

'I didn't see a notice.'

'Well, Finch (the assistant), get Mrs Milburn half a dozen.' Then to me: 'We have just got a case in.'

When I went out, I looked at the notice on the door: 'No oranges, no bananas, no onions.'

Tonight, after an early supper, we both went to the lecture on gas at the Institute. A very able lady, Dr Crosthwaite, spoke very well indeed, and after an hour her Sealyham rose up, put its forepaws on a chair and then raised one appealingly as if to say: 'That's enough, Missie, please.' And so it was for all of us—such a deadly subject, so difficult to realize such horrors can happen.

Saturday 15th February

This is another of Hitler's 'invasion' dates, but up till 9 p.m. he has not arrived. This morning's sun was glorious and the temperature about 45°, with rather a thin wind. A good deal of rain had fallen during the night, but by afternoon I felt a bit of gardening could be done. Jack sprayed the fruit trees with a cleansing wash and I did another yard or two of pear tree border. On the news we heard that we have dropped parachutists in Italy to do a little job. Whatever we dropped them on Italy's toe to do, some of them must have done, for the railway system near Brindisi is out of action at the moment. A very nice surprise for our 'Wop' enemy!

For ourselves, we are longing for another word from Alan. A letter came today with 33s. 0d. from his colleagues in the drawing office to buy something to send him. This has touched me very deeply. I think it is extraordinarily kind of them.

Saturday 22nd February

At 11.10 last night the sirens sounded, so we came down to our bunks—only to get the 'R.P.' when we were just nodding off. But we stayed put and slept soundly till nearly eight. During the morning Jack and I went off to Fillongley to pick up the laundry, and called at the post office, which is also a general shop.

Having bought stamps, I asked if they had any lemons. They had not—nor grapefruit—so we cannot add either of these excellent fruits to the marmalade about to be made from the Sevilles we bought yesterday and the pre-war sugar we have saved for the purpose. On the counter were leeks at 4½d. each! When we got home we had 2s. 2d. worth of leeks out of the garden for a second vegetable—my own growing. A call at the Meriden shop yielded(!) a quarter of peppermints and some salad dressing—but no lemon. The Midland *Daily Telegraph* has printed extracts from Alan's letters I gave them and the photograph of him they asked for is in as well. It would tickle him!

Tuesday 4th March

After an alert last night we decided to sleep in the Bunkhole and eventually settled there about 11.45 p.m. Almost immediately the 'All Clear' sounded, but we stayed put as it was a bright night and it is better to have one's mind made up about this matter. The raid was on Cardiff and was not as severe as many others.

We have now broken off diplomatic relations with Bulgaria. I hope Turkey is strongly *for* us. We have had so many against us—one after another has fallen into the Axis clutches and each one makes the job a little longer in the doing, with more to straighten out at the end. Each day there is a little tightening up of one thing or another, a little less of this and that. The Forces are having their rations cut slightly—they were certainly very generous. There is a suggestion of another hour of summertime from May to August.

Monday 10th March

Jack moaned in the night and, as the noise grew louder, I said: 'What's the matter?' and he replied, firmly: 'Gas attack.'

'Where?' I asked. 'Here,' he replied. 'Don't be silly,' I said, firmly, and he woke up and said: 'Oh— sorry.' So we both were thoroughly wakened and could not settle down again for a long time. When we got up there had been a fall of snow, not very heavy, and half a snowstorm was still descending. But by 1 p.m. the sun was shining and the snow soon disappeared. The air was much warmer, though an east wind still persisted.

When darkness fell—or was it darkness, it was really moonlight—Coventry put up her smoke-screen and we smelt the oily stuff even inside the house. The Dickensons did not come out tonight, as he has to be away by 7 a.m. on a long journey tomorrow. So we listened to an Irish play for half an hour and could not understand it, so shut it off and did the jig-saw awhile. Every day or two we read the diary of a year ago, which we find very interesting. But it seems much longer ago than a year.

A letter came from Florence this morning with a lovely pullover for Alan. I wrote to her during the early evening.

Sunday 16th March

Roosevelt's speech is the great thing of the day: 'The British want ships—they shall have them. The British want planes—they shall have them. Food, arms and ammunition—they shall have them all.' That is the kind of good friend this nation needs now. Food is getting really short, though we are very far from starving, but there is now no choice and even the tinned things are getting scarcer.

Wednesday 19th March

An alert sounded about 9.45 last night, so we slept in the Bunkhole, myself rather heavily and finding the bed hard. The 'All Clear' blew cheerily before we had been there long and I wish we had gone to our proper beds, but once tucked in we don't get up again. I was dressing when Kate called out 'A letter!' and so, of course, I was soon at the door and quickly put my glasses on to read *a letter from Alan*—such an interesting one, too!

We have felt right on top today after receiving this and have read and considered it several times. It is grand to hear of them acting Shaw's play *Captain Brassbound's Conversion* and of Alan reading books and playing Bridge!

The news says there was a heavy raid on Hull. Many houses have been destroyed, but casualties are not unduly heavy. Casualties in Glasgow and Merseyside raids were 1,000 killed and 800 injured. In Africa our troops continue to advance. A few days ago women were told to report for service to their country. We need every bit of help, even if America is doing, or going to do, her utmost to be our armoury and our granary. However long the struggle, we will win with God's help.

VOLUME 6

March 1941 – August 1941

Thursday 20th March

London had a heavy raid last night, but we slept soundly in the Bunkhole, as the 'All Clear' sounded just as we were nodding off. This was the first day of the W.I. entertainment and we were busy getting the stage set for the evening. After an early meal I was across at the Institute by 6.30 p.m.

The tiny cloakroom, where the artistes dress, was made more comfortable by a piece of 'Burleigh' matting, and many were the sights to be seen during the evening! Two or three soldiers complicated matters by popping in and out at critical moments and were generally a nuisance to us—though one or two of the performers seemed attracted by the uniform. We had a good room full and an appreciative audience. Petty Officer Hazel, D.S.M., fresh—so to speak—from a visit to Buckingham Palace, was among the performers and, on being congratulated by Mrs Gorton before the audience, he said: 'Thank you very much,' pointed to his second Palestinian medal, and added: 'I got that for drinking as well!

Friday 21st March

This has been a very sad day for us. This war has now touched our family as well as ourselves. At lunchtime Jack was reading *The Times* and came across an unexpected obituary notice which was a great shock to us. It told of the death 'in hospital', due to enemy action, of Peggy—Colin's Peggy. We could scarcely credit it at first and could not understand the 'in hospital'. I tried to ring up Edith at Altrincham, but was told she had gone to London. Then I thought I would ring up Colin's house at Putney, but was told there would be at least three hours' delay. I left the call on till 5 p.m., but during the afternoon a telegram came saying 'Colin and

Peggy bombed. Colin in hospital. Peggy died later. Just going—Frank.' So Colin is injured too, and it must have been at their own home.

We do not know where to write or ring up as Frank and Edith cannot go to their own home because it is damaged and, anyway, has not been lived in for months. The young go and we old ones are left. They seem the ones so fitted to build a better world after this madness is over. Peggy, so capable and so sane, killed by this ruthless enemy. And what of Colin? If only we could hear more.

All the afternoon I worked in the garden, sowing seeds and digging—one just had to be *doing*. Then the evening came and I went across and did my part with the 'properties' for the entertainment and stood at the end as 'Britannia' with a very sad heart. But it is best to go on, with whatever is one's job at the moment.

Saturday 22nd March
One woke with a feeling of heaviness and the word 'Colin' on one's lips. All day long I have been hoping to hear something about him from somewhere, but nothing has been forthcoming. And so the day has worn away. The morning was spent clearing up after the two nights' entertainments. The furniture was brought back and polished and all the little oddments put away. The railway hut was straightened, the bits of carpet and matting wrapped up, and the cellophane and blue cloth which made the sky carefully rolled and labelled.

During the evening we learned by telephone that Colin had to have his foot amputated. This was a dreadful blow to me. He knows about Peggy and is getting on as well as can be hoped.

Tuesday 25th March
Jack and I went off to Coventry at 2.15 p.m., himself to go to the solicitor and myself to the service at Holy Trinity Church at 3 p.m. Being a little early, I walked down the Cathedral Churchyard to look at the ruined church and met Jack coming up. So we considered it a bit together and then read the wording on the old tombstone which said 'John Parkes, a man of mild disposition, a gladiator by profession, fought in 550 (or 850—the first figure is blurred) battles all over Europe'. I cannot remember it all, but some day must copy it out. I used often to read it on my way home from school as a little girl. Later, at Holy Trinity Church, I was one of the collectors, and remembered the other time when I walked up the nave on Father's arm and came back down with my

new-made husband, nearly 36 years ago.

Yugoslavia has signed the Axis pact—whatever it is. Certainly she has sold her soul.

Thursday 27th March

Great news today! Keren and Harar have fallen and Yugoslavia has imprisoned the two ministers who signed the Axis Pact. Prince Paul, the Regent, has fled the country and by a *coup d'état* King Peter has taken command after the revolution. He is seventeen and was educated in England mostly, leaving here hurriedly when his father was assassinated at Marseilles in 1934. A queer situation for Germany, who had great ceremony at the signing of the pact!

Friday 28th March

A joyous day because Edith was coming. I was up bright and early and got the daily jobs done, went into the village on my bicycle and did a bit of shopping. Edith arrived at 2.20 p.m. and right glad I was to see her. We had a chat about Colin and Peggy and it was good to hear Colin is cheerful. So to odd half-hours of talk with meals interspersed till it came to the 9 p.m. news. There was more about Yugoslavia and rejoicings in this country and America that King Peter and his army had made a definite stand.

Sunday 30th March

A quiet night and we went to 11 a.m. Sunday service and afterwards walked round the Rectory garden in the lovely sun. In the shade last night's sleet still lingered and out of the sun it was penetratingly cold. This afternoon we drove into Coventry to show Edith our poor blitzed town and then had tea with Harry and Ethel at 'Spinney Croft'.

Further news of the naval action in the Eastern Mediterranean is reported: two cruisers and three destroyers are sunk and a battleship damaged in the biggest naval action of the war. Two of our aircraft are missing. A. P. Herbert gave the postscript in tonight's broadcast news and spoke about the 'Top Wop'—Mussolini!

Monday 31st March

Up early, indeed to goodness! Edith was leaving by the 8.9 a.m. and so we were both up and down by 7.30 a.m. for breakfast. Of course we were at the station ten minutes too early, so sat a few moments in the car. By 8.15 a.m. I was home again and nearly ready for the other half of my brekker. The morning was fully occupied and in the afternoon the pear tree border was completed and a little stone path made at the south end.

Good news on the wireless, with more details of the great naval action. Yugoslavia is quietly determined and Germany is beginning to 'lose patience' with her and talking of 'atrocities' in the usual way. Our way of fighting is as humane as such things can be: Sir Andrew Cunningham, trying to pick up survivors after Italian ships had been sunk, was obliged to leave them as German aircraft came to bomb. So he wirelessed to the Italian command to give them the position. Some of the ships, when hit by our gunfire, swiftly disintegrated. 'Not a pleasant sight,' said Sir Andrew.

Sunday 6th April

A very cold morning and, indeed, a bitterly cold day. One simply could not get warm all day. Hitchcock, the verger, caused a little excitement by fainting at the 8.15 a.m. Sunday celebration and had to be carried out. But he was at the 11 a.m. service looking quite cheerful again and walking briskly up the nave to wait on the Rector as usual. After church we had to call at the sweep's and found he could come tomorrow. There was much letter-writing and packing parcels for me all afternoon and evening to try to get rid of the accumulation before spring-cleaning begins.

Germany declared war on Yugoslavia today, but began to fight a little before the declaration! Russia has signed a pact with Yugoslavia for five years, signifying friendship, but rather noncommital. The spring offensive has begun. Our troops are holding the Germans east of Benghazi.

Tuesday 8th April

The alert sounded this evening and almost directly there was a plane over and then gunfire.

As quickly as we could we undressed and went to our bunks. I slept a little, but enemy planes were over continuously for a time. Then there was a lull, during which I went up and looked towards Coventry from the bedroom window. The sky was red with the glow of the fires—poor Coventry again. After five or six hours the raid was over.

Wednesday 9th April

Not much sleep last night and our thoughts are all of our friends in Coventry. It was my intention to go to London to see Colin, but as one did not know the extent of the damage to Coventry, and as I had to go from there, it scarcely seemed worthwhile to try to go and be turned back by road blocks—which I now know would have been the case. We hear of great damage and probably a heavy casualty list. The Grammar School is gutted and much house property damaged. Courtauld's is no more. Nor the Daimler. I rang up Mrs Dickenson, found her phone in working order, and they are safe. But she says the damage is terrible and seems to think it a worse raid than the one in November. I asked them to come out tonight if they wished.

The hospital was very badly damaged, with some loss of life there, but we cannot hear very much and feel far away here, though it is only about six or seven miles from the city centre. Mr and Mrs Dickenson came out just after we had heard the alert—about 9.20 p.m.—and were getting ready for an early bunk night. Planes came over and there was a lot of gunfire, but we slept, and when I woke for a moment about 3 a.m. we heard the 'All Clear'.

The Germans are making great thrusts through Greece and Yugoslavia, as well as Bulgaria, and have reached Salonika. They are also progressing along the North African coasts from Benghazi and have reached Tobruk. This is very trying after all our efforts in gaining them.

Thursday 10th April

A bad night for Birmingham—and Berlin. Each has suffered terrific damage. In spite of gunfire we all slept fairly well in the Bunkhole—we were all tired, having worked hard all day and having had a sketchy night previously. During the afternoon Jack and I were busy in the garden, Jack altering the fence to keep Twink from slipping underneath and I raking and preparing for the seeds I sowed later.

The 9 p.m. news says President Roosevelt is establishing air bases in Greenland, our Army is concentrated east of Benghazi, the Germans claim they have taken 2,000 prisoners and have captured three generals. Greece, in evacuating Salonika, destroyed petrol tanks, warehouses, etc.,—and left little for the enemy when he occupied it.

Friday 11th April

Good Friday. At 9.30 p.m. last night came the alert and we were soon in the Bunkhole after a plane or two had roared over. Then followed very heavy gunfire at very frequent intervals. Once Jack went upstairs to look, but could see nothing. There seemed no time between the planes' arrival, as there was on 14th–15th November.

They were continuous. From time to time we heard a train puffing gently along and wondered why. We now hear that a gun can be mounted on the railway.

It was a dreadful night for Coventry, as well as for Birmingham. We do not know the extent of the damage or casualties, but both are very great. Christ Church is down and the hospital was hit for the third night in succession. Our electric light went out quite soon, probably about 11 p.m., but eventually, about 3 a.m., the 'All Clear' sounded and we all slept till nearly 8 a.m. We found the electric current on again, which was a blessing.

Lunch was early so that we could go to the 2 p.m. service. We had an early tea and took Twink for a run down the lane. Then, just as we got back, the postman brought *the right letter*. Dated a fortnight before the last one, received a month ago, it is very interesting, answers mine and gives us lots of news of the camp.

Saturday 12th April

A quiet night for us, but Bristol was heavily raided. Jack and I decided to go to Leamington this morning and saw Mr Seeley, head teacher at the Council Schools and part-time policeman, on duty at the island. He was stopping people going Coventry-wards, for once again Coventry is burying her dead and clearing her streets. In Leamington—very crowded—Jack got his hair cut and I had an hour at Olave Roy's, tidying up frocks, making minor alterations, etc. Then, after getting a very few things—our wants are so few—we went home by the Birmingham road. We picked up two airmen, Birmingham men anxious to get home as they had had no word of their people since the last raid. Everywhere the men ask for lifts, and one is only too glad to be of use.

Forty-two German night raiders have been lost over Britain during this month.

Sunday 13th April

Easter Day. Another quiet night, and early to bed allowed an early waking after a good sleep. The church was crowded for a splendid, earnest service, which everyone seemed to enter into deeply.

After tea Mrs Richards rang up and gave us some sad news of last Thursday's Coventry blitz. My old schoolfellow and dear friend Ethel Loveitt and her sister Janet were killed that night. They had gone out to be with an old lady in the next road during the raid. The house was hit and they were all killed, while their own home, where their elder sister Maud was left, was undamaged. This loss is a great blow, for we have been friends for 50 years, and Ethel was a true saint, working at the Cathedral Mission wholeheartedly and untiringly. How greatly she will be missed. A Memorial Service for her was held this evening in the Mission. I am glad they sang 'For all the Saints', for if anyone was a saint it was she, and she worked so hard, I like to think she will rest in the heavenly sense. God bless her and the work she has done.

Tuesday 15th April

Delayed-action bombs explode in Coventry from time to time—we think we have just heard one—and one exploded behind the Hippodrome on Saturday. Alas that an officer of the bomb-disposal squad and four men were killed. This is dreadfully dangerous work. They are known as the 'suicide squad'—vulgarly, I think.

Thurday 17th April

A quiet night for us, but a very heavy raid on London, 'the heaviest of the war', which began soon after dark with hundreds of planes. The damage and casualties are very heavy. We think of Colin at Roehampton when we read of the bombing of eight hospitals. It is easy to be 'grim', but not quite so easy to be 'gay', with these awful raids. Coventry had its second mass funeral today.

The British line in Greece is in contact with the enemy, who is making a heavy attack accompanied by all the horrors of modern warfare, mechanized and otherwise.

Friday 18th April

We went early to bed last night and slept well. By 10.15 a.m. we were off to Leamington and got our shopping done expeditiously. Spring-cleaning was going strong in the hall when we got back and, though there is still a bit to be done, most of the annual upset is finished.

The Allied line in Greece is being hard-pressed. Dive-bombing and every devilish method of warfare is employed, and the line is being flattened instead of being V-shaped, with the apex at Mount Olympus. The situation is quite grave. In North-East Africa we continue to make good, and at Sollum there is a lull in the German attack. We need all our wits about us now.

We made a heavy raid on Berlin last night. The Germans threaten to bomb Athens and Cairo. We shall then make systematic attacks on Rome, we tell them. Strict orders have been issued not to bomb Vatican City in this case, but it is known that an Italian squadron is being held ready to drop captured British bombs on the Vatican, and 'this characteristic trick' is exposed beforehand.

Monday 28th April

Florence sent a letter to us today: her flat has been bombed and her furniture gone. It was to have gone to Oswestry next week—such a pity! Colin rang up to say he would like to come on Friday for a night. News much the same: withdrawal from Greece continuing, assaults on Tobruk repulsed, the R.A.F. bombs enemy in Germany, Brest and elsewhere.

Thursday 1st May

Still a cold wind. Very little enemy activity last night and we now know that 48,000 men at least have been evacuated from Greece. It seems that about the middle of April Greece indicated that she would be unable to go on, and so we had to begin to retire then. We have lost the guns we placed there, but each man brought away his equipment. The Navy and Air Force have joined with the Army in making a successful evacuation. If only our Air Force was bigger!

A full morning getting ready for my visitor, who rang up to say he was spending one night with us and that a friend would motor him here and fetch him again on Saturday.

Just as we were getting ready for bed tonight planes went over, the alert sounded and we hastened to get downstairs. There did not appear to be more than one or two waves, apparently going to Merseyside, and after that we heard no more.

Tobruk has been heavily attacked and the enemy penetrated the outer defences.

Friday 2nd May

Colin came about 10.30 a.m. and we were soon sitting down together having a comfortable chat. Colin manages very well in getting about, and we have greatly enjoyed having him here today. We walked round the garden together into the sun. Blackout is not till 9 p.m. and soon we shall have another hour's daylight, when the time is altered again.

Saturday 3rd May

Up early and Colin was down to breakfast at 9 a.m., looking rested. His friend, who had also lost a leg, came early and chatted with me till Colin was ready. I was 'Jeeves' and packed up for him. He entered his name in the visitors' book as 'Colin—or most of him'!

Merseyside was raided last night. There are thrilling stories of the evacuation from Greece—marvellous doings of the Navy and heroic work of nurses and doctors. The endurance of them all was beyond praise.

Monday 5th May

This morning a letter came from the War Office Casualty Branch reporting that Alan had been transferred from Oflag 1XA to Stalag XXA—the camp where he was supposed to be last year. It gives a report from the camp doctor at Oflag 1XA saying: 'Lieutenant Milburn had a bullet lodged under the right knee which was extracted, leaving three wound scars. Good joint, no join, looks very well.'

It is a long time now since we had Alan's last letter and we thought he might have been moved. But I do hope he has received some parcels, and perhaps he will get all the letters I wrote last year. He feels very far away now, for Stalag XXA is in Poland, alas! Still, it is lovely to have been in touch with him and to have had replies to my letters. So now we must be patient again.

This afternoon I replied to the War Office letter and wrote to G. W. Lambert, my W.O. 'friend', to tell him about Alan.

Thursday 8th May

A letter came today from G. W. Lambert explaining that Stalag XXA is now an officers' camp, having been changed by the Germans in order to carry out a quite unjustified measure of 'reprisal'. He says the Germans complained that some of their officer prisoners of war in Canada had been put in a camp which did not conform to requirements, and retaliated by moving a number of British officers to Stalag XXA. He adds: 'At first the conditions there were far from satisfactory, but certain improvements have been carried out and I do not think you need now have any anxiety as to your son's health there. We do not regard the present position as satisfactory and the Government are trying to get the return of our officers to their original camps.'

We are longing to hear from Alan himself.

Friday 9th May

And this morning we heard—a letter and a card from Stalag XXA. He begins the letter with 'We are all in high spirits' and later says 'As

94

you will gather, we are quite happy here.' He gives a brief account of a rugger match, says he is continuing his German studies and then describes the games they have. I went to Coventry about 11 a.m., called on Harry Spencer and told him the Alan news, then went to the Constitutional Club in Priory Row, where the Midland *Daily Telegraph* offices are now, and gave the chief reporter a few details of Alan's letter in case it was interesting news. He said it certainly was.

Coventry looks much more shattered and is a sorry sight, but was full of shoppers—where they shopped I do not know—and people busy about their daily work among the few whole places and the ruins.

Sunday 11th May

I slept very soundly after being very tired—indeed we were both over-tired—but Jack and Kate heard alerts and bumps. There has been a very heavy raid on London and considerable damage done, with many casualties. Oh, dear, this is really terrible. And among the places damaged was 'a club'. I do hope it wasn't the R.A.C., where Colin was probably going yesterday. We brought down 33 planes, a record for our night fighters of 31, and two by A.A. fire. Other places were raided in a minor way. Westminster Abbey and the House of Commons have been hit, we hear, and the latter is reduced to ruins. Big Ben is scarred, but functions bravely.

Tuesday 13th May

All day I have been thinking of *Alan, for a missing letter, dated 17.4.41, arrived this morning.* It is the first from Stalag XXA and describes conditions in the camp, with its underground passages dimly lit, its small windows with no view and the country dull and flat. Most depressing it sounds. But the letter we received the other day says they are in high spirits, and in today's letter he says they are as good a crowd as one could be shut up with. So, since it must be borne, I am glad that this is so and that the food seems good and he had plenty to do.

The great news today is that Rudolf Hess, Hitler's runner-up, who was supposed to have gone out in an aeroplane and been killed, is now known to have landed by parachute in Scotland! A story of the film type it sounded, but apparently it is true. Someone of high standing who knows him has proved that he is the real Rudolf Hess and he is not mentally deranged, nor suffering from any disease, as the Germans put forth yesterday. His ankle was injured and he was seen by a crofter to be coming down by parachute in a lonely spot in Scotland. Truly dramatic!

Wednesday 14th May

A quiet night over England, except for a few bombs on the east and south-east coast. Rudolf Hess is in a secret hospital and is progressing (as if one cared) and having a hospital diet of chicken and rice. He is reading and listening to B.B.C. news. His arrival here, according to the B.B.C., is having a great effect on the Germans. America is asking the reason of his flight to Britain and thinks it shows dissension in the Nazi party. What we have to remember is that Hess is the second arch-villain and not a hero of any kind, in spite of his dramatic flight to Scotland.

Thursday 15th May

No further news of Hess that is authentic, except that he is supposed to have been hoping to land at the Marquess of Clydesdale's and to have brought peace proposals, but I think that idea is washed out now. An intelligence officer is keeping an eye—or two—on him and he is talking a bit. I think he knew a 'purge' was coming in Germany and he has come here to save his skin. Gross impertinence, considering his criminal record!

German planes are flying to Syria and we are going to attack the aerodromes as Germany takes them over, although Syria is (or is she now?) under French mandate. Petain has let us down, with Darlan as accomplice, and we are having no more of this shilly-shallying, but taking a firm hand with these Frenchmen who are not behaving as they should under Armistice terms.

The House of Commons, Westminster Abbey, Queen's Hall, the Criminal Courts are all badly damaged by the last raid on London. Irreparable damage also to other places—St Clement Dane, etc. I wrote to Colin and he replies that he came safely through. Little if any enemy activity over Britain last night. Many are the conjectures about Hess, with everyone offering their views by word of mouth and letter. But does anyone but Hess really know?

Sunday 18th May

Today is Alan's 27th birthday and I got a letter written to him during the morning. The news is that the Duke of Aosta has sent an emissary to the British H.Q. asking for surrender terms in North Africa. Lord Simon has denounced Hess as a 'gangster' and says the British people will remember this, and the Government certainly will when the time comes for a reckoning. Tobruk news is that further defences have been taken and prisoners captured. The R.A.F. during the last few days have attacked aerodromes in Syria.

The extraordinary noise we heard last Sunday as a plane came down less than a mile away is one I shall not forget. It was much too near to be pleasant and it came down in flames, I am told. The two loud explosions were not land-mines, but 1,000 lb H.E.s and they were dropped near the decoy fire and fell in open ground, causing comparatively mild damage to the cottages. All the inmates had been evacuated at five minutes' notice.

Thursday 22nd May

A quiet night, but I was wakened at 6 a.m. by a plane very low down. With the experience of the other night, when a plane went right over us and crashed in flames less than a mile away, I was quickly wide awake. And though nothing else came as close as that, there was tremendous air activity all around.

We now hear that a mock invasion took place last night, for Mrs Bradley came in this evening and told me she was driving a police car all night and finished at 7 a.m.

Saturday 24th May

The wireless news at 9 p.m. gave a sad piece of news: the *Hood*, operating in a naval action off Greenland, received a direct hit in the magazine and blew up, so that there can be few survivors of the complement of 1,300 men. The hit came from the *Bismarck*, but as yet we do not know full details. Heavy fighting goes on round Maleme in Crete, where the Germans hold an aerodrome. On the rest of the island the parachutists have been accounted for 'decisively'. Our cry to the Americans is: 'How Long?'

Sunday 25th May

Heavy showers continued at intervals since lunch-time and all the afternoon and early evening I wrote and wrote and wrote. Jack was out with the M.G., running the engine and giving it a bit of attention. I told Alan this, but said, though I wished he could hear it too, he could take comfort that no-one could go very far these days. Just now the time seems *very* long since we saw him and I am longing for another letter to hear something of him. The garden is enjoying the rain, the onions are growing well and the sets improving. All the plants I have put in look very flourishing, but I do so wish Twink would not help to water the shrubs. All the new little ones I have put in are suffering from his attention.

The Germans are simply pounding Greece, we gather, and those of our army who are there must be having a dreadful time. Life is very hard just now. The part of the fleet in Greenland where the *Hood* was sunk is endeavouring to bring the enemy to action.

Tuesday 27th May

The great news of the day is that we have sunk the *Bismarck*, one of the two new battleships which were the pride of Germany. A most determined hunt was kept up for the *Bismarck* by aircraft, aircraft-carriers and ships till at last she was brought to bay and finally, after damage to her steering gear, was eventually sunk. The *Ark Royal* had a hand in this, which is very satisfactory considering that the enemy has supposedly sunk it more than once. The battle for Crete continues fiercely. The Germans have a hold on Canea [Khadia] in their endeavour to get Suda Bay, which is the best harbour. They continue to land troops, though they have lost thousands of men and more aircraft than we could count at a time. Troop-carriers and small craft full of troops have been sunk. We have lost two cruisers and four destroyers, but there are many survivors from five of these. H.M.S. *Gloucester* sank not far from the mainland and, though no news is yet available of her, it is known that ample boats and rafts were there.

Wednesday 28th May

One more quiet night. The morning sped swiftly away and at the W.I. this afternoon we were glad to welcome evacuees, three of whom had been injured in air raids. One young woman, a native of Coventry, rode here on a bicycle with plaster cases on her legs! Her husband was killed in the raid on Coventry. He was on duty that night, but looked in for a moment to see how his wife was getting on in their shelter. When a direct hit was made there, he threw himself upon his wife and saved her life, but lost his own. Poor girl, she does not want to go back to the house again. It is too full of memories.

Rejoicings over the sinking of the *Bismarck* continue. It was a tremendous hunt and was not *very* far from home (for a battleship). It was a good thing our forces were powerful enough to overwhelm her. The fierce battle for Crete continues, with the enemy landing further airborne troops. And so to bed upstairs, hoping. . . .

Thursday 29th May

But we hoped in vain. At 2.30 a.m. we were wakened by the alert and soon went downstairs and tucked into our bunks. In about

20 minutes the 'All Clear' sounded (no-one ever calls it 'Raiders Passed', it seems) but we stayed there and eventually went to sleep till 7.30 this morning. By 10.30 I was out with the car and soon picked up my two hospital out-patients and we drove gently to Leamington.

Having parked them, I did a good morning's shopping and went to Olave Roy's as well. We got home at 1.15 p.m. but, alas, without Jack's tobacco, for the shops bear many notices: 'No tobacco or cigarettes', 'No sweets or chocolates', 'No saccharine', 'No onions or oranges'. But the one thing that does not fail is bread—and, one might add, *carrots*. Often we see 'No cakes', or else a long queue for them. Vinegar seems to abound in the shops at the moment, and sauces and all kinds of condiments—but not the wherewithal to eat them with.

Sunday 1st June

The great surprise of this Whit Sunday morning's news is that clothes are to be rationed. It had been a well-kept secret, and the rationing has begun! Of course one did not walk Twink today in silk stockings and best suit, and by the time I had changed it was near lunch-time. A piece of pork *and* a chicken! What a grand meal! Such a wee chicken though, and the pork was a surprise which our laundress, Hilda, had got for us on Friday.

It was not until supper was over that I gardened—and only because I felt I *must*—and put in the rest of the snaps after raking out the rest of the tulips in the dining-room bed. I kill all the wireworms, calling them first Hitler, then Goering, Goebbels, Ribbentrop and Himmler. One by one they are destroyed, having eaten the life out of some living thing, and so they pay the penalty.

Crete has been evacuated and 15,000 of our troops have come away. I wonder how many were there? Irak has signed an Armistice with us. What next, one wonders? Our poor men must have had a terrible time in Crete with airborne troops and dive-bombers in endless invasion.

Monday 2nd June

Last night we heard an occasional plane, but no alert sounded and we slept mostly. The onions were due for thinning and hoeing and, as the day was dull with an east wind, not too bad for gardening, I went about 11.15 a.m. and got the job done. Jack helped by cutting back the invading grass and edging next to the ditch, and later we put sticks to the sweet peas.

On the wireless we heard a recording of the evacuation from

Crete and of a bomber or two down by night and day. There is far too much said of what we do and what we are going to do. It seemed foolish to us to hear that a consignment of food had arrived at a British port from America—one thought 'Liverpool'—and of course that was an invitation to bomb Merseyside that night. There is far too much said on the wireless at times.

Saturday 14th June

A rather dull day, decidedly chilly for June. The sun broke through for an hour or two, but at 8 p.m. double summer-time it is grey and unpleasant. Nothing of flaming June about the weather we are having now. The crack in my thumb which recurs every winter is still with me and refuses to heal properly—such a nuisance.

Last night's raids were widespread with comparatively little damage and we brought seven raiders down. Our wonderful R.A.F. is giving the Ruhr a terrific bombing, doing considerable damage and losing in one night six of our planes. That sounds bad, but when one thinks of the works put out of action, the loss has to be borne. But one thinks also of the homes from where these men come and what it means to their families.

Wednesday 18th June

The Dickensons rang up today to know whether they could come along about 8 p.m., and we were very glad to see them. We sat out in Birch Corner, for the day has been terrifically hot. Then we took Twink down Needler's End. Bed was very welcome to our aching legs and we are both complaining of our hands. Mine are swollen and aching and clumsy and feel like two small hams! A message was broadcast to the French in Syria asking them to surrender so that Damascus need not be damaged by warfare. If not, the town would be subject to gunfire at 5.30 a.m. tomorrow. No reply has yet been received.

A letter from Alan today, after more than a month's pause. No parcels yet, alas! He gives us the order of his day, which is most interesting. It *is* good to hear from him!

Friday 20th June

Another letter, dated 24th April, from Alan! At last he has received two parcels and now has the good battledress made last year, pyjamas and underclothes, to say nothing of pullover, socks, etc. I am happy. He sounds well and is apparently taking life philosophically. It is great to feel in touch again. When we had looked at the summary of all the letters he had received (eight or nine) which I keep in a special record, we took eight photographs of ourselves so as to be able to send some to him later.

News is much the same. There is hard fighting against the Vichy troops in Syria and it is stiff work outside Damascus. Mr Roosevelt has had his say over the sinking of the American ship the *Robin Moore* by the Germans and says the Nazis must not be allowed to dominate the seas.

Sunday 22nd June

This time last year we were dreadfully worried and unhappy about Alan and, though one can't be really heart-happy till he is safe home again, at least he is as well and contented as one can expect in the circumstances. No early church for me this Sunday and very nearly cut out the 11 a.m. service, but managed to make the effort and greatly enjoyed it. The church was beautifully cool and airy.

The big news today is that Germany, after having her forces massed along the Russian frontier for weeks, began hostilities, with all her usual claptrap and protestations. So now Russia will get a bit of what she gave Finland—and perhaps a lot more. Mr Churchill broadcast tonight and said we must stand by Russia. I suppose we must, as she is now against the enemy of mankind. But I wish we need not when I think of her ways, which are not our ways. America is sending the goods, though it is time she came in properly. It is difficult to know what is keeping them 'shivering on the brink' fearing 'to launch away'.

Saturday 5th July

Before I went to sleep last night I heard a plane or two dashing round and thought 'Ours'. But later I was wakened by more of them, and then sirens sounded and we were soon up and in a few minutes were in our Bunkhole beds. We heard a few thuds and bumps and many planes over. There was some gunfire, too, but we thought they were going over to Merseyside. However this morning we hear bombs were dropped in Duggins Lane, Tile Hill, and that houses were damaged but no-one hurt. The raid (by the wireless news) was 'not extensive', but we do not yet know just where it was except vaguely 'the Midlands'.

This morning a letter came from Alan—a bright and cheerful one, too. He is 'looking forward to getting back to the Midget', and says: 'I am feeling extremely fit and finding plenty to do.' So that is splendid.

I took the car to get petrol this morning. The prospect of a smaller basic ration is rather depressing, but will have to be borne along with other things, remembering many bright and wonderful things that we still may do, and this with deep joy and thankfulness.

Monday 7th July

I spent most of the day in Leamington and it was extremely hot. Shopping was trying in the heat, but going to the hairdresser's was enjoyable. We got home about 4 p.m., and tea was unusually welcome. Everywhere is terribly dry and we are longing for rain. We have worked so hard in the garden and a lot of it is in vain, it seems. I am particularly vexed with the onions, which have onion fly badly, and my own seedlings are dying off one by one.

The Russians are fighting manfully and making great counter-attacks and beating off the Germans. Our bombers fly by day and night without any let-up and bombard Germany inland and on the coast, not forgetting Brest. Our air losses are greater than formerly now that we send large forces overseas to Germany, but the German losses are higher always than ours. The wireless tonight says that prisoners of war in Germany are to be moved from the 'reprisals' camps, so Alan is probably moved already.

Sunday 13th July

Though I woke at 7.15 a.m. after a peaceful night, I felt very disinclined to get up and bicycle to church, and sank down for another nap before Kate brought the Sunday cup of tea. Miss Evans, the M.U. Diocesan Secretary, rang up about 10.15 a.m. and gave me sad news of the Winser family: the second son, Freddie, who was in the R.A.F., was killed in action in the Middle East.

Thunder began to roll just after lunch, the rain came down heavily, thunder crashed and lightning flashed for an hour or more. The great heat continued till late in the evening, when the sky cleared and we had a cool, restful night.

The birds seemed quite oblivious of the thunder and lightning and a bedraggled thrush hopped up and down the lawn and two equally soaked starlings prodded and probed the grass without taking the slightest notice of the storm.

Monday 14th July

A pleasant night was enjoyed greatly and the morning broke bright and cool and fresh. There were letters from the War Office Casualty Branch advising us that it was likely Alan was now back again at Oflag 1XA.

After lunch we listened to a speech by Mr Churchill—nothing very exciting, though we had an amusing moment when he chuckled in a sinister, melodramatic, un-Premierlike way as he grew a bit bloodthirsty in his expectations of what we hoped to do to our enemy in the future!

Tuesday 15th July

St Swithin's Day—and there were several showers! *There was also a letter from Alan from Stalag XXA, dated 30th May*, when he was very well and said they were probably going to move again: 'Actually we have enjoyed our stay here'. He really is amusing and seems to enjoy whatever comes! I am getting his parcel together as I want it to go as soon as I get definite confirmation that he is at Oflag 1XA.

It is good to know that an armistice with Syria is signed and sealed, so that fighting is ended, but it cost us 1,500 men. We are now definitely allied to Russia. They are fighting well and giving the Germans hard work for their advance into Russia—not far yet.

Friday 18th July

In Leamington this morning we had a good deal to do and shopping takes a long time. People take their ration books to the shops and they have to have the coupons cancelled as well as being served with bits of this and that.

Red currants are 2s. 6d. a lb, cherries 4s. 6d., dessert gooseberries 3s. 6d. (and Mr Malins said to a customer: 'They're not worth it! Wouldn't pay it', as he emptied them from the basket to a punnet). Potatoes are very scarce, and when I asked if I could have two pounds, Mrs Malins said: 'Have three.' So I did. Life is certainly queer now, with coupons for clothes (margarine coupons at that) and very ordinary commodities like potatoes kept in the shops for regular customers only!

Russia seems to be keeping Germany from rushing along into her territory, though Germany is penetrating very slowly and there must be dreadful slaughter going on.

Sunday 20th July

And up for the 8.15 a.m. Sunday service, thanks be. *That man* was not there, so it was a peaceful service. Afterwards Kate went out with friends and Jack and I set to work to get the living-room ready to be distempered and painted tomorrow. Together we carted our 400 or so books into the dining-room, where we stacked them beneath the dressers. We carted furniture here and there and by bedtime had had quite enough laborious work. I managed to write to Alan after supper and also did a bit of tying up in pear tree border.

The V campaign (. . .—) was launched by Mr Churchill today. V for victory, the opening notes of Beethoven's V (fifth) symphony. Britain's Victory Campaign, orders given by 'Colonel Britton'.

Tuesday 22nd July

A good peaceful night for us, Jack in the Bunkhole while our bedroom is upset with window frames being painted, and I in the little spare room. I was late getting off to Berkswell, but I had Alan's parcel to re-pack and put in the gym shoes he asked for. Then there was the excitement of a *letter from him today, dated 19.6.41 and from Oflag 1XA*, as we expected.

Thursday 24th July

A quiet night for us, though night raids were more widespread than of late and Merseyside was visited. Our bombers sweep over France and Germany sometimes twice in a day, as well as at night. This is a dreadful war, but I do feel the enemy deserves this battering when we look at our poor towns and know what murders they have committed here.

It is different from a few months ago, when we were always having daylight alerts. At present there are very few, but in the last month or two our own bombers and fighters fly over continually—singly, in three, sixes and nines—often several times a day.

Nevertheless we still expect invasion, more especially if the Russians cannot hold out till the bad weather sets in. They have done very well so far, as on Sunday it will be five weeks since the Germans made war upon them and no spectacular advance into Russian territory has been made. It seems strange that 16 months ago we were aiding, or hoping to aid, the Finns against Russian aggression, and now we are giving help to Russia against Germany.

Indo-China and Thailand (formerly Siam) are now in the news. Japan wants to bomb the Burma Road and prevent supplies reaching China. The world is really war-mad. The U.S.A. is very quiet just now. The sensation caused by her landing troops in Iceland has subsided, as well as the news of the air base being constructed in Northern Ireland by them.

The workmen finished here yesterday and the paint is dry today, so we are beginning to tidy up and hope to get the living-room carpet down on Saturday morning. It will be nice to be straight again and have a sitting-room as well as a dining-room.

Saturday 26th July

We have had a great fight in the Mediterranean, protecting a large convoy from enemy air attack. In spite of continued attack, only one merchant ship was damaged, but all got to port safely. Malta suffered this attack in one of her harbours. E-boats were also part of the attacking force, and we sank 12 by R.A.F. and shore guns. Besides the merchant ship damaged, the *Fearless* (destroyer) was lost, but casualties were not heavy.

The attack was continued for four or five hours next day, during which one cruiser and one destroyer of ours suffered damage. We also lost three aircraft, but saved the crews. Nevertheless the convoy was safe and fresh troops and munitions of war, etc., were safely landed.

Wednesday 30th July

Russia and Poland have signed an agreement to show a united front to the common enemy: Germany. Diplomatic relations have been resumed and ambassadors will take up their duties afresh. As far as Polish territorial rights are concerned, it is a case of 'as you were' in August 1939, though the land is at the moment in German hands. It sounds a surprising agreement, considering the past quarrels of the Poles and Russians, and it is to be hoped it is a firm and lasting pact.

The freezing of Japanese assets by us and ours since their seizing of places in Indo-China has been copied by our friends in the U.S.A. No trading is to be done with Japan and it is hoped this will prevent her obtaining the supplies she would need for this new aggression.

Tuesday 5th August

At the Red Cross workroom today we finished off shirts, made lavender bags and began new work on blue dressing-gowns. The lavender bags are to be sold in America, and someone suggested putting the victory V on one corner. So they were stitched and embroidered and some of them filled. We also had a Victory raffle, for last week we suggested saving for an outing of some kind after the war—just for the workroom members. So I took two tablets of nice bath soap and we had a 3d. raffle which realized 3s. 6d.

Sunday 10th August

We had an extra hour in bed last night, as we put the clocks back to ordinary summer-time and went to church at 10 a.m. G.M.T. or 11 a.m. S.T., though it would have been 9 a.m. by double S.T. Later I had a good three minutes with Joyce on the telephone and settled my going to her for 9 days, which was perhaps a bit impertinent, but she was a dear, as usual, and sounded as if I should be welcome.

The Queen spoke to the women of America at 9 p.m. and we all listened to her broadcast. She was her very charming and womanly self. Later we heard Quentin Reynolds giving a plain talk to Hitler under his own, not his assumed, name. It is an ugly name, too—Schickelgrüber.

Thursday 14th August

A letter from Alan today, dated 14th July. He speaks of the heatwave at that time, of sunbathing, of a tiny pool and of a sports meeting: 'In spite of living inside barbed wire, you will gather that we are keeping pretty fit.' They took an eight-mile walk one day, which he greatly enjoyed.

By 2.15 p.m. today I was off to Coventry for a M.U. meeting and, after a few inquiries, reached St Francis' Church hut, beside the pitiful little bombed church. It is a tiny hut, built up from the Scouts' Hut with £30 sent from Lincolnshire by sympathizers when Coventry was bombed. The meeting was finished at 4 p.m. and I came away, looking very sadly at the little homes with their blank windows, damaged roofs and fences, and here and there a pathetic huddle of bricks where once had been a home. Poor, poor Coventry! It is all so much worse since the April raid.

Something impelled me to go up Grosvenor Road, where my dear Ethel Loveitt met her death in April. I saw the ruined house and thought I would call and see Maud Loveitt. But as I drew near the house I saw her talking at her gate to someone whom I did not know. As she did not notice me passing by, I drove on.

Great news on the wireless at 3 p.m. of a pact signed by President Roosevelt and Churchill somewhere on the high seas. It is called the 'Atlantic Charter'.

VOLUME 7

August 1941 – December 1941

Friday 22nd August

A day in bed with a very aching back, moaning and groaning. Colin's letter arriving today gave us a great surprise, though we certainly feel it is a good thing for him to be married again. The wedding is to be in October, and I hope by that time 'George'—as he calls his artificial leg—will be working satisfactorily with his master.

Saturday 23rd August

A letter from Alan today dated 28th July, so it has not taken quite as long as usual. He has had several of mine, the last dated 22nd June, with those from 1st June till then not yet delivered. I expect the change of address from Stalag XXA to Oflag 1XA/H has accounted for this. It is an especially personal and interesting letter and very welcome after a night of aches and pains. It was very difficult to get up this morning, and getting to the bathroom and back and washing made me feel very shaky. The doctor came at 1 p.m., just as my lunch tray came up. He soon ran over the details and prescribed bed and a change of medicine.

I then enjoyed writing to Alan—a day earlier than usual—and told him of Colin's news. It has been an exceptionally wet day and never ceased raining—at any rate till blackout, which is now at 8.45 p.m.

The magnitude of the losses of men and equipment in the Russo–German struggle is almost beyond belief. The Russians say they have lost over 5,000 tanks, but that the Germans have lost more than 7,000! It sounds incredible. There are pincer thrusts round Odessa, and in Leningrad the civil population is learning how to help defend the city.

Wednesday 27th August

Kate's 61st birthday! And if I look as fit and am as able as she is when my 61st comes, I shan't grumble! Breakfast in bed once more and then the infra-red rays for half an hour with a rest to follow, though I am much better today. Downstairs at 12.30 p.m., having made my own bed, dusted my room, cleaned two pairs of shoes and done a little washing!

Just after six I walked Twink to the doctor's to fetch my medicine. It was very windy and not pleasant walking, with dust and bits swirling up in spite of a heavy shower during the afternoon. It is soon time to blackout after supper now and I like an hour or more of darkness before going to bed.

Stubborn fighting goes on between Russians and Germans all along the Eastern Front. The Russians have penetrated well into Iran on a 120-mile front and we are not encountering a great deal of opposition, though there is *some* apparently.

Tuesday 2nd September

Off early to Leamington to get a bit of shopping done before going to the station. I found a corner seat, waved farewell to Jack and got out my book. It was a glorious day and hot, too. A nannie and two little girls filled up the carriage—the younger one, Joanna, very entertaining till, at the end of the journey, she grew tired and cross. No wonder, for it was a long, wearisome time.

Joyce was waiting at New Milton and we were soon in the Standard speeding away to 'Redscar'. Tea in the garden was very pleasant, and so was the evening spent together. I read Alan's letters to Joyce and we listened to the wireless news at 9 p.m. and the talk afterwards.

Sunday 7th September

Joyce got the Sunday dinner all prepared and then she and I went to church at 11 a.m. to join in the National Day of Prayer. We came out immediately after the blessing, before the choir and clergy, and so got down the narrow walk—which is a short cut to the church—before it was thronged with people. Then the duckling was put in the oven (this had caused us much merriment earlier when it was being stuffed!) and by 1.30 the feast was ready. It was a feast, too! In the afternoon we went for a glass of sherry with a friend of Joyce's who dashes in and out, hovers, telephones, chatters, at any hour of the day, and is certainly a live wire.

Monday 8th September

A siren in the night was soon followed by the 'All Clear'. Joyce and I went into the village this morning, and in the afternoon took our tea on to the marshes and, to our surprise, there were *no flies*. A long-legged spider was the only insect I saw all afternoon. We left the car near a gate and walked a quarter of a mile to a bank, where we spread rugs and had tea. Looking through binoculars to the Solent, grey ships moved to and fro or lay-to by Yarmouth pier. The Lymington–Yarmouth ferry was plying to and fro—a queer contraption somewhat like a Noah's Ark. And then, after sitting with warming sun tempered by a gentle cooling breeze on our backs for an hour or more, we packed up and came home. The colouring of the marshes was lovely and fresh. There was every kind of delicate colour on the one hand and rich, full shades of colour on the other as we walked back to the car.

Tuesday 9th September

This morning I packed up and Joyce and I set off in the car for New Milton, which I left at 11.40, and after an interesting journey arrived at Leamington at 4.50, a bit late. Jack and I then had tea at the Stores, and so to our precious home. Twink was very pleased to see Missie and whined a little song of welcome in between leaps and kisses.

The Germans are making a great bid for Leningrad and the Russians are stubbornly defending it.

Saturday 13th September

A good day! *A letter came from Alan.* He speaks of a walk through woods with grand views of rolling country, but 'nevertheless we shall be damn glad to see old England again'. Ending his letter, he wrote: 'We are all patient and keep smiling.' God bless the dear and keep him so till all this turmoil is over.

The doctor came to see Jack, gave him a thorough examination and said his arteries were those of a young man. He appeared to be quite sound, but had taken liberties with himself after a temperature of 102° last Sunday.

Tuesday 23rd September

Not too early at the workroom today, but soon we were turning our machine handles and wagging our tongues while making green dressing-gowns. I won the raffle—four delicious-looking pears. Jack had gone to Birmingham to settle about books to be sent to Alan, and so I went part way to meet him with Twink.

The Russians fight bravely and counter-attack fiercely, and the Germans lose thousands of men dead and wounded. All British tanks made this week are to go to Russia. People in the occupied countries are being treated very harshly by the Germans. Wholesale and outrageous shooting goes on day by day.

Saturday 4th October

Off to London today for Colin's wedding. A sleeping tablet last night gave me a good rest and I woke at 6.15 a.m. thoroughly refreshed. Jack wasn't too good, but rose manfully, and by 7.20 we were all ready for our journey. Having carried our gas masks for a year or more, we quite forgot them on this journey, discovering they were missing when we arrived at Coventry station—just the place we should have carried them. People had been known to be refused admission to a railway carriage in 1940 without gas masks.

At Euston a taxi was soon found and we drove to St George's, Hanover Square. It is a beautifully kept church and the sanctuary lamps—six or eight of them—and the huge chandelier brightly lit made the altar flowers stand out cheerfully in two yellow clusters in front of an old painting forming the reredos. Soon the family came along in twos and threes and then the bride, Rona, with her father. Colin rose up from somewhere in front and the bride gave him a smile as they met. She looked very sweet in a dove-grey princess dress (made by Norman Hartnell), quite plain except for long pipings of cerise—or a softer shade—round the neck and straight down the sleeves, with a hat of the same material and trimming on her dark-brown hair. Very charming indeed. She seems a very sweet girl and Colin is a lucky man. 'George' did his work well today and only a limp was apparent as Colin and Rona came down the nave. We then drove to Brook Street, where about 30 or 35 people were present for the drinking of champagne and to eat the delicious sandwiches and dainties provided. About 1 p.m. Colin and Rona left for Taunton and we all departed. We had tea in the train back.

Monday 6th October

A busy home morning after a long and good sleep. Clean covers were put on the living-room chairs and settee—a tough job—and then it seemed to be lunchtime.

Arrangements for the exchange of prisoners of war go on—the Germans are already waiting on the south coast—and a dramatic announcement was made on the wireless today. A broadcast from Germany was picked up: 'Hello England, Hello England, Hello

England', and a message in English which asked for the time of departure, number of sick and wounded, etc. We listened, very thrilled, and it is now hoped all will be well.

Tuesday 7th October

Alas for the wounded prisoners, the Germans are not playing the game, but want to make alterations and not keep to the international law. So negotiations are now over and the German prisoners are being moved back to their former hospitals, homes and camps. What a pity it is, and how sad for our men, but one felt suspicious of German arrangements.

Saturday 11th October

I woke early to the sound of pouring rain and, with the darkened sky, it was not a pleasant prospect. But at 8.30 a.m. the whole aspect was changed by a ring of the bell—the postman with *a letter from Alan*. A snapshot pinned to the letter shows him looking fit and determined or, as Jack says, 'quite pugnacious'. Edward Greenslade is on one side, Eric Snowdon on the other, and on either side of them two men of the R.A.F.

This snap was very welcome and was just what we had wanted for a long time. Alan says he has plenty of clothes to last for a bit and gives a short list of articles he would like to be sent in the parcels. Our hearts are at rest for a while now. We gather that the badly wounded were being sent to hospital and then hoped to go home. But alas, *we* know they have not come.

How many times today have we looked at Alan's photograph! I have the magnifying glass on my desk and look at it about once every hour!

I rang up Mrs Greenslade and told her that Edward's photograph was on the snap, and so now I must send it for her. She must be aching to see him, just as we were. She says her other son had a bad accident in the mock invasion last week, being thrown from a motor bicycle and suffering concussion, broken ribs, damaged leg, etc., and is in hospital at Newmarket.

The German thrust for Moscow continues and the wireless says no important change is indicated in spite of terribly fierce fighting on a 700-mile front.

It is very chilly indeed tonight.

Saturday 18th October

The equinoctial gales have been demonstrating their power, flinging a large branch of ash into the Bigg's garden, sweeping the rain down the windows, and through them in some places! Birch leaves and branches and twigs strew the front lawns, pine needles cover the drive beds and the whole place is thoroughly untidy though Batchelor swept it this morning.

No more news of Alan and we are longing to hear where he is. Meanwhile I go on scribbling my bi-weekly letters and addressing them to Oflag 1XA/H.

There is severe fighting on the whole of the Russian front except perhaps round Leningrad. The Russians resist fiercely and the slaughter is terrific.

Wednesday 29th October

I never remember such a cold wind in October. When we had gathered Alan's bits and pieces together for his parcel and been into the village in the car for a bit of shopping, Twink and I went out by the hedge gate. Goodness me, the wind was awful, and when I got into Jones's fields I just couldn't bear it and had to turn round and go into the lane and across to Bungalow fields instead. It was a tearing gale—one tried to lean against it, and surely one's clothes were made of paper!

When I weighed the things for the parcel I found it would not be possible to send the gumboots. I think he would prefer to have the little oddments and a space left for a bit of chocolate.

Friday 31st October

Cold today, though not with the strong wind we had a few days ago. Every newstime we hear of the Russians' 'stubborn', 'stiff' or 'tough' resistance to the enemy and Moscow is finely defended, though we hear of some progress in the south. Rostov still stands and attacks are fierce near the Crimea. The Red Cross is making a great effort for Russia and all money collected from the 'Penny-a-Week Fund' from now till Christmas is to go to the Russians.

De Gaulle broadcast a few days ago that Free Frenchmen everywhere would stand in silence for five minutes at 4 p.m. today as a token of their sympathy with hundreds of hostages already shot and those awaiting trial at Nantes for the killing of three or four German officers. German reprisals are fierce and out of all proportion—just savagery.

Friday 7th November

A dark early morning. We got off for our shopping in Leamington before 10.30, sat down to our lunch at 2 p.m. and then, with one thing and another, I was busy till 3.45, when we expected the Whitakers. We had a happy hour having tea and keeping warm in the living-room, for it was a cold day. They left at 5.45 as the Rector has to get the blackout done while it is still light. Heavy indoor shutters have to be put in place and there are plenty of large windows to darken.

We have been sorry to read in the local paper of the death of Mr Bealt, our teacher evacuee of 1939, a very kind and thoughtful man. He was only 32, I think. I remember that when he was asked to gather roses for the house he carefully 'de-thorned' them, and always now when I arrange roses I think of his kind, gentle ways.

Saturday 8th November
Rather raw and cold today and bicycling was chilly. The first collections for the Red Cross Penny-a-Week were made and people were very willing. They gave the 1s. 1d. for a quarter most willingly—only three were out and only one gave 4d. for a month. As usual, being matey, I learned a good deal about my neighbours. At one house I was told they had been there a bit less than a year. Their home in Coventry had been lost entirely and a son of 23 and a daughter of 15 killed. No wailing, though.

On the B.B.C. tonight we had a sound picture of the ground Air Force men getting the bombers ready, and tidying them up when they get back from raids. The Air Force has a lingo of its own: 'Get cracking', 'A good party' and plenty of 'Cheerio'. Last night our bombers went over Germany and though, as usual, they did a good job, they encountered unexpected and difficult weather, so that we lost 37 planes. This is an outside figure, as we never minimize our losses or keep back the truth. It was also a very big raiding party.

Stalin has made some clear, concise speeches on the occasion of the commemoration of the Revolution. Lord Beaverbrook has revealed that much aluminium and other commodities required by Russia have been sent. He calls for bigger and bigger output of war necessities.

Sunday 9th November
A raw, cold day for Remembrance Sunday. Church was full of Home Guards, British Legion, school children and 'casuals', so 'regulars' took the side aisle seats.

The wireless news reports a successful action in the Mediterranean in which two enemy convoys were sunk.

Monday 10th November

The post was late this morning, but about 11.30 a.m. I saw letters lying on the hall floor. When they were gathered up we found a letter from War Office Casualties in Liverpool saying that officers interned in Oflag 1XA/H have been transferred to Oflag VIB. So now we know. Now we want a letter from Alan very badly. From the map of prison camps in Germany we think that he is at Kassel.

Jack says the wireless news was thrilling, though we are sad at the loss of the *Cossack*, Captain Vian's ship, which scorned the *Altmark* and rescued our imprisoned men from below hatches with the words 'The Navy is here'. Rear-Admiral Vian will be sad to hear this. The Italians report that the convoy ships sank 'one by one' and that *two* destroyers were sunk and one damaged.

Mr Churchill made an excellent speech on the time-honoured Lord Mayor's Day luncheon—not in the ancient Guildhall, which has been laid in ruins by enemy bombs, but held elsewhere, after a procession of present-day honoured men and women of the Civil and other Services had marched through the City. He reviewed our progress through the past year, spoke of our fleets, now in strength, and our Air Force, equal to—if not greater—than the Luftwaffe. He spoke plainly to Japan, lauded America's Lend and Lease Act, gave a cheery word for Chiang-kai-shek and China, praised India and her works and gave us a heartened feeling, though he bid us bend our backs again to the task.

Friday 14th November

A year since the big raid on Coventry. I got up very early and by 9.20 had started for Leamington, for the permanent wave was due and it behoves one to be early at the hairdresser's. The deed was done by 12.45 and during shopping we talked to a nice woman in the Stores who was in charge of a stand showing what was sent in prisoner-of-war parcels, till she told us her own *only* son had been missing for nine months. He was in the R.A.F. and came down in the sea. I had to walk away to hide the tears—she was so splendidly brave. Back home, we gave ourselves a treat this rather mouldy day and opened a tin of cheerful yellow apricots for our tea. Very good indeed.

We have heard today the sad news of the loss of the *Ark Royal*, so many times previously reported by the enemy to be sunk. She was torpedoed in the Western Mediterranean and was taken in tow, but eventually had to be abandoned and it is thought the casualties are very light. There is a personnel of 1,575.

We also learn that 262 people were killed by air raids in October and 361 injured. Last October the casualty list was 6,335 killed and 8,690 injured.

Strikes in America are serious, but the Neutrality Act is now amended, passed by 212 votes to 194. One would like to have seen a bigger majority. Nevertheless, it is passed.

Saturday 15th November

An east wind today—very cold. But the sun came out and the day was dry and good. Good news at 1 p.m. saying about 16 or 18 are missing from the *Ark Royal* and may yet be found.

Later: Hurrah and hurrah! There is only *one* casualty on the *Ark Royal*, which is remarkable. One is sorry, though, for the relatives of that one.

Tuesday 18th November

Russia's winter has begun and the Germans are having a hard time. Some have been found frozen to death and some are clad in women's fur coats. On the whole the Russians are holding them and counter-attacking, though fierce fighting goes on all along the Eastern Front. The British forces are closing in on Gondar, the last Italian stronghold in Abyssinia. Japan is saucy and conciliative in turn, mostly the former.

Thursday 20th November

News at 8 a.m. of a British offensive in Cyrenaica, evidently long-planned and launched on the 18th at dawn. It has been a complete surprise to the enemy. This is welcome news now. God speed the 'push'!

We have just heard the 6 p.m. news and are told that adults are going to get two pints of milk *per week*. We have had two or three pints *per day*! Well, well, we shall see, I suppose. It won't be any use buying coffee if that is all we are going to have. Perhaps this evening we shall have our last milk pudding for the duration! Horrible thought!

Friday 21st November

We rejoiced to have *a letter from Alan*, dated 23rd September—nearly two months ago. It intimates a probable move to a camp with many more officers, but asks us to continue to write to Oflag 1XA till we get another address. Two small, clear snapshots were enclosed, showing a boxing match and a little view of Oflag 1XA. It is nice to get a letter, but the news is so old when it comes. The armies have met in Cyrenaica and many German tanks have been destroyed. The R.A.F. is bombing the enemy aerodromes and helping to make way for the Desert Army.

Monday 24th November

Silver cleaning on Monday mornings takes a long time, but I had finished just after 11.30 and then quickly changed to go in the Crowhurst car to the station to catch the 12.24 to Birmingham. Jack came too, which was very nice, and when we arrived about 1 p.m. we went straightway to the Queen's Hotel for lunch. It sounded *so* good. '*Hors-d'oeuvre*,' said the foreign waiter, and when it came it looked quite attractive, though it was mostly the same old potato, cabbage, carrot, parsnip and beetroot with a nice fat sardine. Good thick soup next and then fish—which was not a good choice for us as we ought to have had fish cakes at home this evening—followed by a chocolate mould. The first forkful or two were good, but it soon palled as it needed more sugar. This is a record of a 'five bob' war luncheon!

At 2.45 we took a taxi for me to have my first ionization treatment for hay fever—not painful, but certainly not pleasant.

Not much more news of Libya at 6 p.m. except that the battle still rages. Our air supremacy is maintained and the Germans are trying to get reinforcements across by glider and other aircraft.

Friday 5th December

Our shopping day. We got off without haste just after 10.30, deeply laden with oddments all over the car—gas masks, a fur coat and hat, a pair of shoes and three baskets, among other things. First to be attacked was the cake shop.

Then we took our separate ways for shopping till 12.30, when we met and went to the 'Little Kitchen' for lunch. M'yes, it was called meat in the pie, but . . . However we were fed and came out before 1.30 and began the shopping again. We actually got 5 lb of dessert apples—Mrs Malins treats me very kindly when she serves me at the greengrocer's—and we picked up fish and tinned goods at the Stores with our new 'Points' ration book. My special assistant did what he could with other things, like the single and precious box of matches and ½ lb of sweetened biscuits—things that were 'nothing accounted' in the old days.

Later the wireless gave us the good news that the Russians are still holding Taganrog and have gained villages in a counter-attack elsewhere. Around Moscow there has been a fall of snow which in England would be called heavy, but which is only 'the beginning' there. A corvette which dropped depth-charges on a U-boat (of the newest type) caused it to come to the surface, then closed in for action. The U-boat commander, careless of his men's lives, jumped on to the corvette and saved his own life. Later some of the men were picked up and are found to be a poorly-trained crew for such work. A new action has begun in Libya and hard fighting is continuing. Hungary, Romania and Finland have made no reply to the British note telling them to stop fighting or we must declare war on them.

Every day we hope for a letter from Alan from Oflag VIB, but the days go by. . . .

Saturday 6th December

A tight sleep last night, waking to a dark morning with a threat of rain and a blustering wind blowing. What's the good of *dusting* these dark mornings, I thought? However I flicked round and, with my mind on bulbs, soon got out into the garden and forked and bone-mealed the little bed below the rambler trellis as Jack cleaned the car.

Then I put in 100 pheasant eye and about the same number of daffodils, finishing each end of the bed with seedling forgetmenots. After lunch—delicious fish and a biscuit pudding—rain began and we were both rather glad we really couldn't go out and work again.

On the wireless tonight the new announcer 'Wilfred Pickles' (gorgeous name!) read excellently, though his accent is a combination of Lancashire, Yorkshire, Oxford and I know not what. We have had successes in Libya, the Russians are still chasing the Germans in and around Taganrog, and slight advances and terrific counter-attacks continue round about the Moscow defences.

At one minute past midnight we shall be at war with Finland, Hungary and Romania. It leaves us cold—will it make any difference? Perhaps not now, but at the end we hope they will all be on the wrong side.

Sunday 7th December

Mrs Varley rang up as she had heard from Philip and that he had seen Alan, who was very well. They were enjoying each other's company—that is, all the officers in Oflag VIB, nearly 3,000 of them.

We have just heard that the Japs have bombed islands held by the U.S.A., though no reply has so far been received from the

Emperor, to whom Mr Roosevelt had sent a last-minute appeal to keep his country from war with them.

Monday 8th December

The Japs have bombed many U.S.A. bases while still continuing talks with Mr Roosevelt and their representatives, M. Kurusu and Admiral Nomara, pretending they still wanted peace. In the meantime they collected their troops in Thailand and convoyed war material overseas. We hear tonight that 3,000 casualties are reported in an air raid over the Hawaian Islands. Air attacks seem to have been launched simultaneously on other American bases. Singapore has been bombed and two landings were made in Malaya, one near the Thailand border, but I think one was eventually frustrated. Every American base seems to have been surprised, as well they might be, for, if they had been dealing with a straightforward enemy, war would have been declared before an attack was made. But with these gangster nations one never knows. What a world! We feel very low tonight. I'm tired and the news is certainly not cheering.

The German panzer forces have divided in Libya and one is fleeing to the west.

Wednesday 10th December

I woke late and soon the news was pouring out. We heard President Roosevelt's 'Fireside Chat', and such a title seemed scarcely applicable, with such dire things to tell of—air raid casualties in the Philippines and Japanese landings here and there, and above all Japanese infamy and treachery in conducting 'talks' in a friendly manner while their troops were preparing to fight and sink and bomb the Americans. Then, at 1 p.m., came what Mr Churchill told the House was 'bad news'. The *Prince of Wales*, one of our newest battleships, and the *Repulse*, a battle cruiser, were sunk while carrying out operations with the enemy off Malaya. This was certainly terrible news and we know nothing of the casualties yet. There is fighting in Malaya, where the Japanese have made a landing. The Russians are the bright spot at the moment and continue on the offensive in many places.

I went down to the Rectory this afternoon for our Red Cross workroom party, and what a marvellous tea we had! Plate upon plate of lovely cakes, and we did our very best to enjoy them. Two men were present,—Mr Whitaker and 'Oo-dar', a little evacuee boy who used to say, when going into a blacked-out room, 'Oo-dar!' ('Oo-*dark*'), and the name has stuck.

Thursday 11th December

Over 2,000 men are saved from the *Prince of Wales* and the *Repulse*, but Admiral Tom Phillips is among the missing. There's no denying this is a great disaster and will take a bit of getting over. But nevertheless we shall get over it. We must. It is thought that Japan is quite formidable, with large stocks of oil and other necessities, and that her entry into the war will lengthen it considerably. The bright spot still is Russia, and the Germans are retreating in many places.

It seemed unnecessary for the B.B.C. to broadcast bits of Hitler's and Musso's speeches today, making our wounds ache still more, but the B.B.C. has some deplorable lapses.

The news tells of Japanese air raids in the Pacific war zone (curious phrase), landings in the Philippines and Malaya and the sinking of Japanese battleships and troopships. Japan is doing her best to follow up the first blows and we hear of America's reaction and in the U.S.A. the calling up of men. Russia is rolling into the Germans and driving them back from Moscow. They speak tonight of having killed 55,000 Germans on this front.

Saturday 13th December

Such dark mornings, but in these portentous days we have to be listening to the 8 a.m. news, for much may have happened since the last news we heard at 9 p.m. the night before. The Germans are still retreating before the vengeful Russians and villages are being cleared of Germans. The number of killed is put at 85,000 between 10th November and 10th December. They say also that 1,434 tanks were captured or destroyed, as well as great quantities of other war material. The British advance in Libya is being pressed with the utmost vigour.

Though the dawn was red, the day, though cloudy mostly, kept fine. Twink and I went to Meetinghouse, Sunnyside and the grocer's walk, meeting all the dogs of the village—including the nasty white-and-orange quarrelsome beast (ought to be called *Hitler*) and many evacuee dogs, too. Twink looked his charming, well-bred self and, as Master says, 'A Rolls-Royce is always worth its money', likewise a well-bred dog. We got safely home with only a few bristling backs, an odd snarl or two and an indignant protest from Twink at the unpardonable rudeness of some mongrels.

Tuesday 16th December

A good day, for *two letters came from Alan*, both dated 28th

October, and written in continuation. He has received a batch of my letters of August and September, says what things he would like sent to him and gives lots of information about the camp. A postcard of Oflag 1XA and a small photograph of himself were pinned to the letter. Now we are happy again.

Friday 19th December

Japanese troops have landed in Hong Kong, but part of the island is still holding out. Penang has been evacuated. Dutch submarines are doing good work. We have occupied some Portuguese territory in Timor to prevent the Japanese from doing so, and the Portuguese have protested. Aircraft (enemy) are becoming more active in the Philippines and one Colonel Knox is giving the Americans first-hand news about the attack on Pearl Harbour, after his return from that place. In Libya the British have taken the airfield at Derna and are pressing their attacks on the enemy without cessation.

Thursday 25th December

A very nice Christmas Day. No early church as 9 a.m. service makes it difficult, so we got up for 9 a.m. breakfast, had our few presents, then went to church at 11 a.m.—a full church, too. I did a few odd jobs, discovering bits of Christmas trimmings for the table—two large and several small crackers—then we had an old-fashioned pre-war dinner: turkey, plum pudding, mince pies, crystallised fruits, Cox's orange pippins! It all sounds marvellous, everything considered, but we bought the pudding, there was one Cox's each, and the crackers and crystallised fruits were bought two years ago.

A quiet afternoon (necessary perhaps) listening to the King's broadcast at 3 p.m. Thinking all day of Alan and longing to have him back again. The King spoke kindly of the prisoners of war and sent them 'a message of comfort, courage and hope'. Kate heard the 9 p.m. news and says Hong Kong has fallen.

Friday 26th December

We woke too late to hear the 8 a.m. news and had breakfast just after nine. It was colder today than yesterday and the ground was white with frost early. We dined on devilled and hashed turkey, mince pies and custard pudding and home-bottled fruit—truly royal!

Mr Churchill, eloquently broadcasting from Washington, ended with: 'And so we move together in majesty, in justice and in peace.' He used the word 'together' many times and spoke easily and fluently. No word of Hong Kong in the news at 1 p.m. and 6 p.m. Russia continues her victories and is pushing the enemy further and further from Moscow and Leningrad. The Germans are losing masses of equipment and material and incredible numbers of men in their retreat.

Tuesday 30th December

Laid low for the past few days with aches and pains, chill or cold or whatever unpleasantness I've had.

A thrilling raid on a Norwegian island came off according to plan, with 90 or so Germans captured and a few quisling prisoners too—150 killed, industrial plants, gun positions, etc., destroyed. And all completed in a quarter of an hour, less than the time allowed. A smoke screen was laid while our men and ships did the raiding. Six or more enemy ships were destroyed and the place left useless. The whole raid was well-timed and perfectly executed.

I have re-read Miss McNaughten's *The Gift* and enjoyed her charm to the full. Never was there a more charming writer— womanly, but far from weak; critical but not cruel. The doctor came at 2.30 p.m. and admired 'my hoarse, crow-like voice'! A nap after tea, waking up a little the worse for wear. Jack came in and we heard Mr Churchill's broadcast from the Ottawa Parliament. Marvellously good! Speaking of the British people who refused to break up after the collapse of France (in spite of the French words 'like a chicken with its neck wrung'), he said: '*Some* chicken.' Loud laughter. '*Some* neck.' Just the man for the job and thank God for him.

Wednesday 31st December

Not too bad a night, and no temperature this morning. Only great weakness and delight at being able to lie up in a comfortable room, for the morning was cold and cheerless. Everywhere the doings and sayings of 1941 are being recorded and the hopes for 1942 cheerfully put forth.

A fierce battle ranges in Libya. Rommel is doing his utmost to check the British advance on the borders of Tripolitania lest his force should be encircled. Twenty-two enemy tanks were destroyed and 20 others rendered useless, while we lost 14. We sank five schooners in the Mediterranean, one loaded with ammunition. Malta is being severely raided, though occasionally the onslaught is intercepted. The Japanese press north and south towards Manila, calling on the town to surrender 'to prevent further bloodshed'. The Russians descended on the Crimea and re-captured Kerch and Hodosia, two important towns, while the Germans are still battering at the walls of the fortress of Sevastopol. How marvellously 'the Brown Bear' has recovered from the enemy's sweeping onslaught and is giving Hitler's forces no rest, day or night.

I listened to a few 'Hogmanay' songs on the wireless this afternoon, with that poignant undercurrent which all Scottish music seems to have, and later to 'The World Goes By', when guests from France, Russia, China and Poland told about their New Year customs and Freddie Grisewood finished the broadcast by reading Tennyson's 'Ring out wild bells'. That made me think how very much we miss the church bells. I wish we need not have made the order for them to keep silent for the duration, except in case of invasion. I wrote a letter of good wishes to Alan.

And what of the year that is fleeting fast to its end? In spite of huge losses, undreamt of catastrophes and setbacks, it has been a wonderful year. The loss of the *Hood* was a blow, then the 'old Ark' and later the *Prince of Wales* and *Repulse*. The evacuation from Greece and Crete and the frustrated feeling some had when we did not invade France, while Germany attacked Russia—all these seemed bad. Then one looks at Libya, at Russia, at the wonderful R.A.F., the continued pounding of Germany, the successful convoying of stores and supplies from overseas to England and the transporting of the same with men, equipment and ammunition to the Middle East and the Far East. Also the many unspectacular, careful placing and shifting of our Forces to places of need. For real thankfulness one has to think of a year ago ('I wish myself could see myself as I knew him a year ago'). Personal happiness and satisfaction are derived from being able to write to Alan and to receiving cheerful letters and an occasional photograph from him.

VOLUME 8

January 1942 – June 1942

Thursday 1st January

The year begins with the scribbler in bed finishing off an attack of 'flu', nevertheless feeling very cheerful and full of hope. No doctor today, and with newspapers, wireless at intervals, a little mild needlework, meals and the reading of this diary from 1940 to 1941 the day has slipped away till 6 p.m., when I have just heard the news. There has been a further raid on Norway—the Lofoten Islands again, I think—undertaken with great dash and courage. More German prisoners have been taken and a few quislings, while, as before, Norwegian families have asked to come to England with the raiding parties on their return.

Friday 2nd January

The invalid is much better today—not so 'weak i'th legs' or so light-headed—and able to take a proper bath without feeling queer.

After I had my chop(!) by the fire in the living-room Mr Curtis, the new curate-in-charge of St Peter's, arrived, followed a few minutes later by the doctor. He strictly enjoined me to go slowly and slack for a week at least. After tea my bed was ready, the bottle was put in and the room warmed, and right glad I was to be between the sheets once more.

Jack came up and we heard the 6 p.m. news together. Manila has fallen. Chinese troops are in Burma under the command of General Wavell—good luck to them, say I. Bardia is again in our hands, with 1,000 of our men captured previously by the Germans. Was there ever such a breath-taking business as this war for comparative outsiders like we old 'uns?

Saturday 3rd January

Bettah and bettah! Up to lunch today again, pottering around a bit, resting a bit and being in bed by 6 p.m. in time for the news. There was a great story of a convoy attacked persistently for five days. We lost the *Audacity*, formerly a German ship, and another was sunk or damaged, plus two small merchant ships of the convoy. We sunk three U-boats and as we depth-charged them they surfaced and we took prisoners, and destroyed Focke-Wulfs which tried to do damage from above. A very creditable job.

Sunday 4th January

The Naval service broadcast today was excellent, though unfortunately had to be cut off towards the end of the sermon, for which I was sorry. Also the Senior Service coughed a good deal! I got up at 12 and did a little work of a kind, had Sunday dinner, prepared tea and then sat very comfortably, chaise longue fashion, before the living-room fire and dozed and slept. *Very* comforting! I came up from below after the 6 p.m. news. Bardia has now yielded 7,000 prisoners, of whom 1,000 are Germans. Anthony Eden broadcast an account of his very recent visit to Moscow in a temperature of 58 degrees of frost. Br-r-r-r! He described the inadequate clothing of German prisoners and the vast distances in Russia—almost incredible to an Englishman.

Friday 9th January

Up and out today! By 11 a.m. we were on the way to Leamington with the low winter sun in our eyes as we drove towards Kenilworth. There was a bitter north wind, but Leamington's climate is kinder. I managed to do the shopping while Jack was getting his hair cut. No fish today, but most other things, at a price! A tiny bundle of two sticks of rhubarb was 9d., a tiny lettuce 9d., cooking apples 9d. lb, and a small cake which would ordinarily have been 9d. was 1s. 2d. By 1 p.m. we had gathered all we required, got the radiator mended and set off homewards.

Knitting and wireless as usual tonight. The news is much the same. Russia's good progress, persistence in the Crimea, but never much said until a definite step is made and something done.

Tuesday 13th January

A good day indeed, as it brought *a letter from Alan.* Though he says he had a cold and was in bed two days, he was better and going out for a gentle stroll. A strange girl called Juanita Cain of New

Mexico had written to him and he said 'this . . . was most exciting!' He had received the July parcel two days earlier, 'all complete and very satisfactory' except that three razor blades were missing. He says 'I have got much too fat lately'. Well, better than being emaciated.

Friday 16th January

The Leamington shopping, hairdressing, lunch and more shopping was got through about 3.30 p.m. We did it unhurriedly and I had time to get some books to send to Alan. Jack and I soon had tea when I got home. Mrs Greenslade rang me up to say she has had a letter from Edward. He says they are allowed to be out of their huts till 10 p.m., and this must be very pleasant for them to be able to visit friends in the evenings in other parts of the camp.

The Duke of Connaught, aged 91, died this morning:

'He marched me here and he marched me there.

He made me sweat and he made me swear, did Arthur'

—Kipling's verse of a soldier speaking of his General, the Duke of Connaught.

The Russians are still re-capturing towns and villages, and the punishment meted out to the Germans is severe. Since the sixth of this month 14,000 of them have been killed. The way the enemy is treating the Russian prisoners is terrible, and Mr Molotov calls upon the world to hear of these atrocities, some too dreadful to print.

Saturday 17th January

A postcard from Alan to Jack today, dated 29.11.41.

It is good to know that he has received five technical books and the A.M.I. mechanical engineering syllabus through the Red Cross. He cannot remember whether he took a language in his Matric. He ends: 'Will let you know how things progress in due course.'

Good.

The 6 p.m. news was joyous and told of the Prime Minister's safe return via Bermuda to Plymouth. How nice and free-feeling, even in a war like this, to know that the head of Britain's Government can visit the head of the U.S.A. overland and by sea and air and not have to meet like those two villains Hitler and Mussolini in armoured trains on the Brenner Pass. The news told of the Prime Minister's arrival at Paddington and greeting Mrs Churchill with a kiss!

Also we are delighted that Halfaya has fallen and 5,000 prisoners taken, while 76 of our men taken prisoner by the Halfaya force are now liberated. Malayan news is not too good, but the situation has not really deteriorated in the last day or two. Australians seem to be there in some force and it is to be hoped we do not lose Singapore.

Friday 23rd January

It is strange how different people are. Some get up feeling the world is against them and takes a good breakfast and an hour or so for the good side of life to come uppermost. Jack is of this category, while I am plagued with a gentle melancholy o' nights and go down, as it were, with the sun, waking generally next morning knowing this world is a *good* place and here is a new day, one that has never been before. Who knows what it might bring!

This is really quite irrelevant, for this has been an ordinary day, not too good as regards war news. The Japs are having it mostly their own way in the Far East and Rommel has recovered lost ground. One imagines our line must be rather too long at present and Rommel is taking advantage of this.

Monday 26th January

Aeroplanes were busy around here last night from dusk till 2 a.m. at least, but after that I got to sleep. Daily work filled this morning and at 12.30 p.m. I took Twink in the fields. It was not a pleasant morning. The wind was bitterly cold and I went out in Alan's leather helmet, worn first by him as a little boy, with his green sledge 'Rocket' in the field at Stoneleigh (and what a dangerous place for such a winter pastime—a steep slope with the deep river at the bottom; it makes me shudder to think of it). Since then it has been worn by a succession of girl-friends going out with him in his open car. The old fur coat with collar up, gauntlet gloves and gumboots kept out the worst of the wind, but even then I wept. Twink made his first 'kill' today and didn't enjoy it. He rooted a little mouse out of its nest in a tuft of grass and then feebly bit it, distastefully giving it one nip and later another. Poor little thing! I finally had to help in its dispatch.

Russia is still marching forward through the snow and Germans are being killed in thousands.

Monday 2nd February

Or, as a visitor has just said: 'It's the two-th of the two-th of the forty-two-th!' (2.2.42). The snow which fell yesterday lingers still. It is scarcely freezing and there has been a good deal of thawing during the night. There is news of the U.S. Fleet in the Pacific doing a bit of real damage to the Japs. Rommel and his force are pushing east in the see-saw battles of Libya. It is said that 'substantial reinforcements' have arrived at Singapore. The Russians are fighting back to the Dnieper. I do hope they may take Kharkov again.

Wednesday 4th February

Goloshed and gumbooted, I took Twink to the grocer's and round Sunnyside and Meetinghouse. Walking was trying in parts. Though it was not freezing, it was rather slippery on the sloshy snow. Lord Beaverbrook is appointed Minister of Production and Sir Andrew Duncan succeeds him as Minister of Supply. General Wavell has sent an order of the day to the defenders of Singapore calling on them to hold on till the great reinforcements which Britain and the U.S.A. are sending can reach them. There is bitter fighting in the Dutch East Indies and New Guinea is believed to have been raided for a second time. In the Philippines General MacArthur's troops are repulsing the enemy. In Libya we have evacuated Derna, but are attacking near Msus to the south-west.

Friday 6th February

A letter came from Alan and one from Jon Curtis. Both were very cheerful. Alan gets my letters through well and relates two amusing incidents in Oflag VIB. He also says they do not get up till 9.30! He is now beginning to study, too. Jon says the sand in Libya is awful and one seems sometimes to have swallowed half the Sahara! The news is a little more cheerful today all round and the weather cold, but not freezing.

Thursday 12th February

Breakfast in bed for both of us, Jack having developed a cold now. Later Twink, crossing the main road without waiting to be put on the lead, was just missed by four Army vans and lorries and came back to receive two hard whacks with the lead.

His tail goes down and he looks miserable, but when the punishment is over up goes the flag and I fear his misdeeds are equally quickly forgotten. Incorrigible dog!

This afternoon at 3 p.m. I went across to the Institute and we went through the play we are presenting, *Hide and Seek*. If only the performers would learn their parts we might get on, but everyone's life is so full these days. Jack and I have had a good 'moan' over the war news—nothing very cheerful at the moment.

Friday 13th February

The 8 a.m. news told of the departure of the *Scharnhorst, Gneisenau* and *Prince Eugen* from Brest, complete with a protecting line of E-boats and aircraft overhead. They started early, screened by bad visibility, and as soon as our reconnaissance planes sighted them, out went all available craft to harry and endeavour to damage them—destroyers, motor torpedo boats, bombers and fighters. We pressed the attack home, but it was a difficult job and, though hits were scored, it was difficult to see full results as the enemy laid a smoke screen. For this we lost 42 aircraft. It is supposed the ships are now in harbour in the Heligoland Bight. The bombing at Brest has kept them in awhile, but could not destroy them, it appears.

Sunday 15th February

The fall of Singapore has been announced and this—on top of the outcry in *The Times* yesterday and *The Sunday Times* today on the matter of the German warships slipping comparatively easily through the Channel—has made a black week. Everybody feels thoroughly down, but it is no use staying down. Our pride is lowered and our enemies rejoice. A broadcaster said today, in speaking of St Dunstan's blinded men: 'They turn their trials into triumphs', and we must do the same.

Mr Churchill is criticized for keeping too much power in his own hands. Everyone feels what a marvellous leader he is, but many wonder whether he ought to do quite so much personally and feel he should depute some of his jobs to others. He spoke at 9 p.m. tonight, reviewed the situation calmly, remarked on the vote of confidence recently, and reminded us that a free Press, such as this country has, can be abused. He gave no promises for the future, only spoke of things as they were after Dunkirk and then last year. He felt there was something better now than then. We were then alone, and now have Russia, America and China with us—all powerful countries of unlimited resources. He spoke firmly, not minimizing our difficulties, prophesying more setbacks in the near future, but a hope of the tables being turned eventually. The papers have been very churned up, but Churchill was calm and sane in his words. He is undoubtedly the leader and a Prime Minister to be proud of.

Monday 16th February

Still very cold and, though a little ice and snow disappear day by day, the Burleigh car park is still a sheet of ice and in the fields in

Mrs Milburn and her son Alan in the early 1920s

Second Lieutenant Alan Milburn, 7th Bn, Royal Warwickshire Regiment, at the outbreak of war

A wartime photograph of Mrs Milburn

Jack Milburn in the garden at Burleigh (1943), looking at planes passing overhead

Twink on the tennis lawn at Burleigh

Burleigh: the house and garden

A family group (1939): Richard Bagnall, Alan Milburn, Colin and Peggy Bagnall, and Jack Milburn

The Milburn cars (1939): Alan's MG and his parents' Rover and Morris

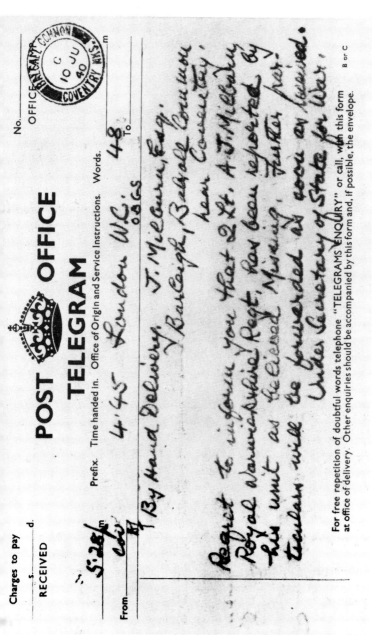

Oflag IXA: *(Left)* Alan, POW 3604 (centre) with a group of friends

(Right) The main entrance to the camp

sheltered places the snow lingers, crisp and crunching as one walks on it. A letter today from Jan Johnson told of a Nazi landing on the south coast and the seizure of two Home Guards, who were carried off! That ought to 'larn' the H.G. to shoot first!

Friday 20th February
Changes in the Cabinet (War) were announced this morning. Sir Stafford Cripps is to lead the House of Commons (Lord Privy Seal); Mr Churchill remains Minister of Defence as well as Prime Minister; Mr Attlee is Deputy Prime Minister; Anthony Eden is Foreign Secretary; Bevin is still Minister of Labour and National Service; Sir John Anderson is Lord President of the Council; and Oliver Lyttleton is Minister of State with general supervision over production.

After shopping and a visit to the dentist in Leamington today, I walked Twink, and I think he killed a partridge in a distant field. But here we say: 'Hush-hush'.

Monday 23rd February
Jack not very fit and so I had the job of going to the Rover Works to take 'Maria' to be decoked. The car was left with Jack's notes, which seemed to amuse the recipient! Then I walked away hugging the rug and eventually chased a bus, landed in it panting breathlessly, and was transported to Trinity Street.

On the train back a little girl in the carriage pointed out 'Daddy's works'—the Standard Company—and presently burst into sobs. The mother and two children had come from Yorkshire to see 'Daddy' and were now on their way back, and the little girl hated parting. The mother soothed her and said: 'Don't cry, love—you'll upset Mummie if you fret.' Oh this cursed war, separating families and destroying home life!

At 2.45 p.m. there was a drama rehearsal. I can't think the play will be ready in three weeks from now. Great changes in the Government today, with Lord Beaverbrook out of office.

Wednesday 25th February
A good day, *for we had a letter from Alan*, written on 24th January. A most cheerful letter, too, telling us how busy he is and how little time there is to write even! There has been a great Russian victory south of Leningrad, with 16,000 Germans killed and the capture of much equipment and material. The question of our night-bombing of the enemy seems to be under consideration now. We hear that the King and Queen were in Coventry today.

Thursday 26th February

Still cold, but not so penetratingly cold as yesterday. We know now that the King and Queen slept in *our* railway siding on Tuesday night, and are proud that Berkswell and Balsall Common shelters the First Gentleman and the First Lady in the land. They made a visit of a few hours to Coventry, the city and some works. Jack was in Coventry and actually went up Stoney Stanton Road while the King and Queen were in the Hospital ruins, but alas he did not know.

Wednesday 4th March

Rain fell all night and up till 5 p.m. today, so everywhere has had a good wash—and it needed it. Snow still lies here and there, but is fast disappearing now. *A letter from Alan, dated 25th January, came this morning*—very condensed and mostly commenting on particular things in my letters to him.

Sad days for Java, alas. It does not seem as if it can be held. The Japs have sunk Allied ships and are swarming into Java, while gathering their forces in Burma as well. Our aircraft were over northern France bombing the Renault works, where the French are working for the Germans. A great to-do about it and a day of mourning proclaimed. It is reported that 400 civilians were killed.

After yesterday's grand 'wash down' we were extremely disappointed to find snow falling when we got up. A thin layer covered the ground and it has fallen at intervals during the day. I enjoyed a morning at home with household work and writing, and after lunch went over to drama and we went into the billiard room and set to work, enjoying our rehearsal greatly.

An excellent war commentary by Group Captain Helmore tonight. He told of five airmen who came down in the sea. There was food and water for four for seven days, and they were seven days from home. During the first night the Captain evidently made up his mind, for when the morning broke he wasn't there. In seven days four terribly exhausted men reached the home shore. This recalls the story of Captain Oates—'a very gallant gentleman'—who, knowing the shortage of food on the Antarctic expedition, went out into the night saying: 'I may be some time', and was not seen again. Nations may rise and fall, wars come and go, but such deeds are deathless. They are for all eternity.

Saturday 7th March

The news from Java is bad. The Japs have cut across the island and the Dutch radio said: 'Goodbye—we are closing down till better days.' It is no use saying 'Alas, alack'. It must just be borne at present. The invasion of Australia is now threatened and the situation at Rangoon is very serious. Oh, America! If only, after all this warning, you could have been ready to guard the Pacific! It is almost impossible, with these gangster nations, to hold one's odd possessions all over the world. They recognize nothing but force. 'Asia for the Asiatics' just means 'Asia for the Japanese'. God forbid that this should be!

Tuesday 10th March

A workroom day, mending atrocious hot-water bottle covers. We stuck to the unpleasant job and tidied up 28 of them. The six or seven of us present also talked of our own work and did a bit of it at lunchtime. The doctor met me just as I came from the workroom and, as usual, was interested to hear what I was doing. He carried the sewing-machine to the car for me. Mr Whitaker had begun gardening and I told him I didn't feel I wanted to do any gardening at all. Then I came home—and worked out of doors for an hour tidying up! Contradictory person!

Japanese atrocities, told by Mr Eden, have made us rage inwardly. Terrible things are reported from Singapore. Fifty British officers and men were bound hand and foot and then bayonetted, and there were other dreadful things which concerned the women. May these wickednesses be properly avenged!

Tuesday 17th March

A letter from Alan. He sounds well and busy. I went off to Coventry in the car at 10.30 p.m. and at two minutes to 11 arrived at the Bishop's house, parked the car safely and spent an enjoyable day hearing M.U. business. Afterwards I called on several people, including Katie Bluemel and her mother, and heard of their *burglary*. A man called saying there was trouble with the main electricity connection outside and could he just look at their plugs and other electric fires, etc. After he had been upstairs a little while (and Katie went up with him first), he came down, knocked on the sitting-room door, thanked her and went away. Later in the evening two cases of jewellery were found to be missing and, a few days later, two fur coats as well. The latter were probably thrown out of the window into a side lane.

Thursday 19th March

General MacArthur has now taken up his new position as Supreme Commander in the South Pacific. American troops have arrived in Australia 'in strength'. Good!

A very wet morning and not so warm as yesterday, and at 2.15 p.m. I picked up Mrs Greenwell to go to Coventry to the Deanery meeting. The dining-room at the Provost's house was full. I was in the Chair and presided over a very satisfactory meeting. The rain had ceased by then and we got home at 5 p.m., had high tea at 6 and were over to the Institute at 7 p.m. We had a good evening. Both plays went splendidly and we had a good audience in a crowded room. The only professional there congratulated the producer on her efforts for *Hide and Seek* and the actresses certainly did their bit and enjoyed it. Home at 10.30 p.m. and so to bed.

Wednesday 25th March

The Daily Mirror has lately come into the bad books of the Government since it has apparently suggested all is not well with the Army and it is calculated this is undermining the confidence of the nation, while there is no foundation for such a sweeping statement. Morrison has spoken very firmly and confidently for the Government and all the cries of 'Freedom for the Press' are unheeded in his speech in the Commons today. Details of Captain Vian's brilliant work in convoying special stores safely through attacks of the Italian Navy from Alexandria to Malta have been published and warmly commented on. A message has been sent to him from the Prime Minister. Malta is suffering from unlimited air attacks and bearing this assault splendidly.

Tuesday 31st March

Very little to do at the workroom today. Kate had turned out the boxroom so, after taking Twink out when tea was over, I turned it in again. Doing drawers in Alan's room is a job I do not like—everything brings back happier days and accentuates present separation—but it has to be borne and that's that. It is good to tidy drawers and cupboards and I am glad spring-cleaning has really begun, though it may be long protracted.

A daring raid on St Nazaire a few days ago in which H.M.S. *Cambelltown* rammed the dock gates. The ship was then scuttled and, having been well-filled with explosive at the bows and time-fuses set, she later blew up. One of the dock gates is reported missing and commandos, under cover of a bombing raid to distract attention, damaged machinery at the docks. The raid occupied two hours. Some of our men could not be re-embarked, which was a pity. The docks at St Nazaire are at present the only place which the *Tirpitz* can use.

Saturday 4th April

A very good day, *for we had two letters from Alan*. He promised a 'domestic' letter next time and we have had *two*. He certainly does get a lot on to one sheet, and very interesting items, too. Thank God he is well and occupied day by day.

At 11 a.m. I managed to get off to Kenilworth and *looked* at the daffodils. They were 2s. 6d. for a bunch of six—5d. each! As the cemetery where I was going is so windswept, it is not worth paying so much for rather delicate flowers as these early ones are. So I found a small pot of spring flowers and took those.

Wednesday 15th April

Searchlights and planes were busy last night—the lights throwing their stiff beams at all angles across the sky and the planes zooming round continually. However, being thoroughly tired, I slept. Today we had perfect weather—cloudless blue sky, sun all day and only a cold north-east wind to make us growl slightly, though it was not too unpleasant.

There has been a nasty accident on exercises with our troops. A dive-bomber got off the target and machine-gunned the company of staff and others who were watching, instead of the dummy collection at another spot. Live bullets were used, unfortunately, and 25 people were killed, with 60 casualties altogether. A horrible mess-up.

I haven't made any remarks on food lately, so I will just say that today I paid 1s. 3d. for a lettuce, and watercress is 2s. 4d. a lb. Sprouts were 1s. a lb. In this village things are generally a little more than in Leamington—sprouts 1s. 2d. and watercress 2s. 8d.

Friday 17th April

Today, on the Birmingham–Warwick road, I saw the first swallow! We were on our way to Brett's, where I left Jack, and went on to Leamington, shopped quite unhurriedly and met him for lunch.

Hairdresser for me at 2 p.m. and at 3 p.m. a bit more shopping. Then we met Mrs Greenslade and had a chat about our sons and read various cards and letters from them. Edward says the hut they 'live, eat and sleep and nearly (!) everything else in' is 15ft square, so it is rather difficult to divide in half and live in one half and sleep in the other. Alan is senior officer in it. We think it is very small for nine men, but what can be done? Mrs Greenslade does not wish anything said about it to the Red Cross. I had thought of writing about it, but she is afraid they might make things awkward for our sons in the camp. I expect that all these things are noted by the powers that be.

Saturday 18th April

At 2.30 p.m. Jack had the car ready for me to go to Coventry to open the St Francis' Fete, and I managed to do my part without getting worried, thanks be. I enjoyed the company at tea of the three bachelor clergy, one of whom, John Lister, lost the sight of one eye and had facial and other injuries in the 1940 raid on Coventry when St Nicholas' Church was destroyed and four servers with him were killed. And so, with a basket of large dimensions nicely filled, I came home.

The great news today is that American planes have raided Japan, and Tokio, Kobe, etc., have been bombed. Horrible as it sounds, this is really a good thing.

Tuesday 21st April

Mrs Bushill came for me today and we had a restful morning mending white nightshirts and blue trousers at the Rectory. We left at 12.50 p.m. and I, at any rate, was very glad of the afternoon at home. More onions were planted, as well as some chives, and after tea I did a little more general gardening. Even after supper we both went out again and put guards over the peas, which are just through.

Coal, fuel, electricity and paraffin are to be put on 'points' in six weeks' time. This has called forth much comment and many questions from Members of Parliament, and a debate will follow in due course.

Monday 27th April

After a refreshing night, it was good to wake to a sunny morning, though the north-east wind still rages. Everywhere is dried up and we need rain—the last fell on the 10th. The news today of air warfare is that we have raided Rostock for the fourth night in succession, and last night the enemy raided Bath again. One of the beautiful old crescents is destroyed, we hear.

Tuesday 28th April

There is much raiding by the R.A.F. Oh dear, what terrible destruction everywhere—a terrible war! Norwich was badly raided last night, while we went for Cologne, and Exeter has had it now and Bristol again. Hitler is surely Satan let loose.

Wednesday 29th April

And last night it was York, but the Minster fortunately escaped. These are called 'reprisals' and, according to Hitler, all our beautiful ancient towns are to be bombed. What an evil mind he has, and what idiots are the German people to allow themselves to be led by him. Our bombing in enemy country grows fiercer. Rostock is flattened out and we hear of the people rushing away from it.

Wednesday 6th May

And another delightful day, warm with a fair breeze. Deronicums are gay in their yellow dress as the daffodils fade from gold to bronze. The birches, which drop innumerable catkins, are putting forth their delicate heart-shaped leaves, and the oaks are budding and bursting at the corners of the garden. The chiffchaff is heard all day long and the blackbird sings the most enchanting lullabies on the tree above its nest. The sparrows are queer, common little birds with a dull 'chip-chip' which is penetrating and unpleasant, or else continually repeating 'Philip, philip', which is equally annoying. They love the projecting eaves of this 50-year-old house and many are the nests all around it.

A little gardening came first on this nice cool morning and half a row of summer spinach was sown.

Later I wrote to Alan while Jack was marking out a spot on the warm side of the toolshed to grow a few tomato plants. We sat out in the Corner again after supper and surveyed the vegetables before finally coming in.

There must be a lot we cannot hear about yet, but the St Nazaire raid a week or two ago was much more than we heard at first. Apparently the French joined in and helped our commandos. Some German officers would not believe that a ship which blocked the dock-gates was filled with explosive, so they suggested that two Englishmen should go aboard with them. The Englishmen consented and all were blown up immediately afterwards. It is marvellous, but terrible.

No news of the Burma fighting for three days. Our Forces are fighting a great delaying action. What a waste of precious lives it seems.

Friday 8th May

Today we hear of a great Naval action taking place in the Coral Sea, with 16 ships (aircraft-carrier, gunboats, cruiser and transports among them) sunk by the American Fleet. Is this the attempted invasion of Australia? If so, the American Fleet seems to be in the right place. Later in the day we heard of more sinkings elsewhere by the Americans.

Sunday 10th May

Unwilling to get up today and Jack felt the same, but eventually we found ourselves in the car going to church. The Sunday service seemed dull to me because I was so dull; couldn't get any 'breff' to sing, so had to be quiet half the time—not at all the proper kind of worship. At 9 p.m. Mr Churchill spoke, and this time he was very resolute and very hopeful. He also threatened the Nazis that if they used poison gas we should do the same. It is regrettable that this is the only kind of talk they can understand—but so 'tis.

Saturday 23rd May

A quiet night, thanks be! I took a skim into the village shops for a few things on my bicycle, while the weather was fine. After a rest (when dinner was over) Twink and I went in the fields, getting back just as the rain began in a half-hearted way. But later it rained in earnest, so there was no gardening—and I was not sorry.

It is difficult to realize that tomorrow, in the ordinary way, would have been part of the Whitsuntide holiday. Some shops—boot shops—are closing for a whole week. Sweets are now to be rationed, which is a good thing, but any suggestion of rationing fuel seems to upset the average Englishman.

Marshal Timoshenko claims that he has fortified the positions captured at Kharkov and is still pushing westward. The Germans claim fantastic numbers of prisoners in the Kerch zone. Poles are now being shanghaied and drawn in to military service, in contravention of international law.

Wednesday 27th May

A letter from Alan, dated 19.4.42. The two special bits that interest me are that he has mastered the art of darning his socks! And that they are often reminded of the Cornish prayer about the 'long-legged beasties'. The end of the prayer is a petition to the Almighty that one may be delivered from 'long-legged beasties and ghosties and things *that go bump in the night.*' So do they hear our bombers o' nights?

Sunday 31st May

The news tells of the biggest air raid of the war (shades of Gracie Fields' 'biggest aspidistra', etc.) in which we sent a thousand bombers, as well as other aircraft, to Germany last night. Cologne was the target. We lost 44 bombers—less than five per cent. The Libyan battle rages and, it is thought, has reached a climax, since there is a limit to what men can stand in desert warfare. Tanks are like furnaces, it is said, and the dust must be terrible. General Auchinleck has sent a heartening message to General Ritchie and his men: 'Well done the Eighth Army'.

Monday 1st June

Great news today of the 1,250 bombers raiding Germany and occupied countries near at hand—1,000 of them went to Cologne and the attack was organized so that one bomber went into attack every six seconds. The Air-Vice Marshall, J. E. A. Baldwin, as well as other senior officers, flew with the crews under their command to see the effect of the first four-figure attack on Germany. It was a terrific raid, the biggest yet, and each of today's broadcast news has had a good deal to say about it, as have our Allies everywhere.

Tuesday 2nd June

Another big raid, with 1,034 aircraft, over Germany. Target—Essen. We lost 33 planes, bombers and fighters in this raid. The Libyan battle is now a great struggle to gain control of the gaps in our minefield which the enemy made, and we are pressing him hard with our troops and aircraft, while he has a large force of anti-tank artillery covering the gaps.

Thursday 4th June

Sitting up in bed at 10.45 p.m. with only a sheet for covering this hot night, with all the windows wide trying to get a breath of air, I am writing this diary. It is not dark, but I have my flashlamp shining on the page to see to write. Birds are chirruping still—they don't get much sleep o' nights at this time of the year—and across the way at the Institute a noisy crowd is dancing . . . that is when they are not shouting outside. And what tuneless tump-tump twaddle the band is playing—or so it seems to me. This morning we both went to Kenilworth, myself to the dentist, but I managed to plant my eight tomatoes before going out and do hope they will be a success. This afternoon I biked to Mrs Gorton's in the heat and it really was baking. Alas for my stockings—a new pair of *silk* ones! The tar was lying in pools along the road and melted in this heat, spattering as one rode along. Oh dear, oh dear—all so very serious these days.

Heydrich, the German Gestapo beast who was shot a week or so ago by a person or persons unknown, is dead. Already 150 Czechs have been shot in connection with this affair. The battle in Libya continues as fiercely as ever. The Japs have been snooping over the Aleutian Islands and from other fronts there is little news.

Monday 8th June

A really chilly wind has persisted all day. Linens and cottons and thin clothes have gone back to their cupboards and drawers and warmth is desired instead of our panting in the heat. This is too great a change to be pleasant, but it was nice for hard work in the garden and I managed to get in a row of purple sprouting broccoli, which was a great satisfaction. Jack stuck peas. Later we had a great blow when we found our potato clamp was growing great sprouts, great shoots pushing forth. Will they be eatable now, we wonder?

Fighting in Libya is fierce, with lots of tanks lost on both sides. The battle is not to our disadvantage so far, but still proceeding. The Midway Island attack is broken off, with terrific losses for the Japs, one destroyer lost for our Allies and very light casualties. We have warned the French to get away from the coast because of our raids to come.

Tuesday 9th June

A chilly day, but nice for working in the garden. The sky was overcast and it looked as if rain would fall any moment, but it never did. Jack sowed a fourth row of peas in the small orchard patch, stuck peas and cut edges, etc. My jobs were hoeing the bird garden and small beds round the house, planting the round beds with dahlias and planting out French marigolds in the trellis rambler bed. Not a good combination of colour, I fear, but the best that can be done this year. We carried on till nearly suppertime, when I walked Twink.

Earlier Jack spent some time getting Alan's bicycle in order, putting on the handlebars which had been removed in case a parachuting Hun should arrive one night and borrow it. After lunch he went off on it to the tobacconist and returned safely!

Wednesday 10th June

Still cold and we went back to three blankets and an eiderdown last night, though the latter was only over my feet. The morning soon passed with a little cleaning of silver and 12 o'clock came. Then I biked down to the grocer, where I stood and waited while long lists of groceries were packed for two women. I finally got home an *hour* later with the small quantity of groceries which our little home requires. This was salvage day in the village, so Kate and I put out the paper, old metal and rubber at the front gates, as well as the piles of books which I received at the Institute yesterday.

Germany is still punishing people in Czechoslovakia for Heydrich's death and today there is news of a village razed to the ground, men shot and the women sent to a concentration camp. The children are taken away to be 'educated'. 'How long, O Lord, how long?' one cries.

Saturday 13th June

Both sides are preparing for attack in Libya. The Russians have repelled attacks round Kharkov with heavy losses to the enemy. Sevastopol's situation is pretty serious. The Japs have made small landings in the Aleutian Islands and the extent of their losses in the battle of the Coral Sea is now made known. They were undoubtedly extensive and America feels herself avenged for Pearl Harbour. Mr Molotov has been to London and Washington and an agreement has been signed, called the Anglo–Soviet Treaty! Great Britain and the Soviet Union will stand in armed alliance, ready to resist aggression at any time during the next 20 years! There is also talk about the 'urgent task of creating a second front in Europe in 1942'.

Wednesday 17th June

Housework soon finished this morning and I hastened to the shops in the village before the best cauliflowers had gone and to take the 'points', previously forgotten, to the grocer—and forgot them again! So I had a second journey—very quick on one's bicycle. Then I got the edging shears and did a good hour's work, while Jack, full of energy and enthusiasm, cut the yew hedge. This evening I was once more at the household mending. I meant to garden later, but did not want to change and thought it might be better to stick to the . . . mending!

Mrs Greenslade rang me up tonight. In Edward's letter he said they had seen a woman pass by the camp—the first woman they had set eyes on for eight months!

Saturday 20th June

A very warm morning, with a thundery feeling persisting all day and a good deal of cloud later. The daily round and a skim down to the grocer filled the morning. We had a restful, lazy teatime in the Corner and then Mrs Gorton rang asking if we could put up some Belgian officers tonight. Two hundred men were arriving and had to be put up at the School (I think) and 19 officers wanted a bed (one each, of course!) for the night, and what about our air raid shelter? 'Yes,' I said, 'we can do it.' So hastily I aired an extra mattress. Presently along came Mrs Gorton with the billeting officer and a sergeant. A click of the heels and in they came and had a look. 'Splendid,' he said, and he would send four youngsters, and gave me the names.

Then Jack and I went for a walk, and in the meantime two officers and batmen had been in and dumped their stuff in the shelter. The officers came again later and got a tidy up, then went off to eat—I suppose at the School. Just as we finished supper the senior officers came, and by that time we had heard that only three were coming. I had decided to put one in the spare room, and he said: 'I am to have a little home of my own—marvellous.' He looked pleased to see a bed ready for him, for he had marched a long way and was very tired. Eventually the three officers arrived and were glad to come in and sit in a comfortable chair. A tall, slender figure was Lieutenant Savage, who had lived in Buenos Aires and had married an American. He was the exact type of King Albert of the Belgians, and very handsome.

After pouring out our last two flagons of cider lavishly upon them and seeing Lieutenant Haes blinking sleepily, I asked if he would like to go to bed. The poor man was worn out. Then the others retired to the Bunkhole and we were glad to get to bed, too. Nice men all, and very appreciative of a bit of home life.

Sunday 21st June

Our wedding anniversary—37 years today. Sleep did not come quickly last night and I woke early. I asked our guests if they would stay to breakfast. They were delighted, and I had to ring up Mrs Biggs, borrow a loaf and some eggs. (Yesterday I dropped half a dozen—bad luck!) Soon, with porridge, Kellogg's and potted meat, we had a meal. It was very nice to have them, but food is a problem. They all left immediately after breakfast and came back for their belongings just before 1 p.m.

In the meantime Mrs Gorton rang up asking if I would have them again on Wednesday evening. My garden party is on Thursday, so I hesitated a moment and then said I would have two of them, but could not manage any meals. This is not expected, and so I said: 'Very well, we shall be delighted to put them up.' I only wish one had the food for them. But they seemed pleased to think they were coming back again.

The news is bad today: the enemy claims to have captured Tobruk, with 25,000 prisoners, much equipment and many supplies. We have no official confirmation of this, but it might well be so as a convoy recently reached Tobruk. Sevastopol still holds out, though the position sounds very serious.

Monday 22nd June

Tobruk has fallen and we are certainly reeling under this disaster—for such it is. We have decided not to have the Belgian officers again on Wednesday, and Mrs Greenwell is having them instead. Jack felt tired this morning, had breakfast in bed and rested a good part of the day.

We are considering keeping a few fowls, but it is getting a house to keep them in that is the bother. The heat is oppressive, but I went to the shops this afternoon and also got Jack's tobacco. We had tea in the garden and did some work in it later.

Thursday 25th June

In order to sleep well I took the last of three sleeping tablets, but no sleep came stealing over me till about 1 a.m. Then, just as I was fading gently out, Jack said sirens were sounding all around. Presently German planes came over and I laid still in bed while Jack stood at the window awhile. Presently a gun spoke, so we got up and went down to the shelter where Kate was already lying on her bunk. There were a few guns and planes and at 2.30 a.m. the 'R.P.' sounded and I was soon out of my bunk and into my bed. The 8 a.m. news reported a raid on a West Midland town. Five raiders were brought down and casualties were not heavy. We hear it was at Nuneaton, but have no definite news yet.

The day was chilly mostly, but fine for the Deanery Party. We got through the preparations without fuss this morning and were ready by 2.30, having had an early lunch. Twenty came and enjoyed the games in the garden with papers and pencils, and then at 3.45 we had tea and they left soon after 4.30.

About 150 Belgian soldiers are parked in the Institute for the night and will be leaving at 5 a.m., so I don't know what kind of a night we shall have.

Friday 26th June

A very good night for me, though I heard the departure of the Belgians very early and then slept again. We all went for our last shopping expedition to Leamington, calling to give birthday greetings to Edie Cramp on the way and visiting Elizabeth at Kenilworth on the journey home. Tea in the garden, then later a little gardening, and after supper a little rest.

A thousand bombers went to Bremen last night. We lost 52. Churchill, Roosevelt and Letoinoff are consulting in Washington and planning a concrete effort to end the war—or words to that effect. Our submarines have sunk two ammunition vessels in the Mediterranean.

VOLUME 9

June 1942 – February 1943

Saturday 27th June

The ninth volume! And what a terrible lot of things have happened since the first was begun. Incredible, awful things; wonderful, amazing things. The evacuation of Dunkirk, the capitulation of the French, our own personal anxiety, relieved at last on hearing that Alan was a prisoner of war. Then the long silence and the gradually growing fear that there had been a mistake and he was, perhaps, not a prisoner, but was lost at Dunkirk, or before. At last the genuine news of his safety, though he had been wounded, and finally the joyous news that the wound had been slight and he was definitely in a prison camp in Germany.

The Battle of Britain stands out as one of the incredible things and the bombing of Coventry as one of the awful things, just as the little ships going across the Channel to bring our men home was a wonderful thing, and the bravery of those who bore the bombing, who lost their homes, and often some of their family, and still work and hope on, is an amazing thing. And now Alan has been a prisoner for over two years and we haven't seen him for two years-and-a-half. So many things that one cannot pretend to prophesy or imagine when the end of the war will come. It looks as if it could go on for years yet.

Today has been grey and cool, and I did a bit of work in the garden till 9 a.m., when we had breakfast. Afterwards I took flowers to Berkswell on the back of my bicycle, and in a basket, and got there safely. A deep hollow in the porch steps at the church sent me tumbling across the gravel as I carried a vase out to empty it, and the vase flew out of my hand with a great clatter. I called out 'I'm all right—no damage' to a man mowing the grass in the churchyard and went back and got on with the job. But, as I had fallen on my knee, I fund it getting stiffer and stiffer, and as I

143

mounted my bike to come home I emitted a fearful groan. But by sticking to it I think the motion prevented the knee from getting too stiff.

Monday 29th June

I woke up with an ache like a chilblain in my toe joint and during the day it became rather awkward, making me limp a little. After dinner I rode down to the grocer, with the foot getting more painful, and when I got home I had to discard the shoe altogether. The doctor came later, as the toe joint was throbbing and swollen, and said it was 'gouty arthritis'. He prescribed a few days' rest.

A letter came from Alan today, telling of hot weather and a great spring-cleaning in Hut 26, just cleaned out and turned in again before a thunderstorm descended.

Wednesday 1st July

Today Sir John Wardlaw-Milne asked the House to pass a Vote of Censure on the Government. His speech sounds very good to us at the first hearing, and also Sir Roger Keyes's request for the removal of the Labour lot—Alexander, First Lord of the Admiralty, Morrison, the Home Secretary, and Ernest Bevin, who does his utmost to provoke class-consciousness and set employee against employer. The reply given by the Minister of Production, Sir Oliver Lyttleton, on the defeat in Libya, etc., was not very satisfactory, we thought. Everyone seems to want Churchill as Prime Minister, but they do not think he has chosen wisely for his Cabinet.

Thursday 2nd July

Still taking breakfast in bed and enjoying it. The doctor came just before lunch and said: 'Don't squeeze your foot into a shoe yet', but later on I gave my foot light-and-heat treatment by putting it on the windowsill on a cushion (myself attached, of course!) and it seemed much better. After tea I got my bedroom slipper on without too much discomfort and wore it till bedtime.

Churchill has spoken after Wardlaw-Milne made his speech asking for a Vote of Censure on the Government. He thinks we are naughty children to 'barrack' him while he was away from home, and asked us to imagine his feelings when he heard in Washington of the fall of Tobruk. This was totally unexpected, but we have all our defeats explained in the same way. And so the sapping of our military strength goes on. He may be doing the best he can—I am sure he is a grand leader—and he always wins over the House. He

talks to them like a grandfather, and in the end the voting was 475
votes to 25 against the motion of 'No confidence'. It is to be hoped
that the Prime Minister takes some notice of the criticisms, for one
feels some changes are necessary. It is true that a vote of 'No
confidence' just now would not show a very sound front to our
Allies and enemies, though at heart we are certainly united and
resolute.

Sunday 5th July

It is a lovely day and such a pity for me to be laid up, and
a general nuisance to everybody.

The news from Egypt is that we have held up the Germans for
four days now and the R.A.F. have made great bombing attacks on
them, their stores and equipment, sometimes only 400 yards from
our own men, without, however, dropping a single bomb in the
wrong place. Six hundred Germans came out of their holes in the
ground and surrendered to us, tired of fighting, dirty and
dishevelled, sick of everything.

Saturday 11th July

A feeling of misery at first, which disappeared later. At 12
o'clock, having begun a fresh pair of socks for Alan during the
morning, I got up and went downstairs for lunch, pottered round a
bit, sat a bit, and then decided to go and look at the garden.

Mr Willoughby came later with a copy of the *Smallholder* and we
looked at an advertisement for a 'Utility Poultry House' and are
going to write about one. After supper—our own lovely spinach,
just gathered, was the main dish—I rang up the Spencers and had a
long talk with Joan, who was feeling a little depressed when she
thought of the years slipping by and Nevill away from her. So we
had a little moan together about the gnawing pain of separation—
then cheered up! She heard from Nevill that everybody dressed in
their best on the King's birthday and that he thought, considering
they were prisoners of war, they were really very smart. Good for
them!

Sunday 12th July

Sunday, but it doesn't seem much like it. Up in good time for
lunch and, having trotted round here and there, I was glad to lie on
my bed and go to sleep till 4.30 p.m. After tea a little potter round
the garden, getting a lettuce and carrots for supper with the
remains of Friday's 'Prem' (one of the many tinned foods prevalent
now—others are 'Spam', 'Tang' and 'Mor'). Then, having

watered the tomatoes, it seemed time to take my ease again. After supper I wrote to Alan and listened to the wireless.

Jack felt yesterday that we *must* leave this place if possible. We are so terribly cut off from everywhere and everybody. So this morning letters were written to three house agents asking if anything was available in Kenilworth, Leamington or Warwick.

Tuesday 14th July

In bed last night, I heard a welcome sound—*rain* pouring down. How I rejoiced—and then the sound died away and I fell asleep. When I got up and looked out of the window, I found that the ground was really wet, even under the laurels, so there had evidently been much more than I knew about. The garden is greatly refreshed, though we still need more rain. Letters came from two house agents acknowledging Jack's letters. One seemed to think there was little prospect of a house, but the other (Locke & England's) sounded alert and businesslike.

The Russians are having a very tough time, losing a little ground here and there, counter-attacking and regaining a village or two. But at the moment things are serious, with the Crimea gone and the enemy attacking fiercely—and losing heavily, too. Our gain of five miles west of El Alamein along the coast is maintained and our Air Force attacking hard in vulnerable spots. We have sunk a few transports and supplies, too. At intervals the people demanding a 'Second Front' get up and shout. One has no doubt that as soon as we can do it, we shall—only, no more Dunkirks for us.

Thursday 16th July

A letter from Alan, dated 19.6.42, telling of the first results of their gardening efforts—a dish of fresh greens, turnip tops, for their evening meal. He also says horses are very popular in the camp now! Their hut is beside the road and they get first pick!

Tuesday 21st July

A busy morning at home for me and Jack, getting out a trench on the small orchard patch to sow, well and hopefully, a last row of peas. Good luck to 'em! I bought my weekly groceries when I biked to the grocer's this afternoon and they came to 2s. 7½d.!!! Many things were not obtainable, and so one just had the weekly ration of butter, lard, margarine, cheese, bacon and sugar—2s. 7½d. And on top of 2s. 7½d. I have ordered a present for Jack at 47s. 6d., but I'm not sure whether I can get it. That was the last price at which this particular commodity was offered, but now I do not know what price it will be! One might say 'What a thing to buy now'. Well, on the principle of buying a packet of white lint and bandages and then finding a use for them almost at once, I am hoping to buy a —— well, I think I'll leave a space.

As before, the Germans push on near Rostov and the Russians are holding on further north. In Egypt there is not much to report, but terrific attacks by the R.A.F.

Thursday 23rd July

We have attacked on the whole of the Alamein front and there is fierce fighting. What a tough job for our men, hastily pushed out and along from Tobruk, and how difficult to get even a bit of the lost territory back again. And we don't want the territory as such, only to keep the enemy from overrunning Egypt and getting to Suez. Russian news is much the same. Our Air Force is doing very well in Egypt, battering the enemy severely. The Japs have made another landing in New Guinea.

Tuesday 28th July

Evelyn Spencer's boy is in the news again—I mean Cunningham —with a bar to his D.S.O. It is hard to realize that such a quiet, unassuming man can be such a skilful night fighter. Evelyn must be very proud of her son.

This afternoon I sadly decided to take up all my beautiful bed of onions, badly attacked by the onion-fly grub. It was no use to leave them to be eaten off one by one, Hitler fashion, and I shall not grow them again. They were a back-aching job to plant out, and I have spent many hours on their culture—all for nothing. Most disappointing. In fact—and I might as well record it—I am at the moment fed-up with the garden. Every year we slave in it, take years off our life with overwork (?), and by July it is dried up through lack of rain.

This year it promised well, with good rains in the spring, and the pear tree border was nice and full, but now the plants are withering up in the drought. Pests of all kinds are rife, but not only in this garden. I suppose one will get over it, but I wish there was a little less to do sometimes.

Fierce fighting goes on at Rostov, which the Germans claim to have taken. The slaughter is terrible.

Thursday 30th July

Coventry has suffered raids, as well as Birmingham we hear, but have not had many details yet. There was certainly plenty of gunfire till nearly 4 a.m., when the enemy planes ceased coming over and we all fell asleep and never heard the 'All Clear'. I rode down to the shops this morning, as well as getting Alan's parcel together, and had a long afternoon in the garden—myself with a severe bout of hay-fever (b-last it, after all the injections and treatments!). Later I got the 'Next-of-Kin' parcel packed ready to go tomorrow. We made a great raid on Hamburg on Tuesday. We lost 32 bombers, but did a great deal of damage.

Friday 31st July

The enemy came over about 1.30 a.m. and gunfire and bombs were heard till nearly 3 a.m. We are told that Walsall, Castle Bromwich and Warwick had it, with machine-gunning in the latter place. We brought down nine planes.

A bought cauliflower, looking delicious when brought to the table *au gratin*, was found to be full of black fly and so we could not eat it! This pest is on everything and we are tired of trying to cope with it this year.

Monday 3rd August

We slept very well, though I was wakened by a roaring plane very low down about 4.15 a.m. Later we heard there had been an alert about 3 a.m. till 3.40. I'm glad we didn't know! Jack's birthday—his present from me was a Union Jack (see 21st July)—has been grey, with messy little showers doing no good whatever. Just 'nuisance' showers. After lunch we had a short alert, but neither saw nor heard anything. Then I tried to garden, but a little rain fell as I tidied the hard, dried-up pear tree border. It was just enough to make me waste half an hour and yet no good came of it. 'Absurd weather!' said she, very annoyed.

The Germans push on in the Caucasus and are held near Voronezh. Something seems to have gone wrong with the Russians, who have had three-quarters of our production of munitions lately. We continue to raid Occupied France, Holland's aerodromes and Germany's cities. Düsseldorf was pretty well laid out with our concentrated effort.

Sunday 9th August

A long, quiet night and, with the change from double to single (!) summer-time, we got an hour extra in bed—at least some of us did. I woke at 7.15 a.m., exactly right for getting up and going to church. It was a warm, glorious morning—bright sun, blue, cloudless sky, simply grand. So out came the bike at 8 a.m.

and I went down to Berkswell. Except for sitting too near *that man*, with his horrible scraping of his throat and cough, the service was lovely and I was so glad to be there again, and came away refreshed.

The Germans continue their pressure on the Russians and claim tonight to have captured Maikop, where the Caucasian oil refineries are, while continuing their offensive towards Stalingrad. Ghandi, his secretary and Miss Slade, his English friend, have been arrested to prevent any disturbance occurring by the proposed civil disobedience campaign. A Government order has been made to prevent shops closing, which was one of the Ghandi proposals. Mrs Ghandi, aged 70, was later arrested. Rioting took place during the day among the natives.

Wednesday 12th August

An American professor visiting England is amazed at the health of the people after three years of war, and says the children are splendid. The health of the nation is better than before the war, says our Ministry of Health. There is no malnutrition. We shall probably have to tighten our belts a bit more this winter, but it is wonderful what has been done in the way of food-growing.

What the Germans are doing in the occupied countries, with the persecution, is frightful. Oh, the wickedness they perpetrate in exterminating people everywhere.

Wednesday 19th August

Exciting news this morning and later bulletins during the day of a great raid on France. French people were immediately warned by wireless that it was not 'the invasion' and advised to keep out of the way. When the time comes they will be told how they can help. It will be a thrilling story when it is told. There have been heavy losses on both sides and 95 of our aircraft are missing, 82 of theirs and over 100 damaged. The biggest air battle since the Battle of Britain.

Great news today also of Mr Churchill visiting the El Alamein front, being restrained from going to the actual front firing-line, lunching within sound of the bursting shells and going here, there and everywhere, smoking a cigar, talking to the men and giving the V sign. Earlier it was told how the telephone rang and the H.Q. were told to be ready for 'Mr Bullfinch'.

'Who's he?'

'Oh, you'll see later.'

It was evidently a great surprise and one Australian who came upon him unexpectedly said: 'Cripes, it's old Winny!' A German would have been shot immediately for *lèse-majesté*!

Wednesday 26th August

This morning the first sad news came at 8 a.m. of the death of the Duke of Kent, killed while flying on active service over Scotland. The Sunderland flying boat crashed into a mountainside and all but one of the passengers were killed. The survivor, the rear gunner, was apparently thrown clear though injured severely. Eventually a shepherd and his son found the Sunderland still on fire. Prince Michael, the Duke's son, is just two months old.

Wednesday 2nd September

Some rain fell this morning, but Batchelor managed to cut the lawns and later did a few odd jobs, such as staking the brussel sprouts, which have grown enormous and are very top-heavy, and weeding the pear tree border cobbled path. Kate, Jack and I gathered many pounds of apples from our Early Victorias in the orchard. I have already given many pounds away and sold many more for the Red Cross. We have had a fine lot this year.

The Russians have had a bad time lately and today we hear that Stalingrad, the city of which they are so proud, is in grave danger. The Germans also advance in the Caucasus. They seem to have endless tanks, aeroplanes and men, and yet they lose so many in the hard fighting in Russia that their strength and military might must surely be sapped. They are like a loathsome disease spreading and spreading over Europe.

Thursday 3rd September

The war begins its fourth year today and it is two years and nine months since Alan went away. It is a National Day of Prayer and special services have been arranged everywhere. Miss Gray, County Organizer for the Women's Land Army in this district, called to see me and we talked over the work—and the matter of petrol. This afternoon at the Institute I sold 20 lb of apples and made 13s. 4d. for the Red Cross. The evening sped quickly away and we both listened to a 'Marching On' programme, a summary of the three years of war.

I wrote nine letters to all 'my' land girls.

Wednesday 9th September

A petrol coupon arrived this morning for land-girl work, so we both took the car out—the first time since 28th June—and it was lovely to be in her again. I have written and offered my services and the car for the W.V.S. pool, whereby one is sent on a job occasionally and petrol is provided. *Anything* to get a legitimate run in the car these days!

Friday 11th September

Glorious weather, lovely and soft and balmy, with a cloudless sky. Warm, but not *too* hot, so this afternoon I decided to take a holiday. I fetched the deckchair from the hut, draped it with a rug and padded it with cushions and snuggled down and enjoyed a lazy hour. Hurricanes, Beaufighters and an occasional Wellington bomber crossed the sky above. I don't think one can get away from the sound of aeroplanes anywhere, but we certainly do get a benefit here.

The Russians have been called upon to fight all out to defend Stalingrad. There is severe fighting in the streets at Novorossiysk, too. The Germans give no quarter and the fighting is the most severe of this war. *Poor* Russians. The Germans push on in spite of violent resistance. We made the heaviest raid ever made on a moonless night and the target was Düsseldorf. We lost 31 bombers. In Madagascar we have been obliged to make fresh landings and get the surrender of other towns than Diego Suarez, as the Vichy French are allowing Nazis and Japs to continue their machinations there.

Wednesday 16th September

Forty years ago today two people became engaged. I thought of it when I woke this morning, and reminded Jack. By 11 a.m. I was able to go out in the garden, forked a long strip in the vegetable patch and planted out cabbages, which ought to be useful in the early spring, if beasties and diseases leave them to grow. I finished at 1 p.m. and came in *vastly* hungry and enjoyed roast pork and all the etceteras.

We raided Tobruk on Sunday night. The disturbances in India recently have been described and the extent of the damage (pretty considerable) at railway stations and communications. Brutal atrocities were committed, too, and much wanton damage. The Canadian casualties at Dieppe are also given today: 3,350 dead, wounded and missing. The Japs are attacking in the Solomon Islands again, bringing up reinforcements to try and drive the Americans away.

Saturday 19th September

This is a good day, for this morning *a letter and two postcards came from Alan*—gr-r-and! He sounds very much his own dear self and there appear to be no extraordinary happenings up to 18th August. The garden is yielding its vegetables and Alan greatly enjoys 'spinnach', with two ns! Well, our tails were up today and everything seemed good. It has been a nice warm day, too.

There is heavy fighting in the streets of Stalingrad, where the Germans (and Russians too, I expect) lie dead in heaps. Terrible! The Vichy French asked for an armistice in Madagascar and then refused the terms, so we fight on. They have delayed our converging march by blowing up bridges, but otherwise the resistance is poor so far.

Sunday 20th September

A cloudy, though warm, morning, and I managed to rouse myself from deep sleep and was cycling down to Berkswell at 8 a.m. The service was entirely ruined by *that man*. Try as one would, one could *not* get any consecutive thought with this continual hacking and hawking. It is too bad that he spoils the service for everyone else. Rain fell while we were in church, but ceased as I rode home, and teemed down again when I got in, so I was lucky.

Tuesday 22nd September

A letter came from Colin this morning. He has bought a farm! The name intrigues me—the 'Dean and Chapter' Farm, at Codrington, near Chipping Sodbury, Gloucester. At the moment, he says, having been extensively modernized, it is rather a flash country gent's house, but 'we hope to put that right in time'. He goes on: 'A built-in cocktail bar will take a lot of living down, but three bathrooms will all be used, as we have the land-girls living in the house.' Well, here's all the luck in the world to him, after the blows he has taken so well in the past.

Thursday 24th September

Joan Spencer rang up to say she had read in the *Coventry Evening Telegraph* that Oflag VIB had been dissolved, and we afterwards found this in *The Times*. Russians are fighting hard in Stalingrad streets and have made a thrust counter-attack on the north-west of the city. They are having a terribly bloody battle, the worst of the war. It is amazing how they hold on. We have made an amazing attack in Libya, hundreds of miles behind the German front line.

Trucks arrived and shot up many aeroplanes and did other damage, and then returned. Tobruk was attacked at the same time.

Saturday 26th September

Mrs Greenslade rang up to say she had a letter from Edward, sent from VIB. They were then getting ready to leave the camp, and packing up for hundreds of men was a terrific job. He was sorry to leave the garden, but hoped they were going to a better camp—anyway, it would be a change and vary the monotony. He said Alan and Philip Varley were going too, so now we know Alan's address is Oflag VIIB—just an extra stroke to the old address. I hope we may hear soon.

The Russians are still fighting their enemy house-by-house and street-by-street in Stalingrad. We have heard more details today of the Russian convoy, in which 75 warships took part. It was a terrible journey, but the great majority of the ships arrived safely—a victory for the Allies indeed. Russia is suffering greatly from the lack of food, clothing and medical supplies and has a hard winter in front of her. The R.A.F. went over Oslo and hit the H.Q. of the Quisling Gestapo. Only one of our aircraft was lost.

Saturday 3rd October

Two letters from Alan today, dated 24.8.42 and 4.9.42. In the first he was very excited at the prospect of a move, and later knew where he was eventually going. Two very interesting letters. Batchelor left us this morning.

Edouard Heriot, former Prime Minister of the French Cabinet, has been arrested by the Vichy Government. An old man, now over 70, he dared to say what he thought. The Russians are doing better in Stalingrad and holding up the Germans, regaining houses and streets and pressing forward.

British production is greater man for man than in any other country in the world, says Lord Halifax. President Roosevelt is arranging for the stabilization of wages to prevent inflation.

Wednesday 7th October

I have just been telling Jack how miserable some of the shops in Leamington look. The shelves are getting emptier and emptier and many other shops space their goods out to look more than there really is. We are getting down to essentials only, though I will say I saw some lovely rolls of tweed in one shop. The coupons keep people from rushing in and buying the lot. Many are the considerations before one buys any garment these days. I have seen women hesitating, weighing and pondering over a couple of vests at three coupons each, when in an ordinary time four would have been purchased without a thought. Hats are to be fewer—I seem to have many, thanks be!

We have made a raid on Sark, where the Germans are going to deport British civilians to Germany. They say we tied prisoners with ropes at Dieppe and they are now going to manacle *our* men!

Thursday 8th October

Our reply was broadcast to the Germans today—in effect that we shall manacle German prisoners on Saturday if they persist.

Friday 9th October

The Germans now have to go one better and say they will now manacle three times the number of prisoners we put in irons. Aren't they really mad! Our raid on Sark was accomplished by ten men (including officers) and none were lost. They took five prisoners but four, proving awkward, had to be shot. We have a proclamation signed by a German officer concerning the deportation of men of Sark, some of whom have already been taken to Germany. This is against all the rules and I do hope we can do something.

Saturday 10th October

The German retaliation to the manacling (or, as Kate called it, 'mangling'!) of the German prisoners of war is that they will manacle double the quantity. However we have given notice tonight that we are going to carry out our word, as they have not withdrawn their threat.

In a raid over Lille by U.S. bombers yesterday 'the complex operation was carried out without a hitch'. Four bombers were lost, but the crew of one is safe. The fighters destroyed five enemy aircraft and none of our fighters—says the *communiqué*—is missing. It is the biggest daylight raid so far—100 bombers of the U.S.A.A.F. and 500 fighters flown by British, Dominion, American and other pilots acted as escort and made diversionary sweeps. Yes, it is all very satisfactory, and one realizes that power is really coming into the Allies' hands at last. Are we just half-way through the war?

Thursday 15th October

Jack in bed today with a hoarse throat and a temperature. The doctor looked in about 10 a.m. and says it is influenza, so he will be in bed for a few days, poor old dear. No letter from Alan yet and we do want to hear from him. It is nearly a fortnight since we had a postcard giving the new address. The painters are around the house and we are beginning to look very fresh and smart.

Saturday 17th October

The patient is still better today. This morning I did a little W.L.A. work, going down to the hostel with some magazines and a note for the forewoman. I also asked if I might see the bedrooms, and found them all spotless and very neat. While upstairs I asked the caretaker what nationality she was and she replied: 'German'. It made me blink a little! However we went on through the rooms and came downstairs again, where I spoke to several of the girls, and we talked of a club-room for them, etc.

Malta has brought down over 100 aircraft in six days, for the loss of 34.

Wednesday 21st October

Off today for a little holiday! Jack was down to breakfast for the first time for ten days and Mrs Gorton gave us a lift to Leamington station, where we waited half an hour for the train. Soon we were in the train for the short journey to Stratford. A taxi took our three small cases to the William and Mary Hotel and we walked, as the taxi was engaged. I unpacked the few belongings and, after lunch, we decided to go the matinee at the theatre for the performance of *Rebecca*, which we enjoyed very much, though the players were distinctly wartime. Dinner and a quiet, pleasant evening followed in the lounge. I wrote to Alan.

Saturday 24th October

This morning we were wakened early by the people in the room overhead, who were evidently making an early start. Our morning was spent, as usual, with coffee at the Cobweb, and then we found a sheltered seat in the Theatre Gardens. I went and bought some rolls and fed the sparrows and the swans. Very reprehensible in wartime.

A letter from Kate today told of news from Mrs Greenslade about Oflag VIIB. Edward has written that the new camp has brick buildings and proper washbasins. Also they travelled 22 hours in second-class carriages instead of cattle-trucks. (I don't think Alan travelled in a cattle-truck!) They were sorry when the journey was over as the scenery was lovely. Now they are surrounded by woods and mountains.

Jack and I got home at 5 p.m. and I spent the evening unpacking and straightening up my desk and belongings.

Sunday 25th October

A cold east wind today with rain in the afternoon, and a wind moaning and howling around the house tonight, now the rain has ceased. It is bright moonlight.

For three nights in succession our bombers went to Italy. The first night they returned without loss after a journey of over 1,300 miles. They bombed Milan—in daylight first, and again the same night. *We have also opened an attack in Egypt*, first of all with a terrific air bombardment, and then tanks. Fierce and heavy fighting is going on now. The Russians have regained a little of the ground they lost at Stalingrad. Their women soak themselves in water to fight the fires in the city. American forces were reported in Liberia a few days ago. Have these a direct connection with the opening of the attack in Egypt?

Monday 2nd November

Today a quick dash round the daily jobs and then Jack, Twink and I walked together as far as the grocer on my way to the station. At Coventry I made my way quickly to the Geisha Café, where I found Alice Richards waiting at a lunch table. A neat little lunch was quickly served and by 12.40 p.m. we were in our seats at the Empire Theatre for a four-hour sit for the film *Gone With the Wind*. Back circle seats ('Upper Circle') were four bob, but I think we had our money's worth of scenery, tantrums and close-ups! I got home just before blackout. Land-girls came for the first of their weekly meetings and there was a good deal of laughter and joking, and the cloakroom pegs were full of land-girls' coats.

We are sinking ships in the Mediterranean and the latest sinkings were two Axis supply ships off Tobruk. The battle in Egypt is increasing in intensity and there is fierce fighting.

Thursday 5th November

Eleven years today we came to Balsall Common. We are getting quite old inhabitants now and don't look like leaving the place—at any rate till after the war. Great news today that Rommel's forces are in full retreat in the desert. Our Air Force is pounding them as they go along the coast road, breaking up their columns, sending the men streaking out sideways through the sand. They know now what we felt like in France in May 1940—only they bombed civilian refugees; women and children, too. I feel grim and sad over this—sad that such things must be, but retribution must follow wicked deeds. The King has sent a message to General Alexander and the Eighth Army congratulating them on their 'great victory', and after the midnight *communiqué* messages came in from New Zealand, Australia, etc., recording their satisfaction at the good news.

Sunday 8th November

Remembrance Sunday, and great news today! American troops have landed in North Africa at several points, covered by the British Fleet at Gibraltar. Tons of leaflets have been dropped telling the population not to resist as the Allies do not want territory, but only to clear the country of the evil Axis forces. They are asked to co-operate, and to show whether they are willing certain signs are to be shown—one American and one tricolour flown together, or two tricolours, one above the other, etc. General Giraud, who has escaped from Germany where he was imprisoned (both in this war and the last) has broadcast that he is in Algiers and is the Commander-in-Chief. He is calling on the people to rally to him as the only hope of saving France is through the Allies. Vichy, with the old fool (and traitor!) Petain, allied with Laval and Germany, refuses to co-operate. They say the situation in North Africa is serious. One hopes so indeed. America is delighted at the news of her forces making the landings. Rommel's forces continue to retreat. Five hundred tanks and 1,000 guns have now been captured or put out of action. This is all very heartening news. May we keep it up.

Monday 9th November

Algiers has signed an armistice, and so troops are continuing to land there, as well as at Oran, Saafi, Agadir, etc., etc. It has been a vast and wonderful organization which has come safely to fruition. General Eisenhower is Commander-in-Chief of the Allied Force and Sir Andrew Cunningham has charge of the British Fleet in the Mediterranean. Gibraltar provided the jumping-off place for, as the enemy says, like Malta, it is an 'unsinkable aircraft carrier'. The way was led by Rangers (we call them Commandos) of the American Army and airborne troops were brought up in support of the landing parties.

Genoa has been heavily bombed again and great damage done. Rommel's Army is in full retreat towards the Libyan frontier. *The Times* says today: 'His defeat has become a rout'.

This afternoon Jack was told by a man who had been speaking to an R.A.F. signals man that Rommel had capitulated. He said he had just got the message. We were thrilled to the marrow but, alas, after listening to the 5 p.m. and the 9 p.m. news, the message seems to be without foundation.

Wednesday 11th November

Things are moving quickly. The Germans have sent airborne troops to Tunisia and have landed in Corsica. The Eighth Army is on the Libyan border. Italians are stranded in the desert, abandoned by their German 'allies', and we are doing our utmost to rescue them. A speech in Parliament from Mr Churchill today says the enemy has lost 59,000 men killed, wounded and prisoner— 34,000 of whom are German—in the Battle of Egypt. We have lost about 13,000 men, of whom many are officers. For the first time in this war, bells are to be rung on Sunday to celebrate this victory.

And now the 9 p.m. news. All North Africa except Tunisia has surrendered. Germans are occupying part of what was called 'Unoccupied' France, and great events are expected within the next few days. We and our American allies are marching on Tunisia, or are already there. Hitler says as usual, in effect, he only 'wants to be kind' to France and is anxious that its beautiful country should not be desecrated—as if the fact that Germans are swarming over it is not the worst possible desecration! The Franco–German 'armistice' is broken. Today we have broadcast to France asking her to co-operate and for ships out on the sea to come as quickly as possible to North Africa or Gibraltar, and if they cannot do this to scuttle them.

Saturday 14th November

We have shot down six troop-carriers and damaged others while they were flying from North Africa to Sicily. Malta aircraft swooped on them and took heavy toll of the 60 craft. Last night we raided Genoa again and for the second time lost no aeroplanes. Poor Norway is suffering badly—everything seems to be forbidden. They may not listen to anything but German broadcasts and the death penalty is threatened for almost every misdeed. This is in order to try to put down the underground news, which seems to get round, to the detriment of the Germans, in spite of previous efforts to choke it. A naval engagement has begun in the Solomon Islands. In New Guinea many Japs have been killed near Buna.

But the great news for us today *is that a letter arrived from Alan.* Dated 11.10.42, it begins: 'No doubt you will be wondering today whether I have had my hands tied or not. Well, so far I am free, though, in addition to the Dieppe party, Hargrave and Sam were among the unlucky ones who were taken away yesterday. However everything went quite smoothly and they are living in Block I and are being humanely treated. I believe some of them tried to play football this morning, though this was rightly considered too dangerous and the ball was removed.' We certainly hope he won't have his hands tied but, if this indignity is forced upon him, that he will bear it as becomes a British officer—and get a bit of amusement out of it, too.

Sunday 15th November
We heard church bells today—the first since June 1940. First the bells of Coventry Cathedral on the wireless 9 o'clock news and then later, at 10.25, they ended a broadcast of bells from the bombed cities. I must say the familiar bells playing the tune 'O God Our Help in Ages Past', followed by a wild peal, caught at my heartstrings. Just before eleven o'clock we both went outside to hear the Berkswell bells ringing out, and they sounded grand, too.

Monday 16th November
Another letter from Alan today, giving a description of the scenery round the new camp. It is dated 20.9.42—a long time ago. Silver-cleaning early today and later I went off to interview a farmer about one of his land-girls. He is very willing to talk and pours it forth in a great stream, catching his breath at intervals for a fresh spate. At last I got away and came home. The land-girls came trooping in between 7 and 8 p.m. and voiced their wants, had tea and buns, laughed and talked and giggled and left.

General Eisenhower's appointment of Darlan as administrative minister in North Africa has not been kindly received either by the British or by the Fighting French, who have now expressed their distaste for Darlan and have refused to work with or under him. Hurrah! This matter has made us uneasy and we are glad it has come to a head.

Monday 23rd November
Not a very good night, so I stayed in bed till 12. It was a very cold night and the thermometer showed three degrees of frost this morning. The doctor came after lunch and prescribed milk and no solids for me for a day or two, and plenty of rest. So I took his advice immediately and spent the afternoon on the sofa. Great are the blessings of a woollen jumper and tweed skirt, combined with a pullover hairnet!

The Russians are closing in round Stalingrad, killing thousands of Germans and taking thousands of prisoners—50,000 Germans have been killed or made prisoner and the wounded are not yet counted. At Dakar the French Fleet has joined Darlan, and French West Africa has put itself under his orders. I find this very confusing, but the B.B.C. announced it with great gusto.

Saturday 28th November

A good night for me—and good war news from Russia, though the waste of human life and effort is appalling. French sailors at Toulon went down with their ships after the Germans had moved into the port—more waste—but a choice of evils, and we are thankful the French Fleet did not fall into German clutches. A talk by a French Admiral on the scuttling of the Fleet was intensely pathetic after the 9 p.m. news.

Nothing to report from Libya. It is suggested Rommel may make a stand at El Agheila, which is a good position strategically. The First Army in Tunisia is getting on slowly towards Tunis.

Saturday 5th December

A dark and dreary morning after a wet night. The daily round was quickly got through and I hastened out just after 10 a.m. to sell flags for the 'Prisoners of War Special Effort'. Such a piercing cold wind there was, and waiting on doorsteps is a cold job. However I did quite well and shall be anxious to know the result of my particular effort. I always enjoy these jobs, which help me to know my neighbours better. Many inquiries were made for Alan and I wished I had more to tell the kind folk. Walking about for three hours and being chatty and pleasant is quite wearing, so after lunch I sat by a lovely warm fire, wrapped all round with the pretty blue rug, and was soon asleep. Tonight a high wind is raging outside and anywhere outside this living-room or the kitchen is *very* cold. We no longer warm the hall owing to shortage of fuel and electricity, but we don't do too badly.

Lately we have sunk much transport of men and material going to Tunisia from Sicily. Things seem a bit sticky near Tunis at the moment and we are having a stiff fight to dislodge the enemy. El Agheila is mentioned as the place where Rommel's fleeing army might make a stand in the last bit of Libya—and we all seem to be stopping to 'dror breff'. Naples has been severely bombed by American Liberators and the 'planes returned without loss'.

Wednesday 16th December

At last a letter and a postcard from Alan, dated 24.9.42 and 24.10.42. He talks of hockey, soccer and touch-rugger, describing the latter game and appearing quite interested in hockey. He does not mention the tying of prisoners, though he says that Nevill 'stayed with us ten days', so probably the two men who were tied came back after ten days. He had a cold after scorning those 'who spent their time sneezing', while he who was so bronzed and healthy 'spent his time in the fresh air'.

Thursday 17th December

Mr Eden spoke in Parliament today about the attempted extermination of the Jews by Germany. The Jews are sent into ghettos in Poland and there they are starved. They are made to work so hard that they die, or are executed in hundreds at a time—women and children too. The Polish Ambassador is speaking of it as I write. It is just wholesale murder. The scene in Parliament was deeply impressive, for after Mr Eden's recital, on a suggestion from a Labour Member, the House rose and remained standing in silence for a minute in deep and eloquent sympathy.

Monday 21st December

This pleasant mild day we both worked hard in the garden. I hastened to polish up the silver and, as the post came late, I just had to skim through letters and cards, leaving some for a period later in the day when one could enjoy them. Even in wartime the post gives one a thrill—and a flood of memories. Some folks write just once a year Maybe it is only a card, but it sends one turning back the pages and thinking of the things that belong to the sender. As one gets older and there is so much background, one can't be dull, but can just open the heart's store, look round the shelves, take down the memory and live it over again. Grand!

Calcutta has had its first air raid by the Japs—not very heavy. Rommel is still fleeing and has already gone as far as from Istanbul to Munich. The R.A.F. made a heavy raid on Duisburg last night, leaving many fires burning.

Thursday 24th December

A morning of Christmas preparation, and such nice things to do. There was the little Crib to be brought out of its box and put on top of the bookcase with all the little animals and birds from the mantelpiece 'adoring' in front of it. Then there was the holly to be arranged, and as there were such elegant branches I put them in large vases, with just a few bits on pictures and in smaller vases. It was nearly lunchtime by the time Alan's photograph was flanked by two little glass vases of yellow jasmine, a bit of yellow-green shrub and some rosemary.

This is a joyous time in peace, and even in catastrophic wartime such as this it cannot be anything but joyous in its implications. It is, however, such a family festival that the thought of Alan in a prison camp in Germany for the third Christmas in succession does put a damper on one's joy. 'May he be with us next year' is our heart's desire and fervent prayer.

Friday 25th December

Sleep did not come easily last night and Christmas Day was more than an hour old before I fell asleep, waking again at 7 a.m. I felt fresh and more than usually ready to get up. Our Christmas Communion service was at 9 a.m., for Berkswell Church has no blackout curtains and does not draw curtains back until 8.47 a.m. today. The scene inside the church was indescribably lovely. The altar and sanctuary were floodlit and the stonework appeared almost white, with huge white chrysanthemums on the altar and red Chinese lantern pods (physalio) with them among the dark-green leaves. It was an arresting sight.

At 10 a.m. we were home again and glad of breakfast. I gathered some nice big, tight sprouts for our Christmas dinner and arranged the table before Jack and I went with Twink to the station to meet our guests, Harry and Ethel Spencer. After a walk round the garden we came in to a comfortable fire, for it was quite raw and chilly outside. We gave our presents—mostly books—and then, while we were looking at Christmas cards, Joan Curtis and Ann came in and we enjoyed seeing them.

The news told us that Darlan has been assassinated and that the Russians are still victorious. The Japanese are now on a strip of land about a mile long and 500 yards wide at Buna, but it is a strongly-prepared position and will not be easily taken by our Forces.

At 1.15 we sat down to a marvellous dinner. The cockerel proved a truly wonderful bird—the size of a young turkey, with a breast of thick meat of excellent flavour—followed by Christmas pudding à la Kate. Next we each took a mince pie, and there were gooseberry fools in glasses to follow, with Graves of an unusually good flavour to accompany all this. Harry brought the sherry, which was our pre-dinner appetiser, so we really have had a lucky day.

At 3 p.m., after a round-the-world programme, the King broadcast a Christmas message very strongly and clearly, seeming much less nervous. He is, alas, now one with those who mourn someone near and dear in the loss of the Duke of Kent this year. We stood for 'God Save the King' and even tried to sing it. All the time we had Nevill and Alan in our minds and hearts, and the King spoke of the thoughts of the Queen and himself being with those 'who have lost their dear ones, those wounded and in hospital . . . the prisoners of war who bear their long exile with dignity and fortitude'.

Thursday 31st December
A letter from Alan again today, dated 19.11.42, and a cheery one too. It tells of him getting up at 7 a.m., shaving 'by feel', working at his studies till 8 a.m., and again after breakfast and lunch as 'the exam' (Assoc. Member of Mech. Engs.) is in ten days' time. Joan Spencer has had several letters, and one tells of 200 officers being manacled. But 'they are quite humanely treated and no-one need worry', he says. The manacling lasts 18 days for 12 hours a day. Of course they make fun of it, but Nevill remarks 'how extraordinary it is that a man's mind should be so like a child's mind'. The German Censor lets this through, it seems!

Friday 1st January
We stayed up last night to see the New Year in! This is wonderful for us, but we felt this will be a momentous year and so we would usher it in with wakeful alertness instead of *snoring* it in! So, having prepared ourselves for bed, we came down in our dressing-gowns and sat before the fire listening to the service on the wireless at 11.45 p.m. and hearing Big Ben toll the last strokes of the old year. Some slept when they went to bed, some lay thinking awhile, but both woke quite fresh to greet 1st January with great hopes for better and better things this year and a heartfelt wish for victory and Alan John home again.

A visitor came about National Savings just before dinner-time, but my time is already fully occupied, so I cannot take on any more work. I imagine everybody worth their salt also has more than enough to do by now. Tonight I got down to land-girl reports and petrol records for the W.L.A. and W.V.S.—a most lengthy and tiring business. I began at 5.45 p.m. and finished at 10 p.m., with intervals for the news and supper.

Wednesday 6th January

With Epiphany the little Crib was stored away and most of the holly has been removed, leaving just a bit for 'Twelfth Night'. Later I had a spare hour in which to poke my nose in and out of cupboards and drawers, straightening, seeking, finding, disposing of things. My nose went into Alan's wardrobe, and I hate seeing his clothes with himself so long away. However I determined to keep the corners of my mouth well up and instead of 'snf, snf' I said, very vigorously, 'Oh, damn and blast!' and then laughed at such idiocy—and felt bettah!

Sunday 17th January

The news today is that the Eighth Army is on the offensive in Tripoli and Rommel is retreating once more—or 'advancing westward', as the Germans say! The R.A.F. are strafing the German positions and it sounds like another big move. As for the Russians, their advance is marvellous—they are now 50 miles from Rostov. They captured loaded guns that have never been fired, a train-load of lorries, great supplies of food, masses of ammunition and have taken and killed 32,000 men. The Germans counter-attack when they are not unexpectedly over-run, and nothing seems to stop the Russian push. Last night our bombers, a large force, raided Berlin and we lost only one plane. War correspondents went on the raid, and tomorrow Richard Dimbleby is to broadcast about it.

Monday 18th January

I did not hear Dimbleby, but Jack said his description was marvellous. We went to Berlin again last night, but the toll of our planes was heavy compared with yesterday. This time we lost 22 bombers. German raiders came to London and damaged mostly houses. We destroyed ten.

The trapped army before Stalingrad is approaching its inevitable end. The offer from the Russians if they would surrender was refused. Poor wretches, they *dare* not surrender lest their families should be killed or put in concentration camps (those German hells!) at home. The Eighth Army is going on well. In spite of Rommel's rearguard action, tank traps and mines, it advances a mile an hour on an average. Also our casualties are light.

The 9 p.m. news gave us something worthwhile! The siege of Leningrad has been lifted after one year and four months. This really is great news.

Thursday 21st January

The raid on London yesterday was bad. Seventy to a hundred German planes crossed the Channel to the coast near Beachy Head and, in spite of heavy gunfire, some were able to come inland, though chased by our fighters. They dropped their bombs indiscriminately and a school received a direct hit from a high explosive bomb. The children—about 150—were having dinner and 30 of them and two teachers were killed and 21 injured, and I think there are also some missing. In other areas women and children were killed, too. Six aeroplanes can do a lot of damage. Fourteen of the raiders were shot down.

This has been a good day for us. First there was *a letter from Alan dated 28.11.42*, in which he said they were having a cold, damp day, and that his exam was imminent. He feared the April parcel was lost, which is a pity as it contained the gumboots and a beautiful pullover knitted by Florence. However he does not seem very short of clothes, which is a good thing.

Saturday 23rd January

Good news! Tripoli is in our hands—the Italian 'Empire' is no more. Hurrah and hurrah! Fourteen hundred miles the Eighth Army has advanced in 80 days, and over what country! Desert sand and scrub, tank-traps, mines and booby-traps, but nothing stopped them. They just went on advancing, doing about 17 miles a day. All this is very heartening and may we soon hear of a good *shove* in Tunisia so that we can take over the whole of North Africa for the present. We manage to sink a good many Axis ships, transport and supply, and I expect the packs of U-boats take toll of our shipping, too. Russia continues her victorious advance and the Caucasus sack, or pocket, is fast straightening out as they get nearer to Rostov. Great efforts are being made to widen the corridor by which Leningrad was relieved.

Monday 27th January

A bright idea struck me as I opened my window just before 8 a.m. The day was fine and surely it was dry enough for digging—why not ring up the Hostel and ask if a land-girl was free to come and start the potato patch? I rushed downstairs in my dressing-gown and seized the telephone and soon had the matter fixed.

Then I listened to the 8 a.m. news, which had just begun, and heard such news! Mr Churchill, President Roosevelt and a crowd of big-wigs have met in conference at Casablanca. They have been there since 14th January, and the whole field of war was surveyed and plans for the 1943 offensive made. President Roosevelt later described the meeting as the 'unconditional surrender' meeting, by which he meant that unconditional surrender by the Axis was the only assurance of future world peace. General de Gaulle and General Geraud also met at Casablanca, and a statement was afterwards made in London that 'the necessary liaison for assuring the unification of the war effort of the French Empire and of the French Forces on land, sea and air would be established immediately'. This is all very good news. Stalin was invited to go, but with Russia so very occupied with the great offensive in her own country it was not possible for the Head of the Soviet Union, Commander-in-Chief of the Red Army, to leave his country at this time! However he has been appraised of all that has been arranged at the Conference. Now we want to get on top of the German U-boats and then victory will be a good deal nearer. The Germans are now telling their people of the hardships they will have to go through during the coming year, exhorting and threatening in turn.

Saturday 30th January

Rain in the night and so no digging for the land-girl today—nor for us. Jack and I, and Twink, went for a walk during the morning, having previously done a little shopping in the village. I got two sandwich loaves and Jack a garden shovel. His slippers, probably 20 years old, had really worn out, and I took them to the local shoemender's to get a rubber sole fixed on so that I could give them away. But the man said he could put a sole on—and did! Now they look so nice and are so well-fitted to Jack's foot that we are giving a much newer pair away instead.

This is the tenth anniversary of Hitler's accession to power and, as a rule, he makes a speech. This time Goering made a speech this morning—after an hour's delay—because Mosquitos of the R.A.F. bombed Berlin in daylight, upset the speech and got safely home! This afternoon Goebbels spoke before reading the proclamation which Hitler had ordered him to deliver, and the R.A.F. went over Berlin again. They talked a lot of twaddle and Hitler's proclamation referred to the Almighty—though he has been known to say that the German nation is Germany's god. How dare he say these things! Hitler is supposed to be with his armies at the front. M'yes, perhaps not.

Monday 1st February

How soon a month of 1943 has gone! And yet how interminable the long separation from Alan seems! Day after day we get up, work, play and go to bed, and yet Alan is still away. However, Hitler and his lot are moaning at present, and we—well—we are feeling much bettah!!

Lots of rain in the night, and the porch temperature at 9 a.m. was 40°. Having suffered much grumbling toothache all week, and a bit extra last night, I rang up the dentist and found I could have the offending tooth out at 4.30 p.m. That changed the whole day, so we decided to go to Leamington this morning. The hairdresser fell in with this, too, so all was managed successfully and we were home at 5 p.m. The land-girls came in for half an hour and then went to the Social at the Institute.

More advances have been made by the Russians and the German Army divisions which were trapped at Stalingrad are now disposed of entirely. There were 330,000 of them attacking Stalingrad! Now this prodigious number is either killed, wounded or made prisoner.

Thursday 11th February

This morning we were thrilled to have a letter thrust through the banisters, as we never can wait till we come downstairs to read *a letter from Alan*. Interesting but rather ancient. It was dated 31st October 1942. Much chat about books and a description of the scene from the camp—all enjoyable to read.

Eastbourne had a bad raid last Sunday, with 26 killed and 48 injured and several public buildings and shops damaged or destroyed, as well as houses. The Japs have been completely eliminated from Guadalcanal. The Russians continue to progress westward at a good pace. Nothing to report from North Africa.

There was a gorgeous sunset this evening—gold and crimson, orange and opal, ever-changing and blending—resplendent glory.

Sunday 14th February

Another nice fresh day and we went to church and enjoyed it all immensely. A good congregation makes a lot of difference, though it would have been better without *that man*.

The wireless announces 'The Russians report the recapture of Rostov.' It is the tenth largest city in Russia and a great industrial town. Our bombers made two concentrated attacks on Lorient last night. They dropped one thousand tons of bombs there.

Typhoons—our latest bombers—destroyed four Focke–Wulfs over the Channel today. We lost two Typhoons.

Sunday 21st February

This morning was rather cold, with a chill in the wind. Rather reluctantly I went out to garden and set to work on the bed on the right of the drive. Two barrow-loads of pine needles and rubbish was raked off it and then one could begin.

When Wilhelmshaven was raided a short time ago there was a terrific explosion which seemed to puzzle our men who had done the bombing. It is now known to have been a huge arsenal which was blown up, and 150 acres were devastated. The Red Army has been having a great celebration today and in English cities the Red Flag has been flown to show what the British think of Russia! Times change indeed, and we with time. Mr Churchill, who has been ill, is on the mend, but still has a slight patch on one lung.

Three years and five months since war began. Three years and six weeks since Alan went away. We go to bed, we get up, we work, we play a little. The daily round goes on. How much longer will it all go on? The light is breaking—how long till the full day?

VOLUME 10

February 1943 – November 1943

Monday 22nd February

Here beginneth Volume Ten, and wouldn't it be grand if it were the last! The morning was rather misty and was considerably cheered by the high polish given to the silver, for it really looked well today. Perhaps it had a specially good do because this morning we had a nice comforting *letter from Alan, dated 10th January 1943*. He sounds as cheerful as ever, is thinking of future cars, while working hard and reading *Fundamentals of Industrial Administration*. They had many degrees of frost and snow on the ground when he wrote.

Things are not going well in Tunisia, where the Americans seem to be thinly spread, and it is a very unsatisfactory state of affairs we feel. Russia is meeting counter-attacks firmly and still going westward.

Friday 27th February

It was very thrilling this morning to get *two letters from Alan, dated 20th December and 31st December*. These tell of his 'holiday' for ten days after his exam, preparation for future work, Christmas Eve and Christmas Day, and a lot about food. He half-apologizes for this and then says he thinks we shall like to know how well the Red Cross does for them since we all subscribe to it! He sounds quite cheerful, thanks be!

We are counter-attacking in Tunisia after pushing the Germans back from the Kasserine Pass, and Kasserine is in our hands. The Germans are threatening the Danes with more terrors. A Bishop has been sending an encyclical from his Berlin Cathedral condemning force in place of law, and upholding the right of the individual, the family and the people. He also attacked the idea of setting up the State in place of God—in fact, an attack on the Nazi doctrine. I wonder where he will be this time next week?

Sunday 28th February

Nice to lie in bed till a cup of tea comes at 8 a.m. on a Sunday morning, and then get down in time to hear the 9 a.m. news. This morning we went to church and for my part I greatly enjoyed it, for *that man* was absent and we could all enjoy the singing. There were enough people to make a cheerful noise, too. This afternoon there was a final fill-up of reports and petrol logs, and then I hared off to the post on my bike by 2.45 p.m. After tea I wrote to Alan in reply to his two letters and shall not write again this week. Also I sent a copy of Alan's 31st December letter to the British P.O.W. Relatives' Association magazine in case they should care to print it.

Today I absent-mindedly signed my name 'Clara E. Bagnall'!

Monday 1st March

How soon we have come to the first of March, and how glad I am we have so far had no real snowy winter to cope with. All day Jack and I have been out of doors. The hen house came this morning and the hefty man who drove the lorry put it into position. Jack has been hovering round it with screws and hammer, screwdriver and nails, tidying it up. I have given advice—not always welcomed, though mostly heeded! The pear tree border was partly forked this morning and afternoon and the iris bed limed. Later I dug and manured four rows of the potato patch. Good business!

Mr Churchill is better, hurrah and hurrah, and no more bulletins will be issued.

Thursday 4th March

This morning we heard that London had several alerts and two raids. People were killed and damage done. There was a terrible accident at a tube shelter last night after the sirens had sounded in London. People were proceeding down the steps when an old woman holding a baby slipped and fell. An old man tripped over her and, with people above continuing to come down, one after another fell and 178 were suffocated and crushed! Sixty others were treated in hospital. Dreadful!

Thursday 11th March

The morning was mild, with a sprinkling of rain early and lovely hot sun later in the day, with an increasingly cold north wind. I worked in the garden on the south side of the house mostly and so did not feel it, but since the holly hedge at the end of the big lawn has been laid low the cold is intense. I dug five rows of vegetable patch, among many other things, and Jack has been working in the garage on a broody-hen coop, to be known as 'clink' (army prison).

I received a letter from A. C. H. Harrison, a friend of Alan, telling me that her elder sister had met someone who had escaped from his camp. This 'someone' had been lecturing and telling about German prison life. This made me remember Alan's words 'Have you heard from "Pip" Newman?' (Major Philip H. Newman, D.S.O., F.R.C.S., whom he knew in Malines in 1940). I could not understand what he meant until we suddenly wondered whether 'Pip' had escaped. I replied, 'No, ought I to have heard from him?' But so far no reply has come to that. Jack looked him up in *Who's Who* and so we had his address, and today I wrote to ask him if he had escaped. If he has not, someone will open the letter and tell me.

Friday 12th March

Raid casualties for February are 252 killed and 347 injured. Raids on the south, south-east and south-west coast seem to be increasing—we brought down several planes and today a Norwegian squadron chased the enemy over the Channel and brought down five out of 24. Kharkov is in the news. The Germans say they are in the town again. Alas if this is so!

The Petrol Controller says we cannot have a further allowance of petrol for 'domestic purposes'. Blow!

Monday 15th March

This has been a thrilling day and a lovely day, too. Mrs Greenslade came to lunch and *brought the hens*! Four nice big cobby Light Sussex, very good to look at, and who soon made themselves at home. We went to look at them from time to time and they seemed quite cheery. They did us well and laid two small eggs, quite a nice surprise for the first day. Land-girls came later and enjoyed a talk and a cup of tea.

Tuesday 23rd March

The battle raging in Tunisia is, so far, going well for us. Four armies are busy there—the First Army in the north, the Americans near Gabes, the French pushing up from the south and the Eighth Army has taken some primary objectives in the Mareth Line. Good luck to them all. Prisoners have been exchanged for the first time in this war—863, mostly Merchant Navy on the British side, for

863 Axis prisoners—25 Germans and the rest Italian. They were landed and exchanged at Mersim in Turkey and are all now on their way to their respective territories.

Wednesday 24th March

The eight o'clock news was a blow. The Germans have re-taken the gains we had made in the Mareth Line. Disappointing! And more to the Eighth Army than us, I expect, after their efforts. Well, we just have to 'treat those two impostors both the same', as Kipling said of 'Triumph and Disaster'.

This morning a letter came from Major Newman, so he *has* escaped from a German prison camp. I was delighted to hear, and loved having a picture of Alan in my mind walking round and round the courtyard at Oflag IXA/M 'wearing a Polish (but *I* think Belgian) greatcoat', as Major Newman writes. Also he was always fit and cheerful. The idea of pretending he had a T.B. knee when they were in Belgium was a good idea to keep them all nice and comfy in a decent mess altogether. Thank God it wasn't that at all.

The living-room has been spring-cleaned after the sweep's visit yesterday. Very hard work for Kate and me, but well worth it.

Saturday 27th March

A pleasant morning about 11 a.m., when the grey skies cleared and the sun came out, warming up the world. I enjoyed biking to the butcher, and found it so nice to have the afternoon and evening free to garden and 'mess about' generally. Jack was getting up turf round the hen pen and making an ash path, and the hens seemed to enjoy his company. They are not shy. Twink is still frightfully curious about them and puts his nose to the wire and stands and gazes at them. They gobble up everything we give them, and in return they have laid 21 eggs since last Monday week.

Many spring flowers were seen in London today, now that the ban on the sending of flowers by train has been lifted. There are some things people badly need, and flowers do keep up the spirits of townspeople in their wretched bombed cities. I am so glad they can have them. Our forsythia, daffodils, violets and flowering currants are all out now—not many daffs yet, but opening day by day.

Tuesday 30th March

Today's news was given by Mr Churchill in Parliament. We have occupied Gabes and, with El Hamma in our hands too, our

Army is moving through the gap between them in touch with the enemy's rearguard. It would be grand if Rommel couldn't get away. He's a bit elusive, like the imaginary character 'The Scarlet Pimpernel', or the very real enemy of the Boer War who was equally elusive—General de Wet. Our bombers went to Berlin in a large-scale raid and we lost 22. Another force went to the Ruhr.

We have been very cheery all day as this morning we *had a letter and a postcard from Alan*. A very good letter, too. He sounds well and even talks of doing a bit of gardening when he comes home, 'to help us', and suggests a little less garage work. Well, well! They have been having only half a Red Cross parcel a week for three months, but as they pool everything they manage to 'keep up quite a good standard of living'. He is sorry he cannot attend my land-girls parties, but says he would perhaps 'be very shy after three years under monastic conditions'.

Wednesday 7th April

Strong winds and grey skies—stormy like March the lion and nothing of Our Lady April about the weather at all. Planes were going around at 11.30 last night and when I wakened at 3 a.m. they were still coming along, till somewhere about 4 a.m. when I dropped asleep again. Today's news is good. Mr Churchill announced a victory for the Desert Army. It has pushed a wedge into the enemy's strong position and has 'Rommel on the run again'. Six thousand prisoners were taken in this action and the situation is full of possibilities. It is a terrible country to fight in. Our submarines in the Mediterranean are doing good work and sinking tankers and transport. Our R.A.F. go over to France and shoot up locomotives and goods' trains, among many other objectives, in daylight.

Mrs Greenslade has had a letter from Edward, who remarks that Nevill 'is getting tired of being tied'. We did not know before that he was one of the unlucky ones and we shall not pass this news on to his mother and wife. It would worry them and do no good, if they do not already know.

Saturday 10th April

A pleasant if rather grey day. Biking to the butcher (sounds like a modern dance tune) wasn't too bad, and this afternoon I did a job I was glad to have done—sowing carrots, turnips, beet and summer spinach. I enjoyed seeing the seed-bed showing six green stripes—kale, cos and cabbage lettuce, brussels sprouts, purple sprouting brocoli and cabbage. *Tres bon!*

There is great delight today in hearing of the Tunisian Army victories, for we have taken Sfax and are hoping Sousse will fall next. The Forces on the west of the battle area are pressing forward and Rommel is being uncomfortably squeezed. Nothing can avenge Dunkirk, but another of the same kind—only with Germans instead of Allies as victims—is a possibility.

Sunday 11th April

I woke first at 6.15 a.m. when a noisy plane went over, rather close and low down, slept again till 7.15 and with a bit of an effort—but not much—rose up and went to church at 8.15. It was a delightfully warm spring morning and the view from the top of Lavender Hill was as lovely as ever. Lavender Hall looked its prettiest, with the brown branches of a pear tree in dainty tracery over its rosy red walls and all studded with white blossom. Full of delight, I free-wheeled down the steep hill, but was sorry to hear an ominous cough just behind me—*that man*! Alas! However one tried not to let it spoil the service. Home again, cycling with Miss Midgley to the main road, just after nine, and porridge and coffee were excellent.

Tonight we heard Her Majesty the Queen speaking in her kind and charming way to the women of England. Very comforting and sweet to us all in these hard and difficult days. The Eighth Army is 27 miles beyond Sfax. Forty transports going to supply the Axis were brought down.

Sunday 18th April

It was lovely to have tea out of doors today, though a burst of warm weather so early in the year is a bit trying. All the same, to have the freshness of spring with the warmth one hopes for at midsummer—and seldom gets—is a very delightful fusion of seasons. There is a good deal of air activity on the various fronts and war territories, and the Germans and Italians must be feeling the weight of the attacks very much now—Spezzia, Bremen, Duisberg, Essen, terrible damage to them all. Retribution has fallen upon them indeed. I am sorry when we have to destroy their ancient beauties as they have destroyed ours, because such things belong—or ought to belong—to the generations to come, and not have to suffer destruction at the hands of the present one and be gone for ever.

Friday 23rd April

Good Friday. Rain early this morning, clearing about 11 a.m., with sun coming out and going in, and showers in the afternoon. Kate busy spring-cleaning. The last two days have seen staircase, landing and hall made bright and shiny and today I was informed that the scullery was 'for it'. *A letter came from Alan today dated 20th March*. He says he is still finding plenty to do and remarks on their being no room for chocolate in the last parcel. Well, we must see to it that next week's parcel has as much as possible. We are saving all ours for him—and he's worth it—though we are terribly fond of sweets. Food seems a bit of a problem just now. I don't know what to have for meals, but somehow or other we manage to find enough to satisfy us. Alan seems interested in the land-girls and nearly always mentions them.

One of the hens has gone broody, so we have put her in 'clink'. A miserable, humpy wretch she looks, too. The three old ones are unkind to her and give her vicious pecks on her neck, but she is bearing up and manages to lay an egg most days. At 9 p.m. I got her out of 'clink' and put her in the hen house. The old idiot went round clucking and finally sat on top of two hefty stones which I had put in the nest-box! So I heaved her out and put a brick in it. She couldn't sit on that. I left her clucking and hope she eventually went on the perch.

Today 20 Axis transports and 18 other aircraft have been destroyed off Sicily. The First and Eighth Armies are both active and a first objective has been taken in very difficult mountainous country.

Saturday 24th April

A real April day of sunshine and cloud, though up till teatime there were no showers. Biking to the butcher was a tough job against a north wind, but I was mostly blown back. Off to the grocer next and on the way back a call at the ironmonger to ask for a pound of soap—without a coupon to exchange! This was arranged, but never in all my life have I been so short of soap—a nasty feeling.

This afternoon I rang up Joan Spencer to find she was very distressed to have heard from Nevill that he has been manacled since October. They are also segregated from the rest of the camp and are manacled till 9 p.m. at night. One can't think of anything bad enough for these diseased Germans. Their minds are all wrong, and so it is really better that the world should be without this source of trouble. Poor little Joan. I really wish she need not have known, though I can't help thinking how bravely Nevill has concealed it for six months.

Sunday 25th April

Easter Day. A very windy day, later with a cold wind, though not so chilly at first. We hired the Crowhurst 'Queen Mary' to take us to church, which was fairly full with the military on our left in the Lady Chapel. *That man* nearly burst his 'bonds in twain' singing the Easter hymns and we were thankful when he left at the end of the morning service. About 40 or 50 people stayed on to the Communion Service, rather more than usual. Afterwards Twink and I went to see Mrs Sturgess and took our three Easter eggs, laid today, as she so kindly presented us with some soap on Saturday.

After the 9 p.m. news we heard an excellent and most interesting talk by Peter Scott, R.N.V.R., artist son of Robert Falcon Scott, the explorer, and Lady Scott, the artist and sculptress, whom we met at Stratford last October. He was speaking of Robert Hichens, a solicitor from the West Country—also R.N.V.R.—whose courage was an inspiration to all those who knew him and who was lost, or killed in action, recently.

Severe fighting goes on in Tunisia—deadly warfare where our men must take the heights at present dominated by the Axis.

Monday 26th April

Wind blowing strongly all night, but we slept nevertheless. Jack came upstairs after hearing the 8 a.m. news with *another letter and a postcard from Alan, dated 31.3.43 and 14.3.43.* We are glad he sounds 'normal' and not a bit 'cynical'. The daily round went well after that!

Bad news tonight is that Russia has broken off diplomatic relations with Poland. The Germans alleged that there were mass graves at Smolensk filled with the corpses of Poles who had been murdered *en masse* by the Russians some time ago. The Poles wanted a Red Cross inquiry into this (which looks like playing the German game to divide the Allies), with this most unfortunate result.

Friday 30th April

A dash round the house this morning, *very cross* having received the —— petrol officer's refusal to grant even our modest amount of petrol, after further application. Mrs Gorton called for me at 10.45 a.m. and, with Mrs Curtis (and later we picked up her son, the parson here), we were soon at Leamington, myself heartily glad of the lift. It enabled me to shop before going for lunch. All tables were reserved, so I tried the cafeteria—my first experience of this kind of meal. Even wartime difficulties did not make me enjoy this method of serving oneself: pick up the tray, slide it along the bars, receive a slop of meat (not *too* bad, but a bit grisly), far too much potato and gravy and masses of cabbage. Next three prunes and a half and not too bad custard. With these I paid the woman at the end, who spoke in whispers, and walked off to a table—to find I had forgotten my knife and fork, etc.—went back and got them and ate. The coffee was vile, so I left it. Last week I had an excellent meal in the room below for a few coppers more!

Saturday 8th May

The 8 a.m. news described our fresh victory—the Allies have taken Bizerte and Tunis! Now it remains to clear the Germans and Italians from the peninsula with Cape Bon at its tip. Great rejoicing everywhere all day over this good news, which has come earlier than we had expected. Well, though the job is not yet finished, I got the parcel containing the new Union Jack out of the drawer and partly unwrapped it so that one could see red, white and blue. Jack got busy on the flagstaff—it would never do to be found unready when good days come.

Two hundred Axis supply ships is the total sunk off North Africa.

Sunday 9th May

The news on the wireless is full of rejoicing about the ending of the African campaign, and we have just had a 'Marching On' programme describing the victorious push from El Alamein to Tunis. This is Italy's 'Empire' Day. Nuff sed! Thousands of prisoners are being captured and hundreds are surrendering, while pockets remain to be cleared up. What is left of the Axis army is retiring on Cape Bon peninsula. The King has sent a message to General Eisenhower congratulating him and all the Forces under his command in which he speaks of 'repaying the debt of Dunkerque'.

General Alexander, second-in-command to Lord Gort at Dunkirk, was the last man to leave the beaches, and now will see the 'repayment of the debt'. It is very fitting that he should lead the combined armies to a German Dunkirk, three years to the very month afterwards.

Monday 10th May

A letter from Alan this morning. He says April also brought them strong west winds and rain, while rain has only just arrived here. So he says he has been idle as regards exercise for a fortnight.

Nevill S. had been in to see him, so apparently they were not then separated from the others—he may even be free.

We are still thrilled with the North African victories. Leamington has her flags out and it was good to see the old Union Jack on flagstaffs and hanging out of windows, but I couldn't tell whether it was for the victory or 'Wings for Victory' week—perhaps both.

Thursday 13th May

The resistance in Africa is now overcome. The North African campaign has come to a victorious end. The 8 a.m. news gave this welcome word. General von Arnim has been captured and the enemy has had a severe defeat. Our casualties have not been as severe as expected. The prisoners now amount to over 150,000 and there are many generals among them. The Eighth Army engaged the enemy to the south of the fighting zone, but in the meantime sent two divisions to join the First Army by a roundabout route to the north, and the extra weight there caused an unexpected breakthrough, disorganizing the Germans pretty badly and ending their resistance much more quickly. Masses of material have been captured. A million gallons of petrol was found in one place and there were 250 tanks, lorries by the hundred and a good food dump.

Well, Jack soon got out after breakfast and hoisted the flag. 'The flag that braved a thousand years the battle and the breeze' looked simply grand floating out over the orchard. Is there anything more heartening than the Union Jack!

Tuesday 18th May

Twenty-nine years ago a boy was born to the Milburns in Warwick Avenue, Coventry—three months before war broke out in August. Now we are deep into another great war and the little boy, a grown man, is a prisoner of war. I am glad we could not see into the future. It would have been terrifying indeed.

The day has been gloriously fine with a splendid blue sky and a freshening breeze to temper the sun's heat. This afternoon I brought all Alan's coats downstairs and out on to the lawn, brushing them and hanging them in the air, some suspended from the birch tree and others over chairs, etc. I don't think moths will have much out of them for a bit! After supper I nearly forgot the G.T.C. Dance, but remembering, changed and went across to the Institute about 8.45. There I gave prizes, and one of them was mine, for I won a dozen eggs!

The news talks of the damage done by the bombing of two dams in Germany. 'Incalculable damage', it said.

Wednesday 19th May

The Dortmund floods are spreading and devastating vast areas in the Ruhr. The news today tells of 324,000 Axis casualties in Africa—267,000 are prisoners and 224,000 of these have been taken in the last fortnight. General Montgomery has given a message to his Army. Joan Curtis will be sorry that he does not think there will be any leave for them, but he says: 'You and I together must finish the job'.

Friday 21st May

Good news again today: 113 Axis aircraft shot up and down on airfields in Sicily and elsewhere for the loss of *one* of ours. 'Fortresses' did well on our side. The Alan ache is rife today. 'Oh dear, I do *wish* Alan was home,' I say from time to time. 'What's the good of anything while Alan's away.' Really moaning I've been! The only panacea is to work and work and work, and then perhaps one day—maybe. . . .

We continue to bomb Germany by day and night. Italy is getting worried about invasion. Malta had the first bombs dropped since last December.

Friday 28th May

Three years today since Alan was made a prisoner of war—but it's no use moaning. I expect he has thought about it many times today, the darling! This morning, *in the car*, I was really early at the butcher, and how glad I was not to have to cycle! So soon I was back with a nice bit o' beef—round, not square, for once. Then I got the funny little dahlia tubers—such tiny things some were—and found 60 just enough for the three beds. It was a tiring job in the heat, for it has been oppressive today.

News is always of our bombing raids. Essen was last night's target. Our loss was 23 bombers. Mr Eden has warned Italy of what is coming to her and tells people generally that they must not think we shall give up bombing. When our cities in Britain were being bombed, these same people (Spain) laid low and said nothing. Now they want both sides to bar bombing. But if this is one way of ending the war—or helping to do so—horrible as it is, it must be done. One can only deal one way with a dragon. He must be destroyed or he will destroy you.

Wednesday 2nd June

Another letter from Alan, dated 29.4.43, by the morning's post. There was a lot about bird life in the camp. Very interesting, so I wrote a copy of it and sent it to the British Prisoners' of War Relatives' Association magazine in case they would care to put it in. Alan also talks of playing tennis with balls 'not in their first youth', but with a high wind and dust it was not too good. He had a new greatcoat, battledress and boots. Doing very well, methinks. The pinks are nearly out and I have vases in the house—simply heavenly.

An airliner has been shot down by the beastly Germans and the 13 passengers are presumed killed. Leslie Howard is one of them, and how sorry many people will be to hear of this. He had been abroad to Spain and Portugal in connection with his film work and had delayed his return for three days in order to see his own premiere.

Thursday 3rd June

A stormy day. Heavy showers have fallen at intervals and we have both enjoyed having time to work indoors as well as out. At teatime I decided I'd done enough gardening for one day, so a pile of tiresome mending was attended to—much darning of stockings and mending of long ladders, which looked even worse when they were done!

The Axis report that Allied ships have been seen gathered at Gibraltar and that they have now left. They say the invasion is to take place on 22nd June! In the meantime no news of Churchill— except from the enemy, who says he is now going to Moscow. What a lot they know! Sardinia and Pantelleria have been continuously bombed, and one authority says they are practically 'bombed out'. They would make an attack on 'the underbelly of the Axis', as the inimitable Churchill phrases it, a much easier thing. The Russians hit back hard when the Germans took 500 planes to attack Kursk and destroyed 123. They also destroyed another 37 elsewhere—a good bag of 160.

Saturday 5th June

Mr Churchill is home—hurrah and hurrah! He came by night, flying home, and appeared all gay and cheerful walking in Downing Street this morning. The few people about said 'Good morning', and he replied, and then they set up a cheer to which he responded with the V sign. He has been to Tunisia since leaving Washington, going first to Gibraltar and having a good look round. In Tunisia he saw all the places which were greatly in the news day by day when fighting was hardest. He addressed the troops at Carthage and was here, there and everywhere in great form and spirits. I hope he will get a quiet weekend.

Monday 7th June

A letter today from the British Prisoners' of War Relatives' Association saying how interested the organizing secretary was in Alan's long description of the bird life at the camp. They ask: 'Is this genuine, do you think, or is he really referring to another kind of "bird" which has been flying about over Germany of late?' Personally I think Alan just means ordinary bird life, but I have written in reply saying what I think about it.

Wednesday 16th June

The King is in North Africa! He attended Divine Service in the improvised Naval chapel on Sunday and was, of course, recognized by an ordinary sailor, who said in an audible whisper: 'Blimey, it's the King!' His journey was made at night, when he flew in a Lancaster. May he soon be safely home again, as he is very precious. Nevertheless I am glad he is to have world-wide limelight as well as 'Winnie'. From what we were told on the wireless tonight he is the hardest worked war-worker of any. I can well believe it. More storms today, though not as bad as yesterday.

Thursday 17th June

Today it has been fine until 9.30 p.m., and so we have both worked quite hard in the garden.

This is a tense time, with everyone waiting for zero hour and the invasion of the Continent by our Allied Armies and everyone wondering just where the attack will be made. The Germans say the date is to be 21st June, and they know where! Do they!

Thursday 24th June

The years roll on, the birthdays come round and here I am celebrating the 60th anniversary. I woke up late, feeling 100 after rather a tiring week. When Kate wished me 'Many happy returns' I felt so well *down* that I replied 'Thank you—but not *too* many'. However I recovered later, having taken an egg-and-sherry during the morning, well laced with glucose! We had quite a party in the afternoon and the garden was a nice place to sit in, though the lawns are a bit untidy. A lovely bunch of carnations came from

Agnes Sparrow with her usual warmhearted note, and I had three book tokens, some powder, a book, cards and notes, all very nice.

Thursday 1st July

Another lovely day, summer without being oppressively hot. I made a journey to the Hostel today to see the Warden about the dance, where some man got drunk and behaved very badly. However, Leamington office knows all about it, I am told.

The Germans are having a great wail over the damage to Cologne Cathedral, which by the map looks very close to the station. They were glad our Cathedral was burnt and not sorry about the damage to Exeter, Bristol and Canterbury Cathedrals. Nemesis!

I was thinking today of a little boy I took, with his mother, to hospital on Monday. As we walked about the grounds I showed him how a snapdragon flower opened its mouth, and was highly amused when he said: 'Yew moind it don't boite!' As his mother had remarked previously: 'Yer can't learn 'em to talk nice when they're with other children.' Nuff sed!

Saturday 10th July

The great news today is that we have invaded Sicily. British, American and Canadian Troops are taking part, commanded by General Eisenhower. There are masses of ships, British and American, taking part in the operation. Zero hour was 3 o'clock and so far, beyond the information above, no communiqué has yet been received. There are 300,000 Italians and 100,000 Germans on the island. For weeks past we have been bombarding it heavily and now we have made a landing. It will be a difficult business.

Saturday 17th July

And a letter from Alan dated 20.6.43, so this is a good day. It is very hot, too. A very good day for Kate to start her holiday. I hastened out with the car to the grocer and got next week's rations so that Kate could take hers with her.

The news is good. The Allies—British mostly, I think—are ten miles from Catania and fighting is fierce. Snipers in vineyards are a trial and pick off our men despatch-riding or on motor-bicycles for other purposes. A Press correspondent nearly got picked off as he got out of a trench to write up his despatch.

Ten-thirty and I am in bed, full of aches and enjoying the cool room and the fresh feel of the sheets. How hateful it must be for Alan never to feel a sheet next to his face.

Monday 26 July

The eight o'clock news said Mussolini has 'resigned'. This is very good news; it looks like the rot setting in. Marshal Badoglio is now taking the lead in the country, which is under martial law, and the curfew is in force from dusk to dawn. The ex-Duce is reported to be in prison, to be gone to Germany, etc., but no-one seems really to know what has happened to the bombastic idiot.

There has been great perturbation on my part all day about the loss of my ration book. I knew it must be about the house or the garden, but had to get my rations today without it when I went on my bicycle to the grocer. Such a heavy basket, it made the bike wobble a bit. This evening, when getting the cushions out of the oak chest for the land-girls to sit in the garden, there, deep down in the chest, was my ration book! Thank goodness that was found.

Prisoners from Sicily now number 70,000!

Saturday 31st July

Oh, what a hot day! Developing into two peals of thunder and a sprinkle of rain, but nothing worth mentioning. We walked with Twink to the grocer during the morning and just after lunch motored about *three miles*! All these domesticities faithfully recorded day by day while Italy's fate hangs in the balance and Hamburg has been bombed seven times, almost non-stop. The place has 100 miles of works, docks and quays, and builds U-boats. The Allies advance a little in Sicily, but there seems to have been a lull there—perhaps waiting to see what Italy is going to do. Our wireless calls on her to surrender, and I expect Germany is doing her utmost to keep Italy in the war. So, a week having gone by, the bombing of Italy will now begin relentlessly.

Thursday 5th August

Rain fell in the night and everything is refreshed. Messing about in the orchard, I found one of the Early Victorias with scarcely any apples on it—and all three have been bowed to the ground with fruit. Someone has been stealing, we think, so we have put a few bits of wire netting to trap the unwary one if he comes again tonight. We have also put the peg in the gate.

Great news today. Catania has fallen and the Russians have taken Orel. Three cheers! Another one on the nose for Hitler!

Friday 6th August

Not only Orel, but Bielgorod! The Russians had great jubilation, rang bells, fired off a hundred guns in a salute and were generally 'merry and bright'. Of course, the Germans 'evacuated Orel and retired to prepared positions', straightening the line on purpose! M'yes!

I rang up the police to tell them about the apples being stolen, and then we got all the Early Victorias, dozens of pounds, and stored them in the railway hut.

Sunday 8th August

A grey day, cool with a little rain or drizzle from time to time, and later some wind. Jack has worked on the hen pen and I have written many notes and letters, including one to Alan. Last night we bombed Turin, Milan and Genoa. Hitler and the military lot have had a special meeting.

I read in the Prisoner of War magazine this evening that Oflag VIIB is overcrowded and the conditions are not good there. We thought it was pretty good. Apparently they are even short of plates and mugs and utensils for the table and cooking. I do hope we don't treat our prisoners as if they were lords, but, being what we are, I expect we are too kind altogether.

Tuesday 17th August

A hot day indeed. I seemed to be at my desk all afternoon. The room was dark and cool and I had a lamp lit. Then we had tea in the garden. It was still hot, and has remained so till blackout at 9 p.m., when we sat in the dark by the open window and listened to the good news of the occupation of Messina by the American 7th and British 8th Army. The occupation of the island is now completed. Another little campaign over! That sounds very casual, but I don't really take it lightly. The Germans say they have won a great victory! Quite insane they are. The evacuation was wonderful and one would think they hadn't lost a man, a tank, a gun or an aeroplane! Whereas the last known number of prisoners was 130,000, and the booty hasn't been counted yet.

Monday 23rd August

Today's great news is that Kharkov has fallen, the Russians are having salutes of guns and great jubilation, while the Germans try to minimize their own defeat by announcing a few hours previously that they had 'evacuated' the city 'according to plan'. I hope they are out for good and all, as this is the fourth time it has changed hands. We are all anxiously awaiting news of a further move on the Allied part.

Sunday 29th August

Martial law has been declared in Denmark and King Christian is reported to be a prisoner in a castle. From Sweden we learn that some of the small Danish navy has been destroyed off the coast. Much sabotage has been going on lately and Denmark has not been conforming to the Nazi 'New Order' at all well. Now there is to be 'ruthless punishment' for offenders—probably the death penalty. Typically German!

Wednesday 1st September

A happy and mostly wet day. Jack has gone to and from the garage to the hen house, sometimes in a lull when the rain ceased—or almost ceased—and says he is satisfied with his day's work. I meant to have a bonfire, but just as all the daily chores were done, down came the rain. Both toolsheds had a bit of tidying done, peaguards stacked and tied and hung up, boxes and tins rearranged and my little tool shelf swept down. These jobs, with a few letters written and forms filled in, were finished by teatime. The rain stopped, I biked to the post and then we had tea in the hall for a change.

It is four years this evening since the telephone rang and when I answered it a voice said: 'Will you take a telegram, please?' It was Alan's call-up. What a long time! How we long and long to see him. There is never an hour of the day he is not thought of in one way or another. Kate has been bottling pears today and both Jack and I were wondering if he might be here next year to eat them with us. Such funny little things draw him near. I tap the table mats on edge to remove the crumbs—Alan always did that. Something specially nice is served for dinner. I can hear him say: 'This looks a good meal, mother.' Ah, may it not be too long before we are together again.

Friday 3rd September

We begin the fifth year of the war! Italy was invaded by our troops this morning—the first invasion on the mainland of Europe—preceded by a great bombardment. Good luck to our gallant men.

Wednesday 8th September

A nice pleasant day with the usual Wednesday morning's work and an early lunch. This evening I meant to garden a bit and changed just before 6 p.m. Should I listen to the news or not? Perhaps I'd better hear the headlines: 'This is Stuart Hibberd reading it. There is good news—the best news of the war, and John Snagge will read the account.' '*Italy has surrendered*,' he said, and then gave General Eisenhower's message of her unconditional surrender. The National Anthem was played and I had by that time got Jack in to hear, so we stood to attention. In the 9 p.m. news we heard that the Armistice was signed on 3rd September, but for special reasons was kept a secret until today. So it was signed—dramatically—just four years to the day of the outbreak of war. Joan Spencer rang me up after the 6 p.m. news to rejoice, and said: 'Do you think they (Nevill and Alan) will be home by Christmas?' Then Jack hoisted the flag for an hour or so.

We read over the Diary for 3rd September for five years—from 1939 to 1943—and what a change there is year by year.

Friday 10th September

The Germans are now fighting the Italians and Hitler has spoken once again after a long, long pause. His broadcast this evening was rapidly read and attacked the King of Italy and Marshal Badoglio. It has been a dramatic day, with one event after another broadcast from Italy. The Germans have bombed Rome and are fighting Italians in the northern half of Italy who will not deliver up their arms, but are now fighting their former ally. The Allies are advancing and have today occupied Taranto, an excellent harbour. Other landings have been made besides the first landing on the toe of Italy.

The Russians are still taking fresh places and advancing, with salutes of guns telling of their victories day after day in Moscow.

Saturday 11th September

A letter from Alan this morning, dated 10.8.43, telling us about Edward Greenslade being in hospital, and then about the books he had read. All quite satisfactory. Joyce has arrived to stay, and she and I were amused to find ourselves walking out together this afternoon in the same summer frocks we wore in Nancy in 1938 on our holiday, when we heard the whisper as we passed along the street: '*Les deux Anglaises*'. We seemed taller than most French-women, and so were noticed as we were there for a fortnight, walking in and about the town.

The Germans have occupied Lombardy and are in Rome. The Italian surrender does not mean that we now possess Italy—the Germans mean to make it a battleground. Italian ships are coming in to Allied and neutral harbours. There is a lot happening just now, but the events are rather confused.

Monday 13th September

Much rain fell in the night and there was a good deal of lightning. All day it has been hot and steamy, with sun very late in the day and ending with a clear moonlit evening. There is great excitement on the part of the Germans, who say they have 'liberated' Mussolini, and call upon the Facist party to rally to him. How they love to be dramatic, and Hitler, having said he has no need to lie any more, has probably sent forth a great big whopper. And, anyway, it doesn't seem to matter much.

The Russians still progress. The Allies are pushing on in Italy, too, and meeting stiff resistance near Salerno.

Friday 17th September

Apples and pears, apples and pears! We have a great harvest of both, and eat them both in great quantities daily. Everywhere there are baskets of fruit, as well as tons of tomatoes. This is really a wonderful year for everything and, to quote General Montgomery once more: 'Let us give thanks to Almighty God.' It was sad to be taking Joyce to the station this morning and to feel that her visit was so soon ended. We have had a most delightful week together. At the station we had a quarter of an hour to spare. It was soon gone and the train bore her away and left me waving my hand and feeling quite bereft.

Tuesday 21st September

Much cooler today. We went to Leamington by Fletshamstead Highway, where one of the duel roads is packed with Bren-gun carriers—more every time we go. At the Stores we soon saw Mrs Greenslade, and a nice fat cockerel was transferred from her car to ours, plus a glorious bowl of dead-black blackberries, while a basket of pears and a few apples went from our car to hers. Barter indeed—though it's just fine to be giving something away that one has grown in one's own garden.

The 9 p.m. news gave a report of Mr Churchill's speech, which took two hours, with an hour's rest between them. John Snagge has just read the principal extracts, which covered the Sicilian campaign and the Italian beginning, with the story of the Italian surrender. Also we were told about Mussolini. The story of the parachute landing to rescue him was actually true. It was hoped he would be delivered into Allied hands, but the dramatic rescue from his mountain prison thwarted our hopes. I hope he'll like Germany!

Wednesday 22nd September

My goodness, it *was* cold in the night. In fact, there was quite a sharp frost. I couldn't keep warm at all in bed, and no wonder. By 10.25 a.m. I went to Kenilworth to the dentist's and was glad to find the filling I expected was unnecessary. So the teeth were 'treated' and a few other oddments attended to and I was soon in the car to come home.

Why did Hitler's deputy, Rudolf Hess, land in Scotland? This question was answered today. Hess arrived with a string of peace proposals. They were then sure of winning the war, and so, if we did not agree to deliver up the former German colonies, give up Iraq, etc., etc., then Germany would beat us eventually. The blockade would help to do this—if not at once, then in two or three years' time—and we should be kept under after the war, a subservient nation! M'yes? The Germans would not deal with Churchill, they said. Well, they have had to deal with him very seriously since then.

Monday 27th September

The letter from Alan came this morning (dated 30th August). There had been very few letters at the camp for a month and then he had three from me, one from Jack and one from Kate. He sent his thanks to the latter and said he was 'looking forward to the first suet pudding'. It was a sane and cheerful letter and we felt very bright all day after its receipt.

We also heard unofficially that Alan had passed the examination taken in June. We are delighted to hear this and thought we would write and tell him, but decided to get the official intimation first.

Wednesday 13th October

Mr Churchill's speech in the House in connection with the coal-miners and their strikes was partly reported on the 6 p.m. news, and very good it was. But the great news is that Italy has declared war on Germany, to take effect from 4 o'clock this afternoon. Rejoicing today I am! And why? Because I was born an Englishwoman. It's *good*—and marvellous!

Saturday 16th October

So busy this morning that I nearly forgot to go to the butcher for the meat, and when I did . . . well, it very nearly would have gone through the hole in a tram ticket if one had wrapped it in one! This afternoon I managed to gather some of the Bramley's Seedlings, and Wilks tidied up the drive after the carrying of the pine logs yesterday and swept up the leaves from the lawn. And so to blackout.

Thursday 28th October
Mr Churchill has been making a speech about the proposed new House of Commons. Some desire a circular building, but Mr Churchill favours the oblong style, which he thinks best suits our form of government. He thinks it a good thing not to have a seat for everyone, as it is only on special occasions that the House is crowded and on many other occasions it would be half-empty if it were larger. This would make a wrong atmosphere. There is a sense of urgency and intense interest in a crowded House, etc., etc. Maxton had to get up afterwards and suggest that a grand new House of Commons be built 20 miles out of London. 'Ye men of the Labour Party, what fools ye be' at times!

We progress in Italy, though slowly.

Thursday 4th November
Most of today was spent in the garden. Jack washed the car—and found it quite hard work—while I cleared away yellow leaves from sprouts and kale and staked where necessary. Twink and I filled the notice-board in the village as it was just growing dusk. Later I rode to the School Managers' meeting on my bike and found it not too bad, as it was not a very dark evening. When I got back Jack told me Simon Green, repatriated from Alan's hut in Oflag VIIB, had rung up and would I ring up at 7.30? So of course I did, and a very nice voice answered the few questions I asked. He says Alan is putting on weight, but not because he is not energetic, because he is always taking exercise and plays a lot of hockey.

The biggest raid of the war took place last night and yesterday, in daylight, when Fortresses were over Germany—a thousand of them. The R.A.F. was over Dusseldorf for 27 minutes and dropped 2,000 tons of bombs. Flares are dropped by the first planes to show the target to the bombers, and then the enemy lights up the whole place with searchlights. It all sounds frightful—but marvellous.

In Italy we have gained the Massico ridge, which gives us the advantage of looking over the German positions. The Germans in Italy are very strong. No wonder our progress has been slow. It looks as if Turkey might be coming in on the Allied side.

Saturday 6th November
A very interesting day. I got busy on the telephone and asked Captain and Mrs Keens if they would come here on the 2.10 train.

We would then meet them at the station with the local taxi and afterwards take them on to Kenilworth, where they were to go to tea with Joan Spencer. They very kindly said they would do so, and Captain Keens told us a lot about the campaign in France, Alan's wound, etc. Apparently he had a pretty bad time with his knee, worse than we thought, but is now marvellously fit and has broadened out and looks quite different. There is plenty of food in the camp and the Germans are behaving better than at first, knowing they will not win the war. We had a very interesting hour and we thought Mrs Keens charming.

The Russians sweep on in the south and have taken Kiev. They have also landed and made bridgeheads in the Crimea, which looks as if it had been cut off from the land movement and was only held from the Black Sea. Mosquitoes have bombed Germany hard during Friday night and Fortresses took on the daylight attack which followed. No peace for them now.

VOLUME II

November 1943 – April 1944

Sunday 7th November

A good day to begin what one hopes will be the last volume in this fifth year of devastating war. With the Russians forging ahead, the masses of equipment they take as well as prisoners, and the huge number of killed and wounded, the enemy must surely feel the Allies' might. According to the repatriated men, and other sources, the Germans realize they are not going to win. If our—and the American—people could put aside private differences and keep off strikes it would be another step nearer the end. In Italy we are now advancing at a quicker rate, but going is necessarily slow in a mountainous peninsula and the Germans are adept at laying mines and placing booby-traps. They also carry off natives for slave labour and have no pity on civilians or women and children. A nasty race indeed!

Monday 8th November

Sir Walter Citrine seems to think so much Home Guard work and fire-watching is unnecessary, and said so. He thinks people are getting weary of it! Of course they are weary, but that is no reason for slacking off—how foolish it would be to let up now. What a fool the man is! Typical Labour Party mentality!

Tuesday 9th November

Lord Mayor's Day and Churchill has made an excellent, gripping speech. As usual, he takes the long view. Our efforts are not for this generation alone, but for the happiness and peace of mankind in future. No-one should talk, or think, as if the war were already almost finished, for the Germans are still powerful. Nor should the fire-watchers and the Home Guard be discouraged in any of the work they do, which is still wholly and entirely necessary, and anyone who thinks this too hard and says so is doing a grave disservice to the nation. In fact, one in the eye for that idiot of a blatherer Walter Citrine! A direct answer for him! We notice there have been no comments on Walter Citrine's remarks. It looks as if these had been suppressed in our newspapers, perhaps at the Government's instigation, and now the Prime Minister has replied in public—and I shouldn't like to be Walter Citrine this evening, openly rebuked at the Lord Mayor's banquet for all the world to hear.

Wednesday 17th November

Major Lloyd George is appealing for less use of gas and electricity. Too much is being used, he said. Isn't it that the miners are out on strike again that needs stressing? And also that *this* is the end of the matter that must be tackled! When one sees electricity being used extravagantly night after night in places of entertainment and amusement, one feels like being comfortable—but certainly not extravagant. Our cutting down (further than at present, for we have done it) would just make us miserable, but public places don't seem to do anything about it at all.

Saturday 27th November

A cold, damp, murky November day. I pondered whether to go out or stay in, as I suspected I had a cold (only too certainly confirmed by evening), but in the end I went out to do the hens. Changing the birds over to the new hen house, with all the attendant jobs of clearing up the runs, making new nests, burning the old chaff and putting in fresh chaff and oak leaves, took us until 1 p.m.

Then we came in to lunch—lunch!! Perhaps I was pernickety today, but toad-in-the-hole is *not* what it was. That lovely pork sausage in a yellow batter, shining with fat, has given place to a beef (save the mark) beast, flavourless and tough-skinned, in a heavy khaki batter made with milk powder. Mine went down slowly and reluctantly. Later the situation was saved by an excellent steamed pudding with an overcoat of sweet jam.

Just now everything seems scarce. What is a pint of milk a day for three people! Kate visited her friends yesterday—mother, father, a little boy and a babe a month or so old. They can have seven pints a day! This because of the nursing mother and the children, but they do not want so much. The husband can also have extra cheese, which they do not want, so Kate came home with cheese, a tin of dried milk and four boxes of matches—and how glad we were of them all. Well, well, times change.

London was raided last night by two aircraft which caused damage and casualties, some fatal.

Monday 29th November

Storms of rain, cold wind and bursts of brilliant sunshine, though mostly grey skies. After spending the day in bed yesterday, I felt much better this morning, with a temperature of 96°. The doctor came in the early afternoon—and later I wasn't feeling so good. But I slept and woke, always feeling very comfortable and glad to be at ease again.

Tuesday 30th November

Still grey skies and a strong cold wind. Bed is comfortable, but food dull and uninteresting, even though the lunch egg was lovely and supper was a bit of fish! I have begun *Our Mutual Friend* today, but I find Dickens very dreary on the whole. I refreshed myself with an occasional story from *Blackwood's Magazine* and found the crisp, terse writing exhilarating after so much long-windedness— 'in a manner of speaking', 'if so be' and 'if it's all the same to you, Mr. So-and-So,' of the Charles Dickens' characters. Kate had a postcard from Alan saying she 'would be amused to think of my doing washing-up, sweeping and dusting these days. My activities don't extend as far as cooking, but fortunately we have one Mr Betts who enjoys doing it and produces some very tasty dishes—he runs the catering very well and has served up enough porridge (oatmeal?) for us to have for breakfast every day during the winter.' Food news, to one whose activities run greatly to the preparation of food.

The Eighth Army is on the offensive in Italy and has pierced the German 'winter line of defence'. More power to their elbows, say I.

Wednesday 1st December

Och! What a grey, dark and gloomy day! Sleep was far away last night and I lay comfortably, first in one position and then in another, thanking the powers-that-be for my warm and cosy bed. Having the curious hallucination that my bed's head was tight up against the door, occasionally I switched on my torch to assure myself that it was still in its right place. In the darkness, the bed head swiftly returned to block the door! Sometime after 1 a.m. I slept, wakened later to find it was only 2.30 and what was this noise of gentle growling? Only my tummy protesting it was very,

very empty. There was no way of satisfying one's hunger except by going downstairs, where less than a dozen biscuits reposed in a box. Couldn't be done. Three o'clock: it must be done. Should I try to be ultra quiet? Would Twink bark? No, I would just be ordinarily quiet and hope no-one would wake, no dog bark. Neither did, and I came safely back into the warm bed (once again in its proper place), put on the torch, made a warm, light, white cave underneath the bedclothes, ate four small, sweet biscuits, switched away the crumbs—and lay down to two more wakeful hours. Then: 'Are you awake—it's a quarter past eight?' Kate, asking about breakfast. I had already made up my mind. Coffee and bacon. At 9.15 they came. Was ever any breakfast so relished as this? I can't remember *one*.

Jack feels he has a cold and so he is also staying in bed, but he was the lucky one today and received *a very interesting letter from Alan*. He says he has bought himself a new Rolex watch! Ye gods and little fishes! I didn't know prisoners of war could *buy* anything from this country. Or did he buy it from a fellow prisoner?

Friday 3rd December

A really miserable-looking, cold, frosty and foggy day outside and difficult to keep warm inside, too! Jack's temperature was still up, but I am much better, I'm glad to say, and got up about 11 a.m., dressed and stayed up! In the bedroom. It wasn't worth warming up the downstair room, so I went down at intervals and fetched up anything necessary.

Good news of the Eight Army, definitely getting on with the attack over the Sangro River. The Russians are also doing quite well, and we bombed Berlin again last night—heavily. We lost 41 aircraft—it sounds a terrific loss, but we know we must expect this. Monty has said the Germans in Italy were going to have 'a colossal crack'. He has such a boy's way of putting things.

Men are to be 'directed' to the mines, as well as the Services now. 'All classes to be treated alike,' says Bevin. 'Public schoolboys as well as others.' Truly Bevinsome! How class-conscious he is! He made a *faux pas* today in the Commons about his own authority and had to apologise for it.

Saturday 4th December

A bright and frosty morning. The 8 a.m. news tells of the meeting in Persia of Churchill, Stalin and Roosevelt! Somehow the news slipped out before it was meant to, but now Moscow has announced that Marshal Stalin has met the other two Powers.

Jack's temperature remains up and down round about 100° today. The doctor came about 11 a.m. and didn't prescribe anything special, having been last night rather late and ordered whisky! Many people are laid low—it's quite a widespread epidemic.

Sunday 12th December
Kate wakened me at 9 a.m. I had slept till seven and then, satisfied I had another *hour*, slept *two*. The day looked grey and cold and later on I found the wind from the north was *very* cold. When one can't sing it isn't much use going to church—and perhaps coughing—so that was ruled out very reluctantly. Getting up late, doing a bit of washing, doing chores and hens, having a trial fork-over of one end of the drive bed, and it was one o'clock. We live now in one room—it saves warming the dining-room—but Sunday dinner is a bit cramped on a small table. 'Flu' is very widespread and causing many deaths, we are told—709 people died in a week, mostly older people 'over 55', says a Ministry of Health official.

Americans were over Germany in daylight yesterday at Emden. Clouds of fighters came to intercept them and the Liberators shot down at least 138 for a loss of 17 bombers and three fighters. Germans are fighting hard on the Kiev salient, 60 miles from the town, and losing very heavily in men and equipment. The Princesses have given a dance. The King and Queen were there, but, though the King is almost well after influenza, he left early.

Thursday 16th December
Peering out into the semi-darkness at 7.45 this morning, I was glad to see it was a clear, though raw and cold, day. I was able to drive away to Leamington at 9.10 a.m. For this was the day! For what? The permanent wave! There was just time to change the library books and I arrived at the appointed time at the hairdresser. Soon we were under way and the morning passed eventually—a boring business. Home again and there were a few calls to the telephone, and how I wish I had it in this room, for the dining-room is like an icebox. At suppertime a land-girl called—a bonny lass with bright eyes and rosy cheeks.

We are all rather perturbed today as we have heard Mr Churchill has a cold and has been in bed four days. Now a patch of pneumonia has developed on one lung. That he could very well do without, as it is not a year since he had pneumonia before, and got over it wonderfully quickly.

Friday 17th December

The news of Mr Churchill is that the improvement made yesterday is maintained and the pneumonia has not spread. There was another heavy raid on Berlin last night. The Russians have made some gains and trials of Germans have begun for the atrocities in Kharkov. Brutes they are! Bevin has been holding forth on the ballot of young men for the Forces or the mines. Rather a mad idea, and capable of wasting the nation's brains.

Monday 20th December

The day began well *with a letter from Alan*, who has been to a cinema! He said it was strange to go out of a little cobbled side street indoors to a modern cinema. The captions were in English and the scene laid in the Tyrol a century ago. The love affairs were rather involved! Also he had seen a play (I imagine in camp) called *Gaslight*, where the scenes were so tense he was unable to sleep afterwards, and he usually sleeps well. Letters were not going through very well apparently, but he hoped to get a batch soon.

My day was very busy with the usual jobs. At 2.15 p.m. we went out in the car on land-girl jobs to Berkswell and I called to see Mrs Whitaker, who has been three weeks in bed. *That man* is not coming to the church any more as he is offended because Mr Whitaker asked him to be a little quieter. That is the best news one could hear, and I said: 'Thank goodness!'

Mr Churchill is getting on satisfactorily. The Russian traitor, and the Germans who killed hundreds of Russians by various atrocious methods, have been publicly hanged in Kharkov today. Russians were put in a gas chamber and killed, while another one had his beard pulled out bit by bit—brutes! Others were beaten when they would not go in to the 'killing' lorry without being forced. Another prisoner was beaten with rubber truncheons and then pricked with a red-hot needle to force a confession. These beasts of Germans and the Russian traitor were tried, found guilty and hanged. Really this treatment was too kind—but public hangings surely tend to brutalize the onlookers.

Saturday 25th December

A clear Christmas Day, rather raw and cold, with some bright sunshine. Jack and I went to the 9 a.m. service and the church looked wonderful, lit up brightly. About 70 or 80 people were there but, thank goodness, not *that man*, so we had a peaceful service. Afterwards we sat down to a lovely chicken, celery and all etceteras, a patent Kate pudding—very delicious—and topped it all off with a glass or two of 1926 Graves with the chill off! Grand! Afterwards Jack had a nice little sit in his armchair and I did likewise and read the book Joyce sent me, *The Snow Goose*, a story of Dunkirk. Then came his Most Gracious Majesty speaking words of cheer, of wise counsel and kindness. After that the National Anthems of our various Allies were played and we just sat listening.

And all day we think of Alan and long to have him here. Every hour of the day one wonders what he is doing. And will he be here next Christmas? May we all be here together.

Monday 27th December

Boxing Day, though just an ordinary Monday as far as we were concerned. But great news on the wireless—the *Scharnhorst* is sunk!! She was attacking a north-bound convoy, but we do not know details yet. Anyway, that's one German battleship less. Also the Russians have advanced 50 miles on a 25-mile front and captured lots of material and killed hundreds of Germans.

I say at the beginning that this was just an ordinary day, but any day that brings *a letter from Alan* is not an ordinary day. This one, date 30th November, tells a good deal about Edward Greenslade, who is in hospital, saying he was cheerful, warm and comfortable and wanted nothing. The rain and sleet prevented gardening, but they had a tidy-up with a barrow. Altogether a sound, sensible letter.

Saturday 1st January

'A nice dry day—and not cold,' said Jack as we stood on Coventry station this evening. We have had a very happy day, for we spent most of it with our friends Harry and Ethel at Spinney Croft. We arrived at about 12.15—Harry dispensed the sherry, we drank to our 'boys', among others, then we sat down to a pre-war lunch and greatly enjoyed it. We caught the 5.24 home and our usual quiet evening followed. I dismembered the Christmas cards and enjoyed them all again. Now the picture part goes to the Schools for the children to use later on.

Russia is again joyous, having occupied 300 places today, and the Germans are in retreat. The Soviet troops have also advanced from Nevel in the north. Zhitomir has been captured by storm. Mosquitoes, Typhoons, etc., have attacked the enemy without loss.

Friday 7th January

The great news today is of the jet-propelled aeroplane, now

flying after years of experiments. This is revolutionary and is one of the greatest steps forward in the history of the aeroplane. And the invention is the work of Group Captain Frank Whittle, whom the wireless tells us is a Coventry man. Hurrah!

Today the porch thermometer has registered 45° and it has been like a spring day, with a glorious sunrise and an even more glorious sunset.

After lunch I did a bit of gardening, forking part of the border, and found it exceptionally tiring. The spirit is so willing, the weather so excellent, but the flesh mighty weak. (Anomalous expression!) Then there was the dog to take before we had a late tea. The sunset was grand across the little valley, with the great molten ball in a golden glow as it sank behind the trees on the ridge of soft purple, while the trees themselves stood out in their delicate tracery against the living gold. A marvellous sight.

Monday 17th January

A letter from Alan today, dated 20.12.43. He has had very few letters lately. He has now heard about his exam. Gardening is occupying a lot of his time and for serious reading he has studied The Beveridge Report—Alan! Gosh!! He had also been out for a walk, 'very pleased to get away from one's fellow-men'. They must get a bit sick of each other.

Wednesday 19th January

A raw, damp morning. Rain began about 11 a.m. and continued till after blackout. I went out in the car, visited the butcher and later three land-girls, with not much result. Near Burton Green a pair of moorhens crossed the road, flying just above the surface. I couldn't miss them both and was grieved to see that one was fluttering in the fairway, so I stopped the car and went back, determined to make myself wring its pretty neck if it was badly injured. When it was placed on the grass verge it seemed unable to stand, but nothing seemed to be broken as far as I could judge. So I left it supported on either side by tufts of grass, and as I walked away I heard its mate call 'Chr-rk, chr-rk'. Ten minutes later I passed the place and got out to look, but it was gone, so I think it must have recovered. It is hateful to kill anything so pretty unnecessarily.

Marshal Stalin says 15 or more miles west have now been captured on the new front near Leningrad, and a victory salvo has been fired to celebrate this. Spanish troops are fighting with the

Germans, and we have had something to say about this to the Spaniards. In Italy the Allies move forward against severe resistance and still with difficulty due to the weather and floods.

Saturday 22nd January

The morning was rather filled with worry about a land-girl's clothing coupons, given me in a registered envelope at the W.L.A. uniform department, put into my bag and not found there this morning. Six telephone calls, all to Leamington, and two visits to the girl at the farm ended in my finding the envelope tucked into a ration book which I removed from the handbag on my return home yesterday. So at last I took a breath of relief! Twink then went on to the farm with me again and we delivered the envelope safe and sound into the girl's own hand.

Russia continues to take town after town, and Leningrad can now have an entirely different life, for after 900 days of siege the 15-inch guns of the enemy which battered them week by week are now captured and displayed in the squares of the city. The great news today is of an Allied landing on a fresh spot in Italy to the south of Rome. Enemy resistance was slight as the landing was a great surprise. Lots of aircraft supported the landing. Fifteen miles south of Rome, at Frascati, is the German Headquarters, and we unloaded a bomb directly on it. The Fifth Army has established bridgeheads, and while the landing was taking place an attack was made by the Eighth Army on the other front.

German raiders came over the south-east coast last night and some penetrated to London. There were two attacks, one about midnight and one early this morning. There were about 90 aircraft and we destroyed ten. Obviously a propaganda raid, as wonderful accounts are sent out by the Germans overseas.

Sunday 23rd January

Our newly-landed force has established its bridgehead more firmly in Italy. Though I seldom mention the Far East, the Allied Army there is advancing, capturing islands hitherto held by the Japanese and gradually preparing for bigger and bigger onslaughts on the enemy. New Guinea is being cleared, many ships sunk and general progress being made. There is some movement also in Burma and we are beginning serious bombing there. Prisoners of war in Japanese hands cannot write much and relations can only send 25 words! So we are lucky.

After the news George Formby gave an excellent postscript telling how he and Beryl went out to entertain the troops. They had some difficult journeys, going right up to the front line in Italy, driving through minefields and seeing men who stepped beyond the safe taped lines blown up, killed or injured. One night they gave entertainments to the men in a great camp and afterwards, as they lay in their tent, men went by saying 'Goodnight, George', and 'Goodnight, Beryl'. This went on till 2.30 a.m. At 8 a.m. they were wakened by tea being brought in, and when they looked outside everybody and everything had gone except the cookhouse. Not a tent or a man left of the great array the night before.

Wednesday 26th January

A commission has been investigating the massacre of Poles in the Katyn Forest in 1941. The Germans said these men were killed by the Russians in 1940, and this statement caused much excitement in Polish quarters at the time and a rupture between them which ended in the breaking off of diplomatic relations in 1943. This investigation has proved that this statement by the Germans was the usual lie for propaganda purposes. The bodies were removed by them from the mass grave, and identification and other papers were removed so as to make their story credible. Now that an investigation of the matter has taken place, it is certain that these people were killed by the Germans when they captured Smolensk and these Poles were prisoners there. Once again the grave has been disturbed and the bodies examined. Papers which the Germans missed have been found on the bodies showing that they were alive in 1941, when the Germans held this territory. Other facts have also come to light. Five hundred Russians (prisoners of war) were made to uncover the graves and remove incriminating documents and material evidence. These Russians were shot on the completion of their work.

Thursday 27th January

Consignments of oranges from Spain have been found to have time bombs in the crates, and so Spain is getting rapped over the knuckles. Two Spaniards—young men and obviously in Nazi pay—have been executed at Gibraltar for being concerned in bomb explosions on the island. We do have to keep our eyes open.

Once when we talked of 'the invasion' it meant probable invasion of England by Germany. Now it is spoken of as a settled plan with the date fixed (but this is a secret, of course) and everything arranged, but it is the invasion of the Continent this time.

Men's suits have been 'austerity' suits for some time past—fewer pockets, no turn-ups to trousers, etc.—but now they are to be as usual. This change has been made because a soldier coming back to civil life was to be allowed an 'unrestricted' suit, so now all men may return to normal. I wish they'd let us have stockings for one coupon—instead of three.

A few months ago one asked for a toothbrush over a chemist's counter as a matter of course. Lately one has not been able to buy them at all. In fact, most things are 'if we'd got some ham we'd have some ham and eggs—if we'd only got the eggs'. Apples are not seen in the shops at the moment at all, cake shops display bread and rolls, and when cakes are coming in there is usually a long queue outside. The cake shop in the village has buns and rock cakes day in, day out, and not too many of them. The second window displays bird seed, pickles and even toilet paper in discreet rolls! Sweet shops also display goods unheard of in their trade, for since they can only sell the ration they must, I suppose, deal in other things to keep their shops going.

Friday 28th January

Dreadful stories have been told in the House today of cruel and inhuman treatment of our men who are prisoners in Japanese hands. The postcards received recently are reported to be written at the instigation of the Japs under threats, and not to be the truth. Thousands of prisoners have died in their hands—they report a hundred. And the state of some of them is terrible—emaciated, unshaven, with long matted hair—just starved. It is *too* awful, and for those who have relations it must be torture. Oh, the inhuman brutes! Berlin was raided last night.

Tuesday 1st February

The morning's work, after the usual duties, was to fill in *forms*, FORMS, FORMS, and records of journeys for the Women's Land Army and the Volunteer Car Pool. Twenty-four forms and two records for the former, detailing every girl and every journey. The Volunteer Car Pool records I fill in after each journey, but still they must be set down again on a summary sheet, and on the back there are a, b, c, d, e, f, g, h and i to be filled in and half-way down the page 'the two totals must be the same', and again at the bottom of the page. What a frown this causes! And sometimes I just *can't* do the sum and, signing my name at the foot and telling the Volunteer Car Pool officer how much petrol I have got left, leave her to fill it in.

Elsie Hesketh wrote a postcard saying she had read Volumes One and Two of the Diaries which I sent her, and sat down and read for two hours on end! Gosh! The scribe is glad she found the homely writing so interesting.

Monday 14th February

A letter from Alan for Jack today, dated 20.1.44 – quite a quick journey for it. He wrote mostly of engineering matters, but at the end says he has begun to smoke a pipe! This at 29 years of age, after never even taking to cigarettes!! We rather hope it continues. A man is so much more companionable with a pipe.

We are threatening to bomb the Cassino monastery which the Germans have made into a fortress. So far we have respected this very ancient, interesting Benedictine monastery.

Wednesday 16th February

There was a big raid on Berlin last night—apparently the biggest ever in air warfare—lasting half an hour. Over 1,000 bombers were out altogether, though some of them were on other attacks. We lost 43 aircraft. Two thousand five hundred tons were dropped on Berlin.

Today has been moderately cold. This morning seemed quite long for once and I got a lot done. The silver was sparkling by 11.30 and there was then time to go to the grocer with Twink and pick up the week's ration of bacon. We have been lucky to have a nice present of 1 lb or so from Mrs Docker and breakfast has been jolly good with a rasher of home-cured bacon for a change. A bit of Volume Eight of the Diary went down well just after tea. We are now reading of the black months when we had defeat after defeat—the loss of Singapore, Java, Burma, etc., My goodness, they were heavy times!

Jack wrote to Alan today, answering the engineering letter of two days ago and rejoicing with him on having taken to pipe-smoking!

The Benedictine monastery at Cassino has now been bombed and the Germans ran out and were promptly caught by our artillery.

Sunday 20th February

Better news from Anzio this evening. Nine divisions of Germans are against us there and we have encircled a great many of them. Aircraft lost by the enemy numbered 26, and we lost three. We are holding firm against heavy counter-attacks.

The encircled forces of Germans at Cherkassy numbered 10,000 more men than at first thought—93,000 altogether—and of these 55,000 are dead. The enemy is still pretending they cleverly got out of the ring, but of course, this is entirely untrue. The Allies are having various successes in the Pacific. Islands and atolls are occupied and held, shipping and transports sunk and many aircraft destroyed.

Buenos Aires has been found to be a hotbed of German spies. This is a report published by the authorities there, now that diplomatic relations have been broken off, though war is not yet declared on Germany.

Tuesday 22nd February

This day the sweep came! It was so cold outside, and not too warm in the dining-room, with only an electric radiator. Jack's spirits were at a low ebb and, though we had planned a day out in Leamington, taking lunch to eat in the car, he felt he couldn't face sitting in the cold car waiting about for me. Kate, from being monosyllabic yesterday, was overcome with the thought of the day's work and the spring-cleaning to come and poured her feelings forth. I felt it wasn't a bad thing to be going off *toute seule* in the warmest of fur coats, the cosiest of gloves and the best of cars, and became quite cheerful when Balsall Common was a mile behind me, bursting forth into song as the car sped along the road. All the people I came in contact with were pleasant, like Mr Malins, the greengrocer (with a knell of a cold, be it said), smiling and inquiring for Alan as he weighed out my 2 lb of *oranges*! Yes—*oranges*. I saw dozens of them in the shops and never missed a heartbeat! So many of them so suddenly, and I just thought: 'Ugh, it's cold for fruit today.' Ungrateful woman! However in the hairdresser during the afternoon, while my head was in the 'hood', drying uncomfortably, I read a good recipe for candied orange peel, and that sent me to Malins'.

I was lucky with lunch, too, and just walked into the Stores a few minutes before 1 p.m. and found an empty place right away. The W.L.A. gave me two gallons of petrol on request, my new coat was tried on and it looks good, the cake shop gave me a *fruit* cake, there was fish at the fishmonger—all was indeed well.

Mr Churchill has made another grand speech, lasting an hour-and-a-quarter, in the Commons. Among other things, he said: 'This is no time for sorrow or rejoicing. This is a time for preparation, effort and resolve. The war is still going on. I have never taken the view that the end of the war in Europe is at hand or that Hitler is about to collapse. . . . We agreed at Teheran to fall upon and smite the Hun by land, sea and air with all the strength that is in us during the coming spring and summer. . . . Victory may not be so far away, and will certainly not be denied to us in the end.'

Thursday 24th February

A grand sunny day with beautiful blue sky. It was freezing early and there was a cold north wind all day. Yet, during the afternoon, the sun brought the porch thermometer up to 70° while, round the corner, the wind seemed to pierce right through everything one wore. The sun has been very heartening and the usual greeting was: 'Isn't it a lovely day?'

Driving up to Meriden crossroads today we found the Straight Mile closed and a soldier guarded the closed entrance. I was told it is packed with tanks (Bren-gun carriers?) all getting ready for the invasion. Many double roads have one side closed, and one sees scores of vehicles massed on either side of the road. We used to pass Fletchamstead Highway previously and saw them there, too.

Russia still continues her victories. Another town has been captured and there are more rejoicings today. The destroyer *Hardy* has been lost.

Friday 25th February

With the thermometer at 36°, and an east wind, I find this a decidedly unpleasant day outside. I planned to call at the Schools today as I had to call and see a land-girl not far away, but when I arrived I found the Schools closed. Bad luck! I came home via the butcher and had plenty of time to go and get a new loaf and other oddments in the village, as well as filling the W.I. notice-board with two spicy *Punch* pictures before 1 p.m.

The Finns are anxious for peace and the British and Soviet governments are—or have been—in consultation about this. What would happen to the seven German divisions now in Finland, I wonder? It is queer to think that Russia is not at war with Japan and that at the celebration of the Red Army anniversary a few days ago Ambassadors from many countries were gathered together at dinner, British among them, and the Japanese Ambassador sat in a corner of the room!!

The Allies send over small-calibre shells to the Germans on the Italian front which contain a weekly news-sheet printed in German. These shells burst over the German lines and scatter the news-sheet, which apparently the Germans read. They tell the truth about the

Russian front and many other truths which the Germans are not allowed to hear from their own country.

Thursday 2nd March

A very cold wind again, a frosty morning and plenty of sunshine during the day. Jack spent the day cleaning and cajoling the very ancient alarm clock, and by afternoon it was whirring its noisy alarm. So Kate won't have to wake up and switch on her light so often during the night to see whether it is nearly time to get up. At 11.15 a.m. I walked briskly to the station and there had to wait for half an hour till the 11.30 train came in at 12, talking to the locals and getting a bit weary of futile chatter. In Coventry I went to the room where the P.O.W. next-of-kin meeting was held and helped decorate the room with a few vases of catkins, daffodils and macrocarpa. Daffodils cost 12s. 6d. a dozen!

The room filled up gradually and people sat at tables with the number of the camp in which they were interested on a card. I talked with one or two and found it interesting, and listened to an escaped prisoner who 'said a few words'. He was a paratrooper who was captured in Tunisia with about 250 others, out of the 600 who made the descent. He disliked the Italians intensely and says they have a cruel streak, but that the Germans 'are like ourselves'. God forbid that we should be as they are—said I inwardly, *à la Pharisee*, thinking of the Polish children of 12 years taken to give their blood-donations for the Germans in such a cruel way, and the countless other devilish traits and sadistic methods they delight in with those in their power.

John Cunningham is again in the news, having now got a second bar to his D.S.O.—triple D.S.O. He is the most modest and unassuming man in the world. Ethel Spencer visualizes Evelyn (his mother) sitting comfortably in her armchair, telephone receiver in hand, listening to the congratulations of her friends! She knows the house, the mother and the phone!

Monday 6th March

A curious buff envelope marked 'O.H.M.S.' and directed to me in block letters was a surprise today. Inside was *a letter from Alan, dated 10th January*, telling all about his visit to Edward in the hospital outside the camp. He went with Dr Williamson, the camp doctor (later referred to as 'Doc. Willie'), starting at 4.30 a.m. and returning at 2 p.m. They had two hours with Edward and were able 'to cheer him up quite a lot', and get a list of requirements from him—mostly books. Two-thirds of the letter concerned

Edward, so I was soon passing the news on to his mother by telephone. Can it be that a ship was sunk or an airmail plane damaged—or how did Alan's letter get into O.H.M.S. hands?

The Russians have had a great victory in the Western Ukraine and have routed 12 German divisions, four of them Panzer divisions. On a front of 150 miles they have advanced 30 miles in two days! Hitler says Soviet forces were advancing with great force and fury—telling the truth for once! Fifteen thousand Germans have been killed in the new advance and 3,000 are taken prisoner. The Lwow–Odessa railway has now been cut, and this is of great importance. For the fifth day running American aircraft have bombed Berlin. Supplies of arms and ammunition to Turkey have been stopped. Oil supplies to Spain were cut off a few weeks ago.

Friday 19th March

A horrible night, with sickness and other miseries—the worst night I have ever had. In the end I collapsed on the landing floor and Kate heard me fall. When I came to she and Jack were both supporting me, and there I draw a thick curtain. But what a kind, loving Kate, and Jack doing his best to lend a hand.

Monday 20th March

All Sunday I dozed and waked—the doctor came twice and the kind little District Nurse came and refreshed me. I drank gallons of water and barley water, slept, woke and drank and slept, and the same all of this day. No interest in anybody or anything. Land-girls were put off, though one turned up at 8 p.m. And so to a night of wild dreams and anxieties, waking every two hours to drink and drink and drink! Vague hearing of 'By Jove, the Russians are pushing on!'

Tuesday 21st March

It isn't often the first day of spring is spring-like. Today has been dull, grey, inclined to fog at midday, though there has been no howling gale like yesterday. With temperature down, the window widely opened is not needed today and the radiator has been on and C.E.M. is beginning to recover. Weak isn't the word, but a slight interest in food has been indicated today—even half a water biscuit in the night. But enuff of sick!

At last we have another letter this month from Alan. It contained two photographs of a Highland Band taken in the camp. Alan had received four of my letters and hoped for more that evening—

30.1.44—as well as from many other kind friends. It is always a good day when Alan's letter comes, and this time he said he had his pipe going at that moment and the letter reeks of it. I like it. A man with his pipe on can sit at home and think in his armchair. It is a good augury for the future, *je le crois*. Shan't I be smoke-dried when he gets home! Two pipes!

More Japanese shipping has been sunk by our American allies, and in some of the islands where they have landed recently Japs are being surrounded and wiped out. The Finns have decided not to accept the Russian armistice terms—another spot of bother for the Russians to clear up. A ban has been placed on the south and east coasts ten miles inland from Cornwall to the Wash. Ominous!

Saturday 25th March
'Our Lady's' beautiful day, warm and sunny. And to make it still more lovely, *two letters came from Alan*, dated 10th and 29th February. More talk of snow and slush, as well as spring-like days. There's a bit about Edward 'much the same', about reading— engineering and novels—and he says: 'My pupil took his first Matric paper yesterday.' Nothing like consolidating your knowledge by passing it on again!

Breakfast was A.1 and spirits were high for my part. I spent the morning on the —— land-girl jobs. 'No billets' was the main cry. A short rest after lunch till the sun called me out, and Jack and I pottered with the hens a bit. Then I got out my wee garden chair—and how it holds me I can't think. It was bought for 2s. 6d. twenty or more years ago at the door from an old man who said he made it. Jack got a box and there we sat in the sun by the hens. Jack had marked out the rows for the early potatoes and Wilks was getting them in. He also weeded and forked over pear tree border and the path at the back, to my great delight—it's lazy I'm getting! And so in to tea, reluctant to leave the sunny warmth of the garden. Then another kind old friend came to the back door—dear old Mr Jones, whose wife ' *'ad 'eard as I was very bad*', and she'd sent him to see. He fumbled in his pocket and brought out a paper bag (it couldn't be eggs, surely, for I couldn't take them as we've had six today). It was delivered into my hand and resolved itself into three oranges: *'And she thought you'd like these.'* And so I did, for I couldn't spoil such a thoughtful, loving gift by saying we already had many more than our share. So I took them gratefully and sent my thanks. *And she said I was to be quick because she did a bit o' washin' yesterday and I've got to do the mangling!'* Oh, dear, aren't they sweet! I shall eat those oranges with reverence.

Thursday 30th March

Lunch was early as a V.C.P. job took me to Coleshill at 1.50. At the Post Office there I picked up three W.V.S. ladies and took them by pleasant roads and lanes to Solihull and a meeting at the Town Hall. Everywhere are Americans and American transport —the khaki jeep and lorry with its tools strapped on the back, the men in their unmatched jackets and nether garments and their pork-pie khaki field caps. They do not walk or march smartly like our men. I saw a few dozen marching today, loose-limbed in a sort of striding march, very arm-y and leg-gy. No crisp tramp-tramp, but just managing to keep fairly in step. Some of their officers are very smart.

Mr Churchill got his vote of confidence for the Government today—425 for and 23 against. Much cheering and much talk from things like Mr Aneurin (!!) Bevan and other such oddments. Shipyard youths are now on strike, as well as 60,000 miners.

Saturday 1st April

A rather dull, cool day. One stayed in bed to breakfast and had a quiet day indoors later. T'other went early to the butcher, then took the Dawg as far as the doctor along with the empty medicine bottles. We got back by 12.30, Twink having been very naughty and crossed all the roads—main and otherwise—by himself in spite of my calling. He was just deaf, and I wasn't sorry to have him home again.

Mrs Biggs asked me to go in and look at the man they had engaged to do *our* ditch (for which I was thankful) and so I went in and looked, and it seemed to be all right. I then came home and spoke very forcibly on the telephone to the assistant surveyor about moving the waste-paper bin from the grass verge in front of the house. I reminded him that last 1st April, after my complaint, a letter came saying they would remove it at once. Nothing was done. A further reply came on 1st July, after a second complaint, and later I spoke to him on the telephone. He now promises to come and see for himself on Monday. They cleared the paper out of the bin on Thursday, but the tins which people will pile outside are now augmented by a child's rusty motor-car, bottles and jam jars. It is really too much. And he said then: 'Of course, you know there's a war on?' I thought of saying: 'No, I haven't heard, is there?'

The Russians are only 30 miles from Odessa and are still sweeping the Germans back on all fronts. General Wingate's plane crashed in Burma on 24th March and he has been killed. He had been specially successful in training airborne troops and his death is a great loss to the Army.

Sunday 2nd April

There has been a slight advance by Italians at Cassino. The French advanced a little between Cassino and Anzio yesterday. The Russians continue to take dozens of small places in their onward surge towards Odessa. Clouds of smoke have been seen rising up from the town as if the Germans were preparing to evacuate it. How they pillage and destroy as they pass over the face of Europe! A postcript to the news tonight tried to show the awful devastation which is spreading over the Continent—*nothing* left, towns destroyed, all food taken by the enemy, everything of value looted. What will it be like when the occupied countries are liberated, their lands laid waste by the ruthless, wicked enemy? Cattle are driven away and slaughtered, all the future sacrificed to the present total war by the Germans. We must *never*, NEVER forget this and let them rise again to devastate our families, our homes and civilization.

Saturday 8th April

A pleasant day after the early morning cold and dull weather. Russia is making great advances on the Ukrainian fronts and Moscow guns are firing great salvoes for the victories of reaching Czechoslovakia and getting through the Carpathians. The Red Army has broadcast to the Czechoslovaks telling them of their intentions towards them and asking them to co-operate with the Czechoslovakian Unit in the vanguard of the advancing army and help to harry the retreating enemy. The Allies are doing well against the Japs, destroying aircraft and shipping and landing on fresh islands.

And here we are on the last page of Volume Eleven and I am not going to hope that one more volume may finish the war. The only thing is to stick it and *stick it*, and STICK IT till the war is ended and Alan John comes home.

VOLUME 12

April 1944 – July 1944

Wednesday 19th April

Cool today, with some wind for a change, and a good deal of sun in the morning and rain by teatime. A poor night was spent by 'dis chile', hearing the hours strike 12, 2, 3 and 4, and so by afternoon a nap was indicated—and taken. We had all been to Kenilworth this morning to pick up the Greenslade hen, and later I went on to the shops and collected six tins of soup, a lettuce, watercress and some black pepper!

Two thousand American bombers were over enemy country in daylight yesterday and a thousand R.A.F. last night. In the latter raid we lost 14. A small force of enemy bombers were over London and the south-east coast. A London hospital was set on fire. We destroyed 14 of their aircraft. Sevastopol is in flames and loud explosions are heard.

Sunday 23rd April

St George's Day, and a day of prayer for the Nation. A lovely day, too—warm, even when cloudy—and I rode off to the 11 a.m. service at St Peter's. Afterwards I decided to thin the parsnips and, of course, went 'hoeing round elsewhere and mucking abart the garden' like Uncle Joe. Already the ground is drying and cracking on top, though moist enough underneath. Kate looks after the hens well and they lay six eggs most days, and occasionally five or eight.

The Union Jack bought for (my) Jack's birthday in 1942—very optimistic I was to buy it then—has been flown for the first time today, St George's Day. It looked grand, and he has found a new way of arranging the pulley and halliard. It flew out beautifully today. I ran the car into the load of wood in the drive yesterday when backing out of the garage and dented in the back wing. So Jack has been talking gently to it with a cramp and pieces of wood and it looks marvellous.

Saturday 29th April

I took Alan's parcel to the post and thought of Jack's words yesterday: 'I shouldn't mind if he didn't get this one'. Meaning, of course, we shouldn't bother about the parcel if Alan came home before receiving it. Oh, wouldn't that be grand! At the moment the war is in a queer state.

There seems very little doing on the Russian front after the almost breathless rush west. The Germans attack, so we have just been told, and the Russians repulse these attacks in the foothills of the Carpathians. Sevastopol is still being pounded by the Russians, as well as the last German airfields in the Crimea. There has been a bit of Naval engagement off the coast of Norway and we have sunk and damaged several ships. Admiral Louis is 'doing his stuff' in Burma and getting some satisfaction. In the Far East our men continue to advance from time to time and mop up afterwards, getting nearer and nearer to the Philippines.

In the post office today there was a rude poster of Hitler, with an evil face, a bulgy nose and lank, untidy hair. He was to be obliterated with savings stamps, so it gave me great pleasure to give him one in the eye with a half-crown stamp!

Sunday 30th April

Not at all interested in getting up this morning, but eventually rolled out and got going, getting down much as usual. We had made up our minds as we went to bed that we would not garden at all today, but have a complete day's rest. I went out to the hens about 10.30 a.m., gathered the purple sprouting for dinner and then decided to thin the spinach. Next I hoed out the footmarks and finally hoed most of the patch, by which time it was noon. But I'm glad it is done.

Joan Spencer rang up just before 6 p.m. tremendously excited because Mr Eden had been asked in the House whether three-year prisoners were likely to be repatriated. He replied that negotiations had been going on some time and have now reached a conclusion. He could not make a statement yet, but will be happy to do so as soon as he is able. Dare we hope? I went out for a walk with Twink, all shaky and thrilly inside. Could such a thing really be? After all these years! Of course I had to ring up Mrs Greenslade and we thrilled together. She had been trying to ring me, as she had had a letter from Edward. He was still in hospital, though expecting to be leaving shortly to go back to the camp.

Wednesday 10th May

So many aches and pains last night that I did not sleep till nearly 3 a.m. I hastened round my daily jobs after breakfast and Jack went to the butcher for me. The Land Army Representatives' Meeting was at 11 a.m. at Leamington Town Hall, so before long the car was speeding along the high road, leaving Kate spring-cleaning and Jack, as usual, with plenty to do.

A broad Scotsman—accent, not figure—tried to tell us about 'Pay as You Earn' Income Tax at the beginning of the afternoon session, but his accent was so difficult to understand, and he spoke so like one of his native rivers in spate, that we did not learn as much as we might have done. A Miss Brew from H.Q. patted us on the back and told us what all good District Representatives should do—a sort of iron hand in a velvet glove—and later we had votes of thanks, breaking up about 3 p.m.

The day began well with *a good letter from Alan*, telling us of Edward's arrival at camp hospital and how they go to see him each day. Sevastopol has fallen and the Crimea is free of Germans.

Thursday 18th May

And are we thinking of him today, his thirtieth birthday? We are, we are, we are! We intended going to the 10 a.m. service at Berkswell, but a V.C.P. job came along and we got away to do it. The first call was at a wartime nursery, where we had to pick up a small baby girl of seven weeks. A little bundle of her belongings was made up and her bottle packed, and then Matron and I went along to the car with the mite. Jack drove and I nursed her, and she soon went to sleep. Arriving half-an-hour later at Warwick, I had quite a long walk through the precincts and corridors and rooms of the County Council buildings at the Shire Hall. Every girl in the offices I passed had to come and see the little girl, and in the final office the baby was soon seized by a woman who knew how to hold a baby comfortably. The business was one of probable adoption, but if the baby was not approved—well, we were to take it back! An elderly and rather severe-looking spinster then appeared, took the baby (and didn't know how to hold it) to be seen by the would-be parents. She came back after a time and said they were going to take the wee thing. I asked if I could see them, but she slurred this over. However, she did allow me to speak to them on the way out. I am sure the new mother would be very good to the baby. She thought she was 'lovely', and I thought she was, too. A little cupid's bow of a mouth, soft brown hair, blue eyes and a little face of character.

Kate had been spring-cleaning the larder and it now looks very nice—not so well-stocked as it used to be, unfortunately, but still with plenty of spare china on the upper shelves. On the news we hear that Cassino has fallen at last and several other places have been taken. The Gustav Line is no more! More sick and wounded prisoners and other personnel are being repatriated from Germany and England.

Monday 29th May

Oh, what a hot night! I tossed and turned and finally slept with only a sheet to cover me and two windows wide open. I certainly didn't want to get up when the time came, but began the day well with *two letters from Alan* (dated 20th and 30th April). Most cheerful letters, too. There was a good deal about Edward and his prospective repatriation. Alan is to plant out onions and seems to take a great interest in the garden and his work on it. Two 'rustic' chairs had been made, 'nice to sit outside in them in the summer'. One forgets they have no chairs except what they make for themselves, and these have been made out of dead wood gathered on their forest walks.

The Italian battles go on with the advantage to our side mostly, and since the action started we have taken 15,000 prisoners and wiped out three German divisions. A cricket match was played at Lord's today—England v. Australia—in a one-day Test Match. The ground was crowded and had to be closed to any further spectators at midday. England won by six wickets.

Saturday 3rd June

Mostly grey today, with some sun at intervals. It is warmer and very pleasant. I'm beginning to think 'It ain't gonna rain no mo', no mo', it ain't gonna rain no mo'.' How badly we need it! The pinks, wandas, London pride and chrysanthemums are flagging badly. My gardening has been varied, a bit here and a bit there, planting snapdragons, weeding the drive and the flower border, watering two evergreens I moved last year and digging a bit. All necessary jobs, but not 'showy'.

The Pope broadcast a message from the Vatican yesterday much the same as usual—a sort of appeal to both sides to save Rome from bombardment. General Maitland-Wilson has replied today to the effect that we hope the Germans will not make the city a place of defence. If they use it for military purposes, the Allies will be obliged to take appropriate measures to eject them.

Monday 5th June

A letter from Alan this morning with a preponderance of matters horticultural. 'There has been a general three-week hold-up of letters,' he says, writing on 10th April, but he thinks there is no need to worry about not hearing from us as everybody is in the same boat. It's marvellous how he manages to keep up his spirits and—apparently—remain in good heart.

Rome has fallen—the first capital in Europe to be liberated, and great was the welcome to the Allies as they passed through the city. Roses half-filled a newspaper correspondent's jeep, and his arm was nearly shaken off by the glad inhabitants in their enthusiasm. Now the Allies have passed through Rome and are over the Tiber, keeping on the enemy's heels and hoping to give him no respite, while our bombers attack him as he goes.

Our Union Jack has been floating bravely over the orchard all day.

There was a long broadcast story of a girl who was practising reporting the beginning of the invasion and inadvertently broadcast that it had begun. The news flashed round the world, but was without foundation. A quite elaborate story, well authenticated—too well, I think. We shall see what 'Joan Ellis' has been used for in a few days perhaps. *Quelle histoire!*

Tuesday 6th June

The invasion has begun! The 8 o'clock news reported that after a terrific air bombardment airborne troops had been landed at the mouth of the Seine. At 1 p.m. we had a most marvellous broadcast beginning 'D. Day. *The* Day'. It told of the assembling of men and material for weeks past in England, of the segregation of the troops from the outside world, then the gathering of ships and boats and landing-craft, and the packing of the guns and equipment in such a way that when the landing was made the things needed at once would come out first. It told of the men's 'trouser-pocket' rations, the last meal they would eat in England, and of the lorries and guns parked by the roadside, in fields, parks and even in private gardens.

Four thousand ships and many thousand other craft have taken part in the assault and landing. For days past the coast of France has been bombarded by air, the Seine bridges have been bombed, the marshalling yards pounded and locomotives and goods' wagons destroyed. There were 11,000 first-line aircraft to support the landings.

General Montgomery is the Commander of the Expeditionary

Force and the landings were made on the coast of Normandy. We hear that life-sized dummy parachutists were dropped (the Germans tell this) which exploded on landing. They also say that the Allies landed between Le Havre and Cherbourg. Our big ships carried out a terrific bombardment to help our armies in 'this greatest amphibious operation of all time'. This began at dawn and then wave after wave of men surged up the beaches. People on the French coast were warned to leave their homes an hour before the attacks began. This message was broadcast from General Eisenhower. They were told to leave the towns, keep off the roads and get some kilometres away, taking only just what they could easily carry. General de Gaulle has arrived in England today and has also broadcast to France this afternoon.

The day has been cold and grey, with a north wind and showers at intervals—but nothing much. Twink and I biked to the grocer and got the bacon, then biked round Meetinghouse and so home, seeing convoys of vehicles going north and other convoys going south on the main road.

The 6 p.m. news says that so far our landings have gone 'according to plan' and in some places we have 'penetrated several miles'. Mr Churchill has spoken in the House this afternoon. Some 31,000 airmen have been over France during the day. There was much less loss in the landing of airborne troops than was expected, though the battle is expected to increase in intensity as the days go by. Caen is the town where heavy fighting is taking place. The air umbrella was spread over 200 miles!!! 'You couldn't see the sky for planes, and the ships looked like a solid bridge across the Channel,' said one observer. The great assault is known as S.H.A.E.F., pronounced 'shafe'—Supreme Headquarters Allied Expeditionary Force.

The broadcast at this time is simply wonderful. We are now hearing the sound of the aeroplanes which took the parachutists over to France, and then the recorded voice of an R.A.F. pilot who took a glider over, and the little chats on the inter-com: 'O.K., pilot?' 'O.K., Skipper'. Bless them, they're fine chaps. Now we are listening to the Navy's work by a man who earned the George Cross. Howard Marshall went along with the troops and landed, and is now back again telling us what happened. He has been twice in the sea and his notes are sodden and useless, so he is just telling us—all impromptu—how his barge arrived. The Germans had prepared pronged obstacles with a mine on the prong, one of which blew up his barge, but the men waded out and the Bren-gun carrier went through five feet of water and on to the beach!

Somehow or another he got to another barge and, after that had sunk, he got on to an M.L. and came back, having 'done his stuff' in time to get home and broadcast.

At 9 p.m. His Gracious Majesty broadcast to his people, and his talk was heard in the United States as well as the Empire. He called us all to prayer on this most historic occasion. His little impediment of speech endears him to us, I think. We grow anxious for him if he falters and rejoice when he overcomes his difficulty of enunciation. He went along very well on the whole tonight. The news lasted till 9.40 p.m., and then we had a service of dedication with the Bishop of London taking the prayers and reading the lesson and the Archbishop of Canterbury giving the address. Three hymns were beautifully sung, too.

I hate to feel Alan is out of all this. It is such a moving thing to be listening to the wireless and seeing in one's mind all that our brave fellows are going through, though really we cannot know what they are doing from such scraps of news. I write this last bit in bed at the end of this day of days—D. Day. A plane is rushing round and round and overhead. This morning, about 5 a.m., I was awaked by squadrons going by, but though I got up I could not see them from the window—part of that wonderful umbrella, I expect.

At last the invasion has started. May God defend the right and bring us to victory and real peace.

Wednesday 7th June

The news says that all the beaches are now clear of the enemy and Allied forces on some beaches have linked up with their flanks, and stores and equipment are being landed. Paratroops landed and captured a village on the Cherbourg peninsula about four miles inland after the Americans had stormed the beaches. Heavy fighting goes on in Caen. From dawn to dusk yesterday the Air Force maintained its guard over the Channel shipping. Over 1,000 R.A.F. aircraft went out last night, blocking the ways by which the enemy would be supposed to bring up reinforcements. All the bridges over the Seine between Rouen and Paris are down and only two road bridges remain.

Apparently we landed 100 per cent. of the men sent over to France. The obstructions in the water close to the beaches had been photographed very low down and we knew how to deal with them. The enemy expected us to attack at high tide, when the cunning obstructions would have been hidden and would have ripped off the bottoms of the boats, but we went in at low tide.

A tank battle was raging in one spot and an air battle not far away, while in between a farmer with a couple of oxen went on ploughing his field, occasionally giving the oxen a flick, but otherwise taking no notice of the history-making battles so near to him.

Thursday 8th June

A grey day, but fairly warm. I managed to deliver my parish leaflets and walk Twink in Bungalow fields by 12.15 p.m. as this was my 'D. Day' for M.U. The Crowhurst bus took me to St Francis' Church, arriving there at 2.45 p.m. I had been so quaky all morning about speaking in church and before t'parson, too! But when I saw all the dear, homely faces of the Mothers' Union members, young and old—and heard a few of the babies raising their voices—I began to feel quite at home.

Back at Burleigh, as a sort of antidote, I suppose, I went upstairs to change and spent an amusing twenty minutes trying on all my hats in turn—and their name is legion! I experimented with a new curl on one side and Twink, who was hanging round, was very annoyed and whined unhappily. However I enjoyed that lazy 20 minutes and then did a bit of stitching on the machine till supper-time. Later I wrote a letter and then we heard the news and the extra war bulletin we are now getting. We have taken Bayeux and the people there are delirious with joy, throwing flowers, embracing and kissing our men, crying 'Vive l'Angleterre' 'Vive l'Americaine', making the V sign and generally (s–sh) interrupting the flow of the troops through the town! We are warned by Mr Churchill not to be too optimistic as 'though a dangerous part of the operation is now behind us, terrific exertions are yet to come'. The Germans will now begin their counter-attacks and we shall have much to endure.

We heard recorded accounts of the landings by sea, land and air and by parachute. Very terrible and wonderfully brave, I thought. A dead parachutist was laid on the best bed in a small French house, his body covered with flowers. That is what they think of us today. Wounded men are back in England and were recording their impressions—somehow it seems *irreverent*! The Bayeux tapestries have been removed, no-one knows by whom or to where.

Friday 9th June

We seem to be gaining a little ground in Normandy, but this is a stiff job, I am sure. We had records tonight of all kinds of things, the landing of gliders and the Germans shelling of them. Somehow

I don't like this much. It makes it into a 'show', and it is much too grave a business for that. What we are having to suffer because of these bullying, arrogant Germans! And an escaped prisoner said: 'The Germans are like ourselves'! They are the absolute opposite, never satisfied unless they are preparing for a war or over-running their neighbours, pillaging, murdering, dominating, pretending and persecuting. We are just too slack and stupid between wars, only too glad to be at peace again and never looking ahead or being prepared. We don't like war and so don't want to think about it unless we are obliged to—with what dire and terrible results! I hope this nation will always keep fully armed and trained and then there will be none; or, if belligerents do arise, we shall have the means to settle them quickly.

Saturday 10th June

A bright morning when we woke, with a temperature of 50° in the porch. It was nice for gardening, so I dug a bit and weeded a bit and felt quite tired by 1 p.m. After lunch a land-girl came and I somehow managed to change and get across the road by 2.45 in time for the British Legion meeting. They have been so dull we decided to cheer them up with more to the social side, with speakers and whist, etc. So, of course, I had to be roped in at once to do a bit in the near future. Afterwards I heard the 6 p.m. news, ate a boiled egg and toast and at 7 p.m. picked up three blood-donors and drove them to Warwick Hospital. A hundred stretcher cases and 40 sitting cases are expected there at ten this evening from Normandy, hence the S.O.S. for special blood-donors.

We are making progress in Normandy, but there isn't a great deal of news tonight. The heaviest fighting is around Caen. Our supplies are being landed in spite of difficult weather. Everybody talks of the invasion.

Sunday 11th June

The battle in Normandy is raging furiously, swaying to and fro, and the Allies have made some advances. General Montgomery is there and has given out his first message: he gave thanks to Almighty God for our good beginning on the Normandy beaches, commended the Navy and the Air Force for their co-operation, then the Army, and wished them good luck. He has his famous caravan there which was so well-known in North Africa. Today there has been the biggest unloading since the invasion. The material and equipment and the men are flowing in to the beaches.

The bridgehead has been lengthened and is now 11 miles deep in one place at the spearhead. There is still heavy fighting in and around Caen, which is the centre of several radial roads, and, of course, the Germans want to hold it. As I write a war correspondent is saying: 'There was no sign of life in Caen' as they passed over in a bomber.

Tuesday 13th June

The Normandy news continues to be good, with more advances, some fluctuating fighting, places lost and gained, but consolidation on the whole. Mr Churchill has been across to France accompanied by Field-Marshal Smuts and General Sir Alan Brooke. Isn't Winston a lad! I wonder what Hitler thinks of that—the little Shickelgrüber!

Thursday 15th June

A nice warm morning, and this afternoon we went to tea with Ethel and Harry. In Coventry, on the walls of a bombed or burnt out building, was a poster headed 'National Service'. It advertised a meeting for 12th March 1939—what a long time ago that seems!! For some time an old pre-war kind of menu was still in its little case outside a café-that-was at the top of Hertford Street. It remained until the present rations were in force and was eventually removed. Perhaps it made everyone's mouth water as they went by! The old chimes of the Cathedral rang out from the undamaged spire as we waited there, and it was good to hear them again.

The Germans are counter-attacking hard and fiercely in Normandy and villages are taken, lost and sometimes recaptured. Carentan still remains in our hands and we are endeavouring to cut across the Cherbourg peninsula. If we could get Cherbourg, we should have a fine landing-place for troops and equipment. There have been questions about the advisability of the P.M.'s visit to France, when the destroyer on which he went was in action part of the time and he remained on the bridge! Later, in a car, he was a perfect target for the enemy as he stood, cigar in mouth, on the journey inland.

Ethel Spencer told us today that John Cunningham was invited, with his gunner, to Princess Elizabeth's coming-out ball. The King danced first with the Princess and John had the next dance. Then, at the fourth dance, John danced with the Queen. A great honour for him.

Friday 16th June

A gil-loomy day!! Very grey all day, looking as if it would rain at any moment, with the wind stirring the leaves on the trees with that certain feeling of rain coming. But beyond a few drizzly spots late in the evening there was no rain. I went out to get up tulips here and there this morning, and the ground is either hard and dry or just powdery and dusty. Awful!

Very few letters come now, except from the Land Army, but today there was nothing at all for me—the first time for months, I should think.

The Germans' new weapon is a pilotless plane which goes so far and then explodes. A bogey—but which does damage.

Saturday 17th June

A nice bright morning, sun shining out of a cloudless blue sky at 8 a.m. Later lovely billowy clouds formed and unfortunately a wind sprang up—just as if everything was not as dry as dust already. The beautiful car bustled to the butcher and then Twink and I walked on our six feet to the grocer, where we picked up one or two unexpected oddments. One was a pound of suet! It's extraordinary how there's never a mite of suet in the winter, but in the middle of the summer out comes a packet of 'Cook's Suet' from under the counter! Then three tomatoes were put in a bag surreptitiously and placed quickly in my basket.

In Normandy the Americans have made progress across the Peninsula and—the King has been over! He presented some decorations while he was there, and then the cruiser *Arethusa* soon brought him safely home again. What about *that* visit, old Shickelgrüber? Do your people know that?

A pilotless plane went over a cricket ground today, but the game went on. No-one can say they are not unpleasant things, for one does not know until five seconds or so before the explosion takes place and that is when the red glow at the end goes out, and then . . . bang. If you're in the way, well that's that. I expect we shall soon find a way to combat them. Real German frightfulness, and of no possible military value.

The French have taken Elba.

Sunday 18th June

Lots of planes over in the night and one hears through one's dream the thunder of squadrons and the roar of the single plane. I biked to St Peter's and stayed for the Communion Service afterwards. It was beautifully taken, and I wish Mr Curtis were not leaving in a fortnight, for he seems to be much liked by the people here.

The 6 p.m. news tells of the American Army's drive in Normandy, which has made a corridor six or seven miles wide and has sealed off Cherbourg on the peninsula. Now the island of Jersey is in sight from the western coast. Wounded men of Allied and enemy forces are evacuated from Normandy by 'sky trains', which carry a flight nurse and two medical officers who give first aid and administer blood plasma.

A few days ago the Americans' new big bombers raided Japanese war industries, while elsewhere in the Pacific they continue to pound the islands and mop up places here and there in a steady advance.

Some 18,000 prisoners have been taken in Normandy since D. Day.

Monday 19th June
   A letter from Alan this morning. He has had no letters for some time from us, but hoped to be lucky the evening he wrote. He had paid two visits to a circus and enjoyed it very much.

Tonight nine land-girls came, did a quiz and were very merry. They ate up all the buns and cakes and drank many cups of tea. Coming into the room, I overheard one say: 'And I hope those perishin' bombers don't come over tonight.' This meant our planes, which seem to disturb our night and make us a bit scratchy in the daytime. For two or three days they have been roaring round all day, and this afternoon one just couldn't get a nap for noise. How our men do on the battle fronts I can't imagine.

Those beastly pilotless planes have been coming over again, last night and this morning, and there has been more damage and, of course, casualties. We are bombing their starting points and have shot down several today. May we soon get the better of them.

Thursday 22nd June
   I sit up in bed with two windows wide open scribbling at the old diary. It is 10.45 p.m. and blackout is at 11.17 p.m. All day long planes have been roaring over, *very* noisy. For a few hours now there have been none, and it is dead quiet and very pleasant to have peace, if only for an hour or two. Ramps for launching the robot planes have been found near Cherbourg, unpleasantly in line with Southampton, and near to darling Joyce, too. They have been sending them over this morning, as well as last night.

Friday 23rd June

No sign of rain whatever. Everything is dried up—grass grey, leaves and plants going brown. Very unkind weather. The lovely plants I put in at the beginning of the month are far from lovely now. The purple sprouting looks the best, but brussels and brocoli are drooping here and there and I find they have the beastly grub at the roots. What a depressing job gardening can be! Tonight I am very fed-up with it—such *hard* work and so little result. Perhaps I shall feel *bettah* another day.

Mr Eden has told what we know of the shooting of the airmen in Stalag Luft III—47 of them. It looks like cold-blooded murder by the Gestapo! Germans are not fit to live, the brutes.

Saturday 24th June

Midsummer Day and, yes, it's her birthday again—she who scribes this page. There was a bumper post from most of the right people, and the rest, I know, are too busy. So I enjoyed all the letters that came and spent the afternoon answering some of them. Jack and I went out in the car to the butcher and the village, where I stood in a queue for peas, potatoes, asparagus and tomatoes, for this evening we had a birthday meal. And didn't we enjoy it, complete with half of the half-bottle of Graves?

Every day and night planes attack the enemy. Launching ramps at the Pas de Calais have been heavily bombed again. Nevertheless there were flying-bombs over in the night and this morning, with the sad toll of casualties and damage. In Italy the enemy's resistance has stiffened near Perugia. Our successes in Burma are being followed up.

Monday 26th June

A little rain had fallen when we woke, and during the morning it fell quite sharply at times. Everything looked freshened up, but we hope there will be more.

We are taking a lot of prisoners in France and now have 20,000 since the invasion. The Americans are through the city of Cherbourg, but it cannot be said to be captured—or liberated—until the Germans are all cleaned up there. We progress in Italy and the Russians have taken Vitebsk and are breaking through the German lines, making three or four deep breaches. And bang-a-bang go the Moscow guns again. They must be getting tired of the noise there. It seems a slow job in Burma.

Thursday 29th June

The Russians have taken more than 1,200 places—it sounded marvellous on the 8 a.m. news—and have made a great breakthrough. This evening they have been wasting more ammunition in Moscow. It seems rather childish to me, but the B.B.C. announcer gives the news quite heartily, and not as if he thought so, too. Counter-attacks in Normandy are being held and we are still thrusting forward a little. Flying-bomb sites have been attacked and many bombs destroyed in flight. There are, nevertheless, casualties and damage each day.

A convoy of American vehicles of untellable shapes, and unidentifiable things on wheels, as well as some 'ducks', went past this house towards Blacksmith's Corner a few days ago. Today they came back again. We never thought we should see the American Army on the war-path—actually going to war—along this road. At the beginning of the war we certainly did wonder what we personally should do if the Germans came prancing along. We were told to hide our maps, not to give them food or drink or anything. We were to hide our bicycles, knock a hole in our car petrol tanks, etc., etc., 'if the invader comes'. And we certainly didn't think it unlikely. I thought of having some pepper ready to throw in their eyes if they came to the door. Mrs Whitaker was going to make them a cup of coffee and poison it if they called at the Rectory. And though we were half-joking, there was more than a touch of grimness about it, too, for were we not almost defenceless in July 1940?

Friday 30th June

At Mrs Gorton's Disabled Soldiers' Sale this afternoon I was introduced to a man who had lost his right arm. After the Germans had taken them prisoner, he said, they put them in a building and threw hand-grenades in and bayoneted some of them. Truly an accursed race are the Germans!

Stiff fighting goes on round Caen and the Russians are what you might call *shoving* the Germans back on the Eastern front. The Americans announce the breaking of diplomatic relations with Finland. Flying-bombs continue to come over by night and day and the casualties and damage are considerable. Mr Churchill has been in the south watching them come over. The King and Queen have been visiting those who have suffered from bomb damage, in hospitals and rest centres.

The last of the Cherbourg forts has surrendered and, oh my goodness, the Germans were apparently settled there for years, for they had bottles and bottles of cognac and wine (all looted from the French, we expect!), tins and tins of food and everything to make themselves thoroughly comfortable. They certainly thought the place was impregnable from the sea.

Monday 3rd July

The Russians have taken Minsk and the German army is retreating in disorder. They are now very nearly where they were three years ago! And I expect Moscow people have been pretty well deafened this evening. The Americans have started a new offensive on the Cherbourg peninsula. In Italy we continue to progress. Near Caen the Germans are battering themselves to pieces against our Army there.

The flying-bombs continue to come over and do a lot of damage and cause many casualties. London is having a dreadful time, I fear. Edith tells us the Guards' Chapel was hit and many men killed there—only the Padre was left alive. Of course, these things are not published, but London is no place to be in if one need not be there.

Saturday 8th July

At 9.30 p.m. we are having sounds and a talk from just outside Caen. It sounds hell on earth. It is dreadful to think how everything possible has to be destroyed in a city before it can be captured. There is a new offensive from the north of Caen from our Army there, and it is going well so far—better than we expected.

In the Cherbourg peninsula the Americans' new attack is also successful. They have crossed the river Vire and are fanning out. We have bombed the store, which is a limestone cave, where the French formerly grew mushrooms, and is the place where the flying-bombs are stored. The enemy soon got a big gang working to get things going, and then we bombed it again next day! Flying-bombs continue to come over the Southern counties and London and there are casualties and damage. People who have no work in London are advised to leave, and many children and others have already left. There are some in Balsall Common.

Sunday 9th July

It was grey when Kate brought the tea at 8 o'clock. I was fast asleep, having been wakened several times by squadrons and squadrons of planes away to the south. However I woke, looked at the weather, lazed another ten minutes just to distinguish

Sunday from other days, and then began the day. Church was indicated, but about 10 a.m. rain began and came down fairly heavily all morning. Many oddments, which had long been waiting, were done and I de-mothed the spare room and packed up the blankets.

Caen has fallen! Hurrah! It was the heavily-fortified hinge of the front in Normandy, and its capture is of great importance to the Allies. There are the usual booby-traps, mines and snipers to be dealt with and small pockets of the enemy to be cleared out. The Americans have now taken La Haye-du-Puits, too. An order of the day message came in at 8.50 from Stalin, as the Russians have captured Lida, south-west of Vilna. They have freed hundreds more places, too.

VOLUME 13
July 1944 – October 1944

Monday 10th July

And the thirteenth volume! The day began well with a letter from Alan after three weeks' pause. He says: 'My news is, of course, all onions—6,000 planted so far and about 19,000 to plant. . . . We went to the cinema again yesterday morning . . . and one morning last week I had a trip to the nursery in town where the tomato plants and onion seedlings are being raised.' This is all to the good. Any change out of camp must be welcome.

Friday 14th July

The Russians are pushing on. Yesterday they took Vilna, annihilating the encircled troops, taking 8,000 prisoners and killing 5,000. An old man, a woman and a small child were the only Jews left in Vilna. Poor wretched Jews, how they have suffered at the hands of the Germans! Today the Russians have captured Pinsk. Normandy news tells of the American advance, slow but steady, towards Lessay, and they are also only about two miles from St Lo. Weather has been bad for flying and, of course, good for flying-bombs. Mr Morrison thinks we shall have to put up with flying-bombs for some time yet, although the defensive measures are having a good deal of effect.

This day did Preece come and cut part of the orchard grass. The grandfather clock came in for a good deal of attention, too. It now has a lovely soft-toned strike, having formerly pierced ear-drums, upset telephone calls and roused our visitors in the night.

Wednesday 19th July

General Montgomery says: 'Yesterday was an extremely good day.' We launched an attack south-east of Caen, preceded by the biggest air attack in history, and are now 12 miles east of Caen. He

also said that since D. Day we have taken 60,000 prisoners and
buried 8,000 of their dead, and estimated that 150,000 Germans,
counting the wounded, have thus been disposed. Our casualties in
this new attack are, so far, extremely light.

The Germans want lorries very badly and in return they offer
Hungarian Jews. Much as one would like to save the poor Jews,
there is not the slightest chance of lorries being forthcoming.
Russia is advancing on many parts of her 800-mile front, and 1,200
Fortresses and Liberators which made attacks on Germany shot
down 53 enemy aircraft for the loss of seven.

Thursday 20th July

Today has been rather restful and no gardening has been done by
me. After lunch we took a rest, and at 2.45 went out in the car. Jack
was left outside the Schools while I went in to visit, drank a little
tea with the teachers and then went through the classrooms. Very
interesting, as usual. I asked who liked gardening in the 10–12 class
and many boys held up their hands. I asked if they liked
weeding—they did. So I said how glad I would be if they would
come and weed a bit for me, and then went on to other things.
Later a teacher came out to ask if I meant it and, if so, when could
two of them come? So it was arranged for them to come at six
tomorrow. At least they will be able to clear some of my pear tree
border.

The 9 p.m. news tells of difficult country again for our men
south-east of Caen, but says they are consolidating their positions.
In Italy the Army is eight miles on from Ancona. In Burma the
Japanese have almost disappeared from the Imphal Plain as they
retire before our Army there. The Japanese Cabinet has resigned.

There is word of an attempt to assassinate Hitler!

Friday 21st July

News of the 'bombing' of Hitler and some of his generals tells
also of the death of some and the injuring of others of his
entourage. It is said he received concussion and slight burns and
that he started work again immediately and received Mussolini for
a long, pre-arranged meeting. All broadcasts in Germany were
interrupted at 6.20 last evening: 'Attention!' a sharp voice called.
'An important announcement! Attempt on the life of the Fuehrer!
The Fuehrer is uninjured.' Then followed the stuff about the
'deepest gratitude and fullest satisfaction' that he had escaped 'the
criminal attack'.

Two small boys, John and Raymond, arrived today to do some

weeding and stayed until 9.45. Very business-like they were. Having had two tiny weeding forks to begin with, one of them soon came to ask for 'two middle-sized forks', and with those they soon made headway in the massive overgrowth of pear tree border. They say they will be here tomorrow at 2 o'clock! Wilkes also came, and so I was in the position of having three gardeners working here at one time. It sounds quite expensive.

Saturday 22nd July

One small gardener, John Kennell, came at 2 p.m. The other had been summoned by telegram to 'Roogby' for the afternoon. So John set to work and soon rooted up my eryngium, or whatever it is called. Anyway, it is an ornamental thistle with a round globe which flowers on every little spike composing the ball, and which I had specially planted in that spot. However, the little fellow in his blue dungarees soon rooted up a lot of wild michaelmas daisies and many weeds and wheeled them away. So I went and worked and kept an eye on him. By 4.30 I had had enough, so I paid him 2s. 6d. (at the rate of 6d. an hour) and he is coming again on Tuesday.

All kinds of messages from Hitler, Goering and others tell one story after another about internal affairs in Germany. There must be a considerable stir going on. An anti-Nazi broadcast from Frankfurt was, after a time, suddenly cut off. There have been shootings and imprisonments, changes of staff, and Himmler—that sadistic murderer—is now Commander-in-Chief of the Army as well as head of the Gestapo. Grim! Everyone is very excited at the turn of affairs and hoping this is the beginning of the crack in Germany. It is said that the attempt on Hitler's life was made by 'a small clique of officers' . . . 'a few generals and colonels stationed at important points of the home army.'

Wednesday 2nd August

Today war news is good. In France some of the Allied Army is now in Brittany, and as we go forward there is more room for our armies to deploy. This evening there is good news of a 'break through' the German lines and hundreds of prisoners are being taken. Montgomery describes this as 'a major success'. The best day, they say, since D Day.

The casualties from flying-bombs are heavy: 5,340 bombs came over from June to July and 4,735 people were killed and 14,000 more or less seriously injured. Some 17,000 houses have been destroyed and 800,000 damaged. Simply terrible!

Tuesday 8th August

A warm and pleasant day—that is if one had nothing to do. This morning Jack had an incinerator fire and burnt up all the rubbish, and I turned over the orchard bed ready to plant out wallflowers this evening. We had tea in the corner and were much worried with one or two wasps till Jack went in and came back again armed doughtily with the fly swat looming like a knight of old. Soon the persistent wasp was slain, we moved the tea things inside the house and then had peace. Twink had a fierce encounter with the last wasp and felt a very brave but much discomfited dog.

The news is good from Normandy: the Americans continue their advance, and the German attempt to divide them from our forces in the Caen sector is frustrated, with a heavy toll taken of their tanks by our Typhoons. The British forces have pushed out from Caen and taken Mount Pincoa, a valuable height, and have crossed the Orme. The *Daily Telegraph* talks of the 'surge towards Paris'. Prisoners taken on the American front since D. Day number 71,801, and since the advance in Brittany another 12,000 are estimated to have been captured—83,000 in all.

Tuesday 15th August

Great news! Our forces have now made another landing, this time on the coast of France between Marseilles and Nice. It was practically unopposed. Airborne troops were dropped by parachute, then came the gliders and the infantry, etc., the place having been well bombarded by the Navy previously. A second D. Day! At the moment one has not grasped it all and so it must all be digested before one can tell of it properly. Anyway, so far so good.

Thursday 17th August

This morning was full of household jobs, much tidying up and moving things round, till at 12 I went out and gardened, forking up weeds in the drive border as well as I could. It was so hard. Having got a barrow-load by 3 p.m., I decided a rest would be good, for though cooler than yesterday, with no sun till late afternoon, it was still very hot for gardening. Having read the *Daily Telegraph* more or less, I fell asleep for a little while and felt better for it.

The 6 p.m. news told of a victory for us: the Americans have taken Orleans, a town with a population of 75,000. Chartres has also fallen and they are now 30 miles from Paris, with the Germans going back to the Seine. In Paris the rumble of distant guns can now be heard. It is said, by the Germans, that the police in Paris have struck, though this may not be true, but just an excuse to pour in the Gestapo. On the Riviera beach-head we now occupy about 500 square miles, are well-established and still moving forward.

In the Burmese campaign it can now be said there are no fighting Japs on Indian territory, only a few wounded and odd ones to round up. (I was surprised to hear a few weeks ago that Japs *were* on Indian soil.) Hurrah, I say to everything!

Friday 18th August

Grand news on the wireless tonight. The Germans are taking a terrific beating and the battle of Normandy is won! The mouth of the pocket near Falaise is closing—it is now only two or three miles wide—and our aircraft is pounding the enemy as he tries to escape. Typhoons bomb him on all the roads as he gathers his armour and men together in the attempt to get away. We are paying for Dunkirk with interest! The Allied forces are only 20 miles from Paris and are reported unofficially to be in Versailles.

Announcers of the B.B.C. cannot conceal their delight at being able to give such good news, and the war correspondents nearly tumble over themselves with the thrill of telling the story of this most spectacular advance. As Robin Duff told his story we could hear the victory bells ringing from the French church nearby.

President Roosevelt has said that if Germany throws in her hand when we reach her borders this will not prevent the Allies from occupying Germany. We fully intend to march in!

Mrs Greenslade came to talk a bit today, very thrilled over my telephone message yesterday. There was a notice in the 'Late News' about the next repatriation of sick and wounded and invalid prisoners of war which is supposed to take place from Gothenburg, Sweden, on 8th September, and it seems likely that Edward would be among the next repatriated. Alan's homecoming seems a little nearer now. I do hope he can be patient a little longer. My patience is wearing rather thin. How we do long to see him again!

Tuesday 22nd August

The Americans are fighting west of the Seine, and fighting is reported inside Paris, with the Maquis on the warpath. Orleans is under fire from the Germans now. The Vichy government has left and gone 'somewhere in the east'. General de Gaulle, visiting some of the liberated towns, is everywhere welcomed with cheering crowds. Flowers are thrown into his car when he enters these places and all seem glad to see him—concrete evidence of the liberation of France. In the south over 2,000 square miles are in our hands and, though there is opposition and it is stiffening now in some parts, on the whole we have been able to move forward unexpectedly quickly and now have 14,000 prisoners. The Maquis have had arms and ammunition, as well as food, dropped from British and American bombers, and have made good use of them, thanks be.

In one place a German colonel and his chauffeur had been captured and were being driven away in a jeep by two Americans. In the square of the town a crowd had gathered. A woman rushed forward and slapped the colonel across the face. Another woman spat at him and others rushed up to do the same. The Americans—and rightly, too—protected their prisoner. It was an ugly incident, and the German would surely have been killed—and he would have deserved it, for he had had tortured and shot men of the Maquis, relatives of those in the crowd, as well as their own townsmen.

At the dentist's today I heard something about 'dentures' and the way one's transition from 'attached' teeth to 'unattached dining-room furniture' is arranged, without the awful m-m-m pause between! Alas that this time is coming so near!

Wednesday 23rd August

This is one of the good days of the war! Paris has been liberated! Some 50,000 Maquis and hundreds of thousands of the people of Paris have been fighting against the Germans in the city—and have won! This was the news at 1 p.m., and before 2 p.m. the Union Jack was up in the orchard. Not that it was *flying*—there was no wind—but it could be seen by all and sundry. What a joy this news is, and I suppose we have let the Maquis inside the city know when it was almost surrounded by Allied Forces and given the word 'Go', so they have won back the city for themselves. A grand way of allowing them to gain prestige again!

Thursday 24th August

A warm day with a good deal of sun. I was busy about the house and then began to garden a bit. It was very hot working, so after lunch a short rest was indicated, and then I went out to finish a bit of forking and weeding, tidying up after removing broad beans, staking the enormous purple sprouting broccoli and brussels sprouts, etc. Then Jack came out and began to weed the path and sweep it, and didn't it look nice! The 'honest sweat' rolled down my face, seeped into my eyes and dropped off the end of my nose! So when teatime came we were glad to finish.

There is much talk today about the 'liberation' of Paris.

Manchester rang its bells yesterday—a day before St Paul's was due to ring—thus justifying its words, so often used: 'What Manchester says today, the rest of England says tomorrow!' As events turn out, the 'liberation' is scarcely accomplished as there is still fighting inside the city.

Russia reports further victories and salutes thunder forth in Moscow. The forces in the South of France have captured Grenoble, liberated Marseilles, the second city of France, and are reported to have reached Geneva. The report from German sources of a landing by Allied Forces at Bordeaux turns out to be a rising of the Maquis. Petain has been seized and taken away by S.S. troops. It is likely that fighting will be confused for some time in France as the Germans do not seem to know what is happening. Some who have been captured thought we were still on the Normandy beaches only.

Sunday 27th August

Paris had a few thrills when General de Gaulle attended the service at Notre Dame today, for as he went in machine-gun bullets spat around him. Inside there was other shooting, and again when he came out, but he just walked straight ahead and mercifully was untouched. Four Germans (in grey flannels and singlets) were arrested. Paris is still in high feather over her liberation. There was very little food in the city, long queues for a weekly loaf, no meat at all and, in fact, very little of anything eatable.

The Germans are getting across the Seine in small parties, it seems, but they cannot take their equipment. Over the Seine a convoy 15 miles long was stopped at the head by our aircraft, which then swept up and down the column for hours bombing the vehicles. Pretty horrible! But the only thing to be done to Germans. Things go well in the South, and at Brest we have made a special attack from land, sea and air. There is also an advance in Italy.

Much aircraft was going by and over last night, and tonight I can hear our bombers in the distance—zump, zump, zump, zump!

Thursday 31st August

The Russians have taken Ploesti. Their guns will be popping 'em off again! The Romanians are busy about Armistice terms and Bulgaria is told she cannot be just neutral. Having seen which way the cat jumps, these half-baked little nations want to be on the right side of the fence. So easy to slip out like that and save their country from war devastation by saying the word, but it can't be done like that and they have been told so. This evening an Order of the Day announced that the Russians are in Bucharest. In France our Armies are over the Somme! Only 30 miles from the Belgian frontier in one place. The Germans seem disorganized and those who are captured seem red-eyed, tired and bewildered.

Friday 1st September
Once more I write in bed after a very full day. We both went to Leamington this morning and had a pleasant run, and were able to get back again just before 1 p.m., scampering in to hear the news. Grand news, too! The Germans are being thrust out of France and in one place we are nearing Germany. Did the announcer say only fifty miles? Certainly Metz was mentioned, and that is north of Nancy, not very far from the German border. Dieppe has been taken by the British and Canadians and the Dieppe raid, so hazardous in 1942, has been avenged. It is difficult to take in and remember all the news as B.B.C. announcers give no pause, but pack every minute full of meat. It is really breathtaking—both for them and us.

This sweep over France is shattering. How well one remembers when first our planes used to go for 'a sweep over France'. It sounded fine, but this wholesale dash, this rout, is marvellous after all we have borne from the 'Herrenvolk'. In the South, too, we are getting on well. The Russians seem to have stopped outside Warsaw, while advancing and capturing important towns elsewhere. Inside Warsaw deadly fighting goes on between the Germans and Poles. It is a pity Russia cannot—or does not—take Warsaw.

There is a V.C. today for a Catalina captain. He took his craft low down to bomb a U-boat, the bombs did not release and so he turned and went back while the flak did great damage to the Catalina. All the crew were wounded by it. However he went in again, released the bombs himself and sank the U-boat. Wounded in 72 places, he somehow managed to bring his badly damaged craft home and, though he was weak through loss of blood and fainting from time to time, she was at length safely landed. Before the captain could be moved he had to have a blood transfusion. He is now recovering in hospital and is just able to get up. As the old countryman said in a play we saw many, many years ago: 'Lard–y, Lardy, these be 'mazin' toimes'!!

Kate has been bottling fruit and tomatoes and making jam. I

hope Alan may enjoy some of it! General Montgomery has been made a Field-Marshal.

Saturday 2nd September

Arras and Vimy Ridge are in our hands. The garrison at Havre has been encircled. The enemy has made a show of resistance in the Compiegne Forest and the Americans are busy there. They are also threatening those two gateways to the German frontier—Nancy and Metz. Brest and St Malo still hold out, rather forlornly. Bad weather has cut down flying today, but Bremen was heavily attacked by the R.A.F. last night, without loss for us. Two composite aircraft—'pick-a-back' planes—were flown over here last night from Germany, a Messerschmidt riding on a Junkers 88, which finally discharges the former and then goes home!

In Italy, with increasing speed and vigour, our forces advanced 15 miles towards the Gothic Line and then, without pause, pierced the line four miles deep and 20 wide. Other forces—the Fifth Army—have crossed the Arno. In Southern France two columns are converging and doing a good work in disposing of the forces they meet, destroying them and capturing many prisoners. In the East the Russians have taken 50,000 prisoners, among them seven German generals. Severe fighting continues in the old town of Warsaw between the Poles and the Germans. Food going elsewhere was diverted to a concentration camp where women and children and old people were starving. The 9 p.m. news tells that Douai is liberated. St Valery has been taken without a fight by the 51st Highland Division. They defended it in 1940 and against great odds they were captured. Now the new 51st has captured it. The *Malaya* has bombarded St Malo today. It is wonderful to know we are only 40 miles from Calais and Dunkirk.

Sunday 3rd September

Five years ago today we entered into the war. After great vicissitudes, many disappointments, terrible losses and more suffering than can ever be assessed, we are now back again in Belgium, the Battle of France is nearly over and the Battle of Germany about to begin. It has been a day of National Prayer and the King and his people have been to their respective churches and chapels to join in prayer and thanksgiving. For our part, we drove to Berkswell Church and passed through the old door where for more than 700 years the Christian people around here have gone to worship in their joys and troubles, and to show their dependence on Almighty God, to ask His help and to give Him praise. It is a wonderful feeling to worship in such an atmosphere. The church was pretty full today, and didn't we sing the good old hymns with vigour!

Fighting is reported on the outskirts of Nancy—dear Nancy! Von Kluge, who took Rommel's place—Rommel is dead—is now reported to be dead, too. Goering is reported to be 'sacked'. Finland wants peace. Disintegration of the enemy is proceeding nicely. The Romanians have seen vast long columns of Red Army troops pouring through Bucharest and realize how helpless they would have been had they not had an armistice.

Monday 4th September
Today's great news is the liberation of Brussels! In Belgium there has not been much opposition and the Allied troops are now only 20 miles from the Dutch border. On the coast our forces are only 10 miles from Boulogne. In the Rhone Valley there are successes, too, but I am not clear about this except that Lyons is now free. General Dempsey says the German High Command has now lost control of the troops in France and Belgium and they are simply trekking eastwards wherever they can find a way through. There is fighting outside Nancy.

Tuesday 5th September
We are now in Antwerp and Louvain and are mopping up the Germans near the coast. Russia has declared war on Bulgaria. We had a little verbal dust-up with the Poles today as one of their number in authority attacked us for not helping them in the Warsaw fighting—how can we?

Sunday 10th September
But not a very Sundayish Sunday! I couldn't face a long, cold ride to church, and it was a very cold morning—42° in the porch. I did a bit of washing—yes, even on Sunday—and after lunch and a rest we both went out and wrestled with nets and raspberry bushes. Long trailers of the bushes had grown through the nets and it was some job disentangling them. More gardening later and then we heard the first of five parts of *Dr Jekyll and Mr Hyde*—and think one will be enough!

And here comes the 9 p.m. news! The Canadians have reached the coast near Calais. The Americans are 10 miles from Aächen. In Italy there have been heavy casualties on both sides. It is terrible country to fight in—a place for holidays, but not for war—and is a very stiff job for our Armies. The Bulgarians, having been at war with Russia for a few hours, have now signed an armistice. The coastal flooding between Dunkirk and Boulogne creates a good deal of delay and the battle line now is the Albert Canal. At Dunkirk the Germans now hold very much the same perimeter as we held in 1940. Epinal, near Nancy, is mentioned today. We had a lovely drive through there in 1938.

Monday 11th September

We both grew very agitated today about the proposed Coventry Cathedral, which ended in my writing a letter to the *Coventry Evening Telegraph*. I said: 'Now that we have had time to consider the plans for Coventry Cathedral, I suggest that we go back to Sir Giles Gilbert Scott's first report that the walls of the former building could be repaired and the Cathedral rebuilt. Is not this what Coventry people want? . . . the beautiful tower and spire would be part of the Cathedral as before, not isolated, but forming one harmonious whole . . . let us not rush into building an entirely new Cathedral on part of the old site, if the rebuilding of the old is what we really need.' The letter was signed 'A Friend of the Cathedral, Balsall Common'.

This took a good part of the afternoon, but I did manage a bit of edge-cutting before tea, then went out again afterwards and meant to clear up. However the thought of lettuce to be sown, hoping it will come along for the early spring, made me rake and sow the seeds before anything else. Then I looked at the little cabbage seedlings and plants and decided they, too, must be put out, and did that next.

The city of Luxembourg is now liberated and our troops are in Holland. Dutch units are fighting in this area. Our forces broke out of the Albert Canal bridgehead and established themselves over a further canal bridge before the enemy had time to blow it up. American guns are now firing into Germany. (Mind Alan, please!)

Evacuees are returning to London and the stations are crowded with people, prams and children. This is against the wish of the Government and people are urged to stay away, but they will not.

Friday 15th September

A warm and rather airless morning, getting cooler later. Jack and I drove to the butcher's and bank, and when we got back we both set to work on our respective jobs. Mine was gardening, and the drive bed was finished off quite neatly and the edges tidied to the gate. Jack has planted one or two raspberries to replace some dead and weak plants. This afternoon, after a rest, I made a cake and baked it so badly it is just wasted—and in these days! Oh, dear, I could have wept.

The Allies have entered Nancy! Hurrah! I wonder if the Girards are all right. Aächen is surrounded and the Allies are a good ten miles inside Germany. Warsaw is in a terrible state, wreathed in smoke and flame, with the Germans and Poles fighting inside. The Russians have taken the suburb of Praga and at last it looks as if the liberation of Warsaw is near. The Germans in Finland are having a bit of trouble and trying to give some. They should be getting out of Finland tonight, but they remain near the east border, obviously to persuade the Russians to attack and so weaken their attacks elsewhere. Heavens, what a world!

'A friend of the Cathedral, Balsall Common' has a letter in the *Coventry Evening Telegraph* this evening. *Oui, c'est moi!*

Saturday 16th September

The Americans have pierced the Siegfried Line in four places, thus chopping it up and making it useless. Our Army has now passed on beyond Nancy and are at Lunéville and have taken Epinal. These are places Joyce and I drove through with Girard. I remember Lunéville very well, a dull little place. Girard told us the Germans were there in the last war, just as they were near another side of Nancy with the Kaiser ready to enter the city when it was captured. On a white horse and clad in white with a flowing cape, he waited many times to ride in, but never did, and Nancy was inviolate.

The Provost has replied in the *Coventry Evening Telegraph* to 'A Friend of the Cathedral'. She is not convinced by it. The letter says, among other points: 'Those who, like the writer and myself, knew and loved the former Cathedral, must face the fact that it is gone and cannot be recovered. We must set our faces bravely towards the new, which will be just as beautiful as the old, and will come to be loved by the coming generations'.

Sunday 17th September

There has been an airborne landing in Holland today— a good landing, too, very skilfully done. Our bombers softened up the defences first and kept up bombing to protect our men. Lunéville has been liberated and Metz is encircled. The fighting for Boulogne, Calais and Dunkirk goes on.

One's own little daily doings seem scarcely worth recording, but this is 'Burleigh in Wartime'. It was a lovely sunny morning and I went cycling off for the 8.15 a.m. service at Berkswell. Not fortified by my usual biscuit, I was glad to get back to a good breakfast, even if the coffee was made with powdered milk! The morning was occupied with letters—one to the *Coventry Evening Telegraph* replying to the Provost's remarks, which took a little time to compose. Then Alan's letter—a feeble effort. The garden looked inviting, so I piled cushions on the hard seat and then lay down for an hour, more or less comfortably—or was it uncomfortably—with a robin piping shrilly, an aeroplane droning in the distance, a far-away bark of a dog, leaves rustling in the breeze overhead . . . and can it really be four o'clock! Well it was. So we had tea in the Corner and then smoked to keep the gnats away till at last they were so gnatzi we were obliged to go in.

Wednesday 20th September

A warm, hazy morning, then sun, and later a dull warm afternoon. This morning Mrs Greenslade rang up and told us she had seen Edward. He is in hospital in Chester and she and her husband went up there yesterday. They found him looking old and thin and apparently his illness and imprisonment has made him hard. He used to weigh 12 stone, and while he was in hospital he weighed 6 stone. He sounds rather a sad case and the tears came into my eyes as I heard what Mrs Greenslade had to say. He is delighted to be home again.

There is evacuation of Germans on the west of the Rhine. Today there are German reactions to the attacks by our airborne troops and they sound fierce, but we hold on. There are two new offensives in Russia, one in south Estonia on a 75-mile front. Crete is being closely blockaded to prevent the Germans escaping from the island. Brest has not yet surrendered, though resistance seems at an end.

Friday 22nd September

We have spent a good part of the day in Leamington, starting at 10.30 a.m., and I went to the dentist for 'making more impressions'. Not a pleasant job, but bearable. We had conversation in between the waxwork business about the Cathedral plans, etc., and I found two people enthusiastic about rebuilding—without any pushing on my part!

The airborne Army at Arnhem has not yet been linked up with General Patton's Army. I think they must be having a thin time, from this evening's war report.

Saturday 23rd September

Some sun this morning and clouds this afternoon, clearing later, although the glass has 'gone up to rain', as Kate says! All the outside jobs were done, the butcher's and grocer's by car, and this afternoon I meant to take half an hour's rest, but by the time a bit of filling in of forms for the Land Army was done Wilks had arrived. So I went out to see him and arranged for him to strip the two 'Rival' apple trees and then went in the hut to make room for them in an already much overcrowded place.

The Germans have been trying hard to cut our supply route to the paratroops at Arnhem and at one time it was broken. But our Typhoons went along and restored the situation and the corridor has since been widened. At present the fighting is confused, though our men in the south of the town have managed to keep the bridge intact.

Sunday 24th September

A most unpleasant day! At 5 a.m. a gale seemed suddenly to spring up, with heavy rain beating against the windows. All day the wind raged and the garden is littered with twigs, leaves and branches, and looks a mess. This morning I packed a bit to get ready to go off for our four days' holiday tomorrow and then got Alan's letter written.

The airborne troops at Arnhem (once in rather a precarious state, we now think) have been reinforced with more paratroops and equipment. We have just heard about the taking of the Nijmegen Bridge—a monument of gallant effort against terrible odds, but it was won and was whole and sound so that our tanks could go over.

Monday–Thursday 25th–28th September

Off on our Stratford-on-Avon holiday. We stayed at The William and Mary, where we found pleasant company. While there we were all very sad to hear about our withdrawal from the spearhead of Arnhem and our heavy casualties—a gamble that did not come off entirely, but which secured the Nijmegen bridge. Stratford still has many Americans about. The women are very smart—but no smarter than our W.A.A.F. officers, of whom we also saw plenty—and the men carry cameras on their off times and are busy taking photographs of Shakespeare's little town. Many swans adorned the Avon and gathered at the water's edge whenever they thought there was a chance of food. The little motor pleasure boat went up and down at times with a depleted load of passengers—sometimes only ten or a dozen people.

Kate rang up on Tuesday to say that two letters and a postcard had arrived from Alan. She read one letter and the card. The other letter was 'all about onions'. We enjoyed every bit of them, very thankful to hear at last.

Saturday 30th September

The last day of the ninth month! The war goes on endlessly, it seems some days. And what has happened to our summer and the lovely sunny September days? Today has been quite pleasant, but definitely an overcoat day. The morning was filled with the daily round and at 2.20 p.m. I caught the bus to get to Christ Church Hall, where I attended the annual meeting of the Friends of the Cathedral. A few of us said our say and voted against the majority of the 'Friends', which wasn't much use, but at least we put our views forward. As a strange person afterwards said to me: 'Do you Coventry people always express your views in such a downright way?' 'Yes, generally,' I said, 'and especially when we think we are right.' We fell into a discussion on the new Cathedral plan and had quite a good time. Then he recommended some sandwich cake, which I took hopefully, but alas it was lightened with vinegar and was deadly stuff. Fetching me a further cup of tea, he again pressed some of the cake upon me, but I frankly said: 'I don't like your recommendation', and hope to goodness his wife didn't make it!

Then the Bishop floated near and we shook hands. 'I am one of the minority,' I said. 'Oh, but don't you like the new plan?' 'No, I am afraid I don't.' Out came my objections and he went off after a final shot, which seemed to say that the proposed 'Chapel of Unity' might bring Nonconformists to church eventually. I was asked point-blank by one man if I were the 'Friend of the Cathedral' of the letters, but when one has decided to write anonymously it is better to remain anonymous, so I replied: 'I think I know who it is.' 'I hoped it was you,' he said. It was all quite enjoyable.

Calais' big guns are silenced at last and Dover is celebrating her release from the shelling by hanging out flags and opening up her shops again. She has had a rough time the last week or so with heavy shelling. There was a truce at Calais for 24 hours while the 20,000 civilians were evacuated. Then the Canadians closed in again and a heavy new bombardment began.

We have just heard a German record of 'Hang up the Washing on the Siegfried Line'. I hope we shall soon be singing it again.

Monday 2nd October

The snapshot, or rather quite a decent small photograph, came with *a letter to Jack today*. Showing a group of men from Oflag VIIB, four or five of Alan's Mess and some others, it is an excellent clear photograph, but very small. Alan has grown a moustache! It suits him well, and he has never told us this. I wonder how many times we have looked at it today! Jack brought it upstairs with a little stereoscope which we have had for a long time, and how we have scrutinized it during the day, leaving it set in the stereoscope ready to pick up at any moment, and how it seems to connect us again.

As Volume Thirteen ends, I express no hopes or wishes now about the end of the war—we must wait.

VOLUME 14

October 1944 – January 1945

Wednesday 4th October

Wednesday. The morning was soon gone and lunch was early because V.C.P. wished me to pick up three women passengers at 1.50 p.m. in Keresley. The most interesting was Mrs Binks ('a Comic Cuts name,' she said!) and her home county was Yorkshire, as I guessed. We went to the Council House, Nuneaton, and arrived in a thunderstorm, with the rain pelting down. It was also very cold, so I decided not to sit in the car and write letters while I was waiting for them, but to go to a cinema. A man sauntering along in the heavy rain directed me to one with a car park. Soon the rain ceased and I walked out in the dry and entered the truly palatial and magnificent modern building to find the picture was *For Whom the Bell Tolls*. Alas, lots of shooting and bombing, though charming colouring and interesting scenery, but as I went late and came out early I couldn't make head nor tail of the story. It was good to get home to tea, and later to do a bit of desk work during a quiet evening.

Warsaw has fallen after a heartbreaking resistance.

Thursday 5th October

The Prime Minister has paid eloquent tribute to the heroism of the Poles who suffered in the battle of Warsaw: 'When the final Allied victory is achieved, the epic of Warsaw will not be forgotten. It will remain a deathless memory for Poland and for the friends of freedom all over the world.' Poor, poor Poles. Their sufferings are dreadful! Tales of German atrocities in Belgium are not to be forgotten by the Belgians. They are keeping the torture chamber and its dreadful instruments as a warning for the future.

Dunkirk civilians have been evacuated during an armistice.

Saturday 7th October

Off to hospital this morning with a bag of apples for Lieut. Edward Greenslade. He was in a sort of verandah room which could probably be a sun-trap in the summer, and we fell to talking, myself asking questions and hearing many things about Alan, as well as about himself. Food is the prisoners' first thought, he said. Then letters, cigarettes and when the war will end. He was very cheerful, everything considered, and says they think they will save his leg, but he must be anxious to have something done now.

Back home for lunch and then I went over to the Institute, where a Whist Drive and Bring-and-Buy Stall was being held. So I brung and I bought, sat and talked for a quarter of an hour and then, dead tired, came home to tea. After a short rest, Twink and I biked to Balsall Street and met Miss Curtis resting a huge box on somebody's low garden wall—she had won the grocery parcel at the Whist Drive! It was much too heavy for her to carry, so it was popped on to my bicycle saddle and we got it to her home, walking gently all the way. After supper I write up this something diary for four days. An awful business. Exercise books seem to be nil, so I have to use this old one.

Today there has been the biggest raid of the war by three thousand bombers on Germany. The enemy has flooded a lot of land in Holland to delay our advance and are threatening to flood much more. They have mined the dykes all ready for this. Just now we are busy bombing dykes and canals. One which we strafed is now drained and empty for 18 miles, and at least 110 barges are stranded.

Tuesday 10th October

The Americans have given Aächen till 10.50 a.m. tomorrow to give in. If not, the town will be destroyed—a *German* town this time. They have destroyed so many belonging to other nations, and now the tables are turned.

Wednesday 11th October

Aächen did not surrender at 10.50 a.m.—though white sheets appeared on some houses, and were later removed—and now the true bombardment has begun. Germany sacrifices her civilians as she does her soldiers. Some gains have been made in Holland. In Italy the rain has almost stopped all action—dreadful weather. Mr Churchill and Mr Eden, who are in Moscow, heard her guns salute Russian victories today—they are pushing forward in Northern Transylvania and captured 3,200 Germans in Yugoslavia. Eastern

Hungary is the new battleground; the Russians crossed the frontier five days ago and their troops have already cleared more than 5,000 Square miles of enemy territory east of the river Tirza.

Telephonic communication between Germany and Sweden has been resumed. One wonders what has been happening. Another purge, perhaps? We always wonder whether Hitler is alive or dead.

Saturday 14th October

One job today was to cut sandwiches for the British Legion tea and then, at 2.30 p.m., booted and spurred, I went to the Institute. Piff, it was rather warm and 'niffy and very dull. So, rushing back, quickly gathering an armful of little michaelmas daisies and some pink snaps, I thrust them into a green bowl and put them on the table. That really did cheer things up. The tea was good—Mrs Whitaker's cakes are always good and sweet—and then someone suggested the flowers should be raffled. They were, but the winner had plenty and put them up to auction. They fetched 4s. 0d.! And so back to Burleigh to do my own flowers and many odd jobs before supper. A mosquito kissed me on both cheeks during the night and I have two high spots on my cheekbones—very trying and disfiguring, but it might have been my nose!

Civilians are braving their own guns, and ours, and coming out of Aächen waving handkerchiefs, or anything else white, to show they want to surrender if the military does not. The Russians and General Tito's forces are near Belgrade, another capital city soon to be liberated. The liberation of Athens by Greek partisans is confirmed. There is little that is new in Holland, though we beat off counter-attacks and gain a little ground here and there. Dunkirk still holds out apparently and Duisberg has had a terrific air raid today.

Sunday 15th October

And yet not Sunday! But a wumman with a swollen face can't go to church, so instead she spent a messy morning pottering in the house and garden doing nothing in particular—getting a few Rivals from the hut and sampling a few nice juicy ones, messing with the hens, cloching a few lettuces, etc., till it was time to snap on the wireless for the one o'clock news.

The Regent of Hungary, Admiral Horthy, has asked for an Armistice. An Order of the Day from Stalin tells us of the capture of Petsamo in Finland, where the Germans were collected. The Germans speak of a Russian penetration north of Warsaw. Ten thousand tons of bombs have been dropped on Duisburg since yesterday morning. More incendiaries were dropped in *one night* than were dropped in 11 months on London. Colossal!

Home news gives a prospect of further cuts in fuel, due to these something miners who won't overwork themselves and so, in spite of increased wages, are continually dissatisfied.

Tuesday 17th October

The first news this morning told of the King's visit to Holland, where he looked at Germany and walked within the sound of German and British guns during a five-day visit to his troops on the Belgian–Dutch frontier. Enemy bombers flew overhead one morning and dropped canisters and anti-personnel bombs near him. He wore battledress for the first time (had he saved his coupons up for this!), arrived by air last Wednesday and lunched with Montgomery. He went to the Nijmegen spearhead and looked out towards the hills of Germany to the south-east. He lived with Montgomery in his caravan and ate Army rations. During his trip across the Channel the Royal Standard fluttered from the nose of the Dakota transport and Spitfires weaved around it, but no German plane was seen.

Wednesday 18th October

Hitler and Himmler, those arch-fiends, have issued an order for all men between 16 and 60 to become a sort of Home Guard. They are all to be armed and are to fight to the last ditch and harass the enemy in every possible way. They are to be trained to fight! A bit late, methinks. The Russians are pouring through the Carpathians into Czechoslovakia. Cologne has been heavily bombed again today.

We are to have extra rations at Christmas—½ lb of margarine and ½ lb of sugar each, sweets for those 'children' who are not over 18 and tea for the old ones over 70. More meat, too, the week before Christmas, and there will be dried fruits for points and nuts without points. It doesn't interest me much as Alan won't get a Christmas dinner this year—and we had hoped he would be with us this time.

Friday 20th October

Belgrade has fallen to the Soviet and Marshal Tito's forces. Aächen has fallen to the Americans and General MacArthur has landed a force on the middle small island of the Philippines, north of Mindanao. It was evidently a surprise to the Japs and so the

American (and some Australian) casualties are very light. Good business! We can do with a bit of good news.

Tuesday 24th October

Not too bad a day, but rather chilly, and I found lots to do before going to the dentist's at 12.30 p.m. Jack had made the car look very smart and clean when he washed it yesterday, so I was proud to be driving it today. After the messy business of 'making an impression' I was able to go on from Kenilworth to Leamington, and at the car park all the parcels and baskets were moved to the front seats, leaving the back one for Mrs Greenslade and me to use for our luncheon together. She arrived just as all was set and we fell to with an exchange of sandwiches, etc. Then we drove to Warneford Hospital to see Edward—and found six of them in his ward fast asleep!

So we came out again and went to Francis' to buy a hat. Mrs Greenslade saw two she liked, and I said: 'I should have them both,' which she did—and ordered a third to be made. I tried on several, but the hats are mostly dull and not at all ravishing! I like to be frightfully keen on a hat. Even if the price is high, it is always best to buy the thing that is right when you see it: 'A thing of beauty is a joy forever', and 'It is our economies and not our extravagances we are sorry for', are both very true sayings.

Having settled the hats, we made our way back to the hospital ward and talked to Edward for an hour. Here and there I heard something about Alan, and how my ears stuck out to hear the slightest thing about him. He was taken prisoner unwounded, but when marched off behind the German lines one of our shells burst near him and he got a splinter in his knee. It was evidently pretty bad, with poisoning later—'tubes sticking out all over it', as Edward said—but he made an excellent recovery apparently. Edward also said that they 'knew everything that went on'. I told him that a repatriated man had said 100 cigarettes would buy a wireless set. 'Oh, a bit more than that,' said Edward. The thing they did not know was how short we are of ordinary commodities, although they knew about our food. It was an interesting hour, and at four we came away and, after a bit more shopping, I got back a bit late for tea.

Wednesday 1st November

And one did not sleep much and by 7 a.m. decided she must get up as she felt distinctly poorly. The morning passed by, the doctor came, the temperature went up, she dozed and woke to doze again.

I heard vaguely that it was very cold, but I was hot and not interested. *Dies non.*

Thursday 2nd November

A bit better today, still starving but for a cup of Benger's. Nurse came and tidied me up and the doctor came and said I looked a different woman. I read practically a whole book called *A Bird in the Tree* and forgot myself, thanks be.

Friday 3rd November

Better still today, though a bad night with a long time tossing and turning before sleep came. I made the most of bed and enjoyed the rest, reading a good thriller. Nurse came before lunch and I felt much better with my temperature down, but would have liked a good sleep. However I decided to keep awake all day so as to sleep tonight.

This Scheldt Estuary is a sticky bit of war. With flooded towns and roads everywhere, and the beastly Hun firmly stuck in some parts, we have had hard work to scoop him out. Landings on the Walcheren have been successful and we ought soon to have him cleared off it. Knocke is now freed and we have taken 10,000 prisoners. It is a great fight for the port of Antwerp, which town is already in our hands. When we have the second port in Europe freed from block ships, mines and all the impedimenta the German leaves in his trail to thwart and hinder us, we shall be able to supply our Armies freely and get a bit nearer the inevitable end.

Saturday 4th November

I meant to get up today, but didn't feel as good as I had hoped and eventually stayed in bed all day, with the doctor coming in to scold me about 4 p.m.

During the afternoon I continued the 'Autobiography of Anthony Trollope', which I began yesterday, and found it so interesting that I nearly finished it by six o'clock. He surveys himself and his thoughts and feelings so dispassionately and is without vanity, though far from being without interest in his own 'thoughts, words and works'. A very refreshing autobiography, and how utterly alien to those books full of footnotes about 'Maisie'[1]—footnote 1: 'Maisie, Lady Highflier'; or 'Ponky'[2]—footnote 2: 'Lord Puddleduck of Pond's'; or whatever their names may be. It is all so simply written, and his sentences flow smoothly along the pages.

Sunday 5th November

After a windy night the leaves were still being blown across the windows this morning. I got up about 11 a.m. and found Jack and Twink thoroughly happy in armchair and on rug respectively, waiting for the weather to clear. Jack decided shortly afterwards to go to the doctor's with a basket of apples and to pick up my medicine. The obvious thing was to walk Twink as well. As they were going I reminded Jack that 13 years ago it was a very wet day—the day we came to Burleigh. 'This is not so bad as then,' I said. Out they went and I went upstairs to tidy the bathroom, etc. Before long I was suddenly aware of a fearfully heavy rainstorm and, hastily closing the bathroom window, I rushed to my bedroom. The rain had soaked the curtain and was pouring down the wall below, and rain spots showed on the carpet half-way across the floor. I mopped up, put the oddments that were damp on the table by the window into the hot cupboard and hoped Jack and Twink were sheltering. Presently they came in, both soaked as to heads, coats and feet. They had come straight through this almost tropical storm. Twink had been quite frightened and crouched against a fence, then ran across the road and made for home. Jack's shoes were soaked through and his hat and coat, so he was soon wringing out his socks and pouring the water out of his shoes in the bathroom, while I dealt with a sopping wet dog. Kate, who never believes in interfering when people get wet, continued to attend to the Sunday dinner! Later we enjoyed the despised piece of pork—'we' figuratively, because 'I' had a boiled egg, being still in the touchy stage regarding food.

Monday 6th November

A lovely bright morning and the consequent colour in the clear air was glorious. After lunch, as the sun was still bright, we both went into the garden. As I came towards the house the gate closed and there was the doctor raising hands of horror at my being out on such a cold day. I didn't think it was very cold, but whereas I was in woollies the doctor was in a thin suit and no coat. So we went in with about three words regarding me and then began to talk of other things. Jack came into the room and away they went with one thing after another, so the purpose of the doctor's visit was scarcely mentioned. He couldn't sit, he must 'run', but he stood propping up the mantelpiece for another 20 minutes! Finally, with a 'Don't do too much', etc., he went. I thought of charging *him* 7s. 6d.!!!

Wednesday 8th November

This is the day upon which Hitler usually makes a speech to his nation, but so far nothing has been heard of him. Our broadcasts have commented on his previous speeches—so boastful and now proved so inglorious and altogether wrong. The battle of south-west Holland is practically over and Walcheren almost cleared of the enemy. Now there is a lull and soon will be the next stage nearer Germany. In the Vosges, General Patton has started a new attack. Today I saw Gerardmer mentioned—the little place Joyce and I drove to with Girard, and so like his own name it amused him to pretend it was *his* lake. Franklin Roosevelt has been re-elected for the Presidency and America has thus elected him for the fourth time in succession, so he has already served for 12 years! Dewey, his opponent, made a friendly speech of good wishes as soon as he found he was out of the running.

Thursday 9th November

An extremely cold day with a N.N.E. wind, and Kate said a few flakes of snow fell during the early morning.

The battle of south-west Holland and the Schelde has now been won. South of Metz 16 small villages have been liberated and General Patton's attack continues on this front. The day has been very cold and fine and there have been many air attacks on Germany.

Mr Churchill (not quite so fluent as usual) was recorded after the news speaking at the Lord Mayor's luncheon. The greatest fighting is yet to be, he said in effect. While our supply route is strained and lengthening, the enemy is falling back on his supplies and, of course, nowhere will he fight as hard as on his own territory. Every man and woman must realize that the utmost effort must now be made, for it is at the last, at the end of years of struggle, that wars are won—or lost! How true that is when one thinks of the Great War. The Germans were so near Paris when they turned and fled in retreat and the war was lost to them.

Friday 10th November

This was our day to collect the patient at Meer End and convey her to the Warneford Hospital. I also did an hour's shopping and called at the Land Army Office Uniform Department. Seated at one of the tables in this office is a little grey-haired woman very keen on Shakespeare. I said: 'The air bites shrewdly, it is very cold ...' Quick as thought, she replied: 'It is a nipping and an eager air—Hamlet!' We always seem pleased to see each other there. A white-haired, becurled and pearled lady in short fur coat and tweed skirt came in talking about girls and uniforms and said, including me in the conversation: 'My husband complains that his smoking-room is always full of land-girls' uniform.'

'Lucky to have a smoking-room,' says I. 'My hall is always littered with clothing, returned gumboots, shirts and socks.'

The 9 p.m. news gave Mr Churchill's words about V2, the German rocket which is now being sent over here. It goes up 60 or 70 miles into the stratosphere, is faster than sound and so cannot be heard. The ones that have come down here have been in widely separated districts. They go in deeper than the flying-bomb. Horrible creatures are Germans.

Saturday 11th November

Twenty-six years today the Armistice was signed, and oh my goodness me what a lot has happened since then! The one thing we did not foresee was this chaotic world, this welter of destruction of life and property, this wholesale division of families. It is as well we cannot see ahead—our hearts would break. Whereas all these things have come so gradually and we have just had to get used to them.

Mr Churchill is in Paris. He arrived there yesterday and was met by General de Gaulle. Today they have driven to the Arc de Triomphe to the cheers of the Parisians along the Champs Elysées. Mr Churchill signed the book for distinguished visitors and presented medals. The people broke through the ranks to cheer him wildly, and later he and General de Gaulle took the salute while sections of the British Navy, Army and Air Force with the reconstituted French Army (*good* eggs) came along twelve abreast.

Sunday 12th November

And what did I do? It was cold and very damp, a raw November morning. Too far to walk to church and too cold to cycle. Well I cleaned the silver and plate—all on a Sunday morning. It had been left undone for three weeks and badly needed a tidy-up. Then dinner and the duck! About 6d. a mouthful, I reckoned. Not worth the bother and the money—a hen is much better—but if one *will* go black marketing, well!

A long supposed-Hitler's speech has been read for him by Himmler, full of the usual stuff and with the usual threats for foreigners and their own people. They hope to win the war with 'the last breath'. Mr Churchill received the freedom of Paris this afternoon. He spoke to the people in French, which he said might put some strain on our friendship! He was obviously very moved and twice brushed away a tear.

Monday 13th November

The German battleship *Tirpitz* has been sunk by a force of Lancasters. Hurrah! Twenty-nine Lancasters sank it yesterday with 12,000 lb bombs. The first of the Metz forts fell to the Americans this afternoon and there was no opposition. The Schelde battle has accounted for 80,000 Germans—we took 40,000 prisoners and the other 40,000 are either killed or wounded. The Russians have made more gains in Hungary and are very close to Budapest. In Italy our forces continue to gain ground in the Adriatic section. The American tactical Air Force has had to vacate the airfields in China as the Japanese have advanced.

Tuesday 14th November

Another rather dull, raw November day. The question before the house was: What time does one go to the dentist? Having got it into our minds that 11.30 a.m. was the time, one did what one could before trundling off with Jack in the car at 11.10. We were nice and early and so I sailed in comfortably and cheerily, was robed in the rubber bib, sniffed up my gas easily, slept and woke up to find no furniture in the top storey. In less than ten minutes a full set of 16 was put in and out we came into the cold, raw morning again.

Mr Churchill got home at 5 o'clock today. He looked tired but cheerful. Indefatigable man! Yesterday he was reviewing troops not far from Besançon. Thirty cars set out in wintry weather to the spot. Ten arrived. Mr Churchill's car was one of them—it would be!

We are to have nuts for Christmas! Almonds (and Stuart Hibberd first pronounced it *al*-monds), filberts and peanuts.

Wednesday 15th November

Yes, I slept, albeit a little uneasily with my face rather aching and swollen. However during the day the stiffness and soreness wore off a little. I went out into the cold, raw air and 'butched', then 'grocered', and very nippy it was going towards the east. Home again by 12 and I did a bit of mending, etc., shortened a curtain for the bathroom and, lo, 'twas one o'clock. 'Works Wonders' were finishing off their rubbishy programme as we switched on the news. A fresh attack has started in Holland south-east of Eindhoven and so far is going according to schedule. We have crossed the canals which were our first objectives. The House was told today how costly the landing on Walcheren proved to be because of unfavourable conditions. We lost 172 killed in this naval attack, and 200 wounded. The loss of ships was about 80 per cent.

Wednesday 22nd November

A postcard from Alan today. Hurrah! He is anxious about his Belgian friends and gives their names and addresses and asks if I can get in touch with them. We were amused when he wrote 'Mlle. L. Verstichelen, (about 35) Rue St Vincent 39'. The 'about 35' showed the same old Alan!

The battle all along the Western Front is going well. The French around Belfort, having reached the Rhine, are now going north. The German armies seem to be rather harassed and are having a beating generally. In some parts heavy counter-attacks occur, but all are thrown back. Major Lewis Hastings, who gave the war report this evening, has just come back from this front. He says our men's courage is superb—and they have already been through the Normandy landing and the campaign in France. He watched them advancing along a road where mines had been cleared—so many different faces and types, yet all were definitely English. They were cool and alert and unruffled. Presently they would come to uncleared minefields and soon the 'hell orchestra' of mortars, guns and shells would begin again.

It is thought that the battle now taking place may be the decisive one for Germany.

P. G. Wodehouse and his wife were taken prisoner in Paris, but have been released on bail. He broadcast from Berlin once and England denounced him as a traitor.

Thursday 23rd November

The French have reached Strasbourg, where the Marseillaise was composed—the ancient capital of Alsace. The French Chamber was much moved on hearing this news this morning. They rose and sang the Marseillaise and the session was dissolved. Along the rest of the front there is progress and we push on, it seems, beyond the places taken yesterday and check and beat off counter-attacks. Grim fighting continues at the northern end of the battle-front, while the Germans are faced with a vast turning movement as the French drive north. The Siegfried Line will most likely prove a very difficult obstacle everywhere. It was meant to be!

Our great news today is of *three letters from Alan*, dated 31.8.44,

11.9.44 and 10.10.44, so it certainly is our lucky day. In the last he says: 'Next month we shall start digging, and so it will go on until we are told "You can go home now".' He tells of progress of the onions, tomatoes and beetroot, the runner beans—with black fly, which were then disposed of by ladybirds—and then a bit about games. 'Are gardening and games all the lad thinks about? No, but it's a good topic for letters!' He sounds just the same 'lad', anyway.

Monday 27th November

A raw November day—and we had the sweep. Add to this that the lady of the house had a cold and one will see that things were not too pleasant. However I have known them worse! With the living-room shrouded in dustsheets and the electric radiator doing its best in the dining-room, I retired kitchenwards and gave my bits and pieces of silver (nominal!) a reet good clean.

During the morning a great explosion occurred—where one could not imagine. I thought bombs, but Jack thought the sound was from a Bofors gun. However later in the day we were told on the wireless that a tremendous explosion rocked Burton-on-Trent this morning. Chimney-pots were dislodged and the steeple of Horning Low Church in a suburb made unsafe. The explosion took place at an R.A.F. maintenance depôt several miles from Burton. The explosion was heard and felt as far away as Coventry (says our local paper), where doors were blown open by the blast, windows rattled and many buildings shaken. It certainly sounded quite near, and Burton is 30 miles away.

Our Armies move forward in their respective battle-fronts and we have captured two German generals. There is a dreadful story in the *Telegraph* of the wholesale killing of 2,000,000 (million!) people in gas chambers in concentration camps. Their bodies were afterwards burnt in a specially built crematorium. One is aghast at such horrors! These were Russians killed by the invading Germans.

Tuesday 28th November

Two letters from Alan today, dated 20.9.44 for me and 20.10.44 for Jack. All bright and cheerful as usual, telling of the proposed study of electricity this winter, of the gathering of four tons of tomatoes, and the lifting of onions and leeks so that new buildings could be put up. It is grand to have all these letters. A cold east wind was blowing as we went to bed last night and I piled on the bedclothes. During the night I grew frightfully hot and miserable. Then when I flung the window wide at 8 a.m. a soft south wind was caressing the garden! What changes we have! The thermometer registered

50 degrees. I had thought I might stay in again today and it was
going to be a nuisance, but when one felt the warmth of the outside
air it was soon decided we should both go to Leamington and leave
poor old Kate to tidy up after the sweep!

So off we went via Warwick, calling at Brett's to get a lining
put in Jack's winter coat. Brett's shop is almost empty—very few
rolls of cloth there now, and it used to be stacked all round. We
saw the most awful old pair of trousers I have ever seen (except
Jack's terrible trousers with the 14 x 7 knee patches) and they were
sent in for repair! In fact Brett said it was all repair work at the
moment. Then we went on to Leamington and I picked up my hat
at Frances' and saw a new one I liked and fell for. Hats are mostly
rubbishy now, but this one was bright and plain. My dress account
was on the right side for the first time for years last month! It looks
all wrong to be on the right side, and I'm so used to the other way,
so bought a hat!

Wednesday 29th November
This was one of the days when I got up earlier, but was ten
minutes late when calling for an old man to go to hospital. Dunno
why, but I was. He remarked that most of the ladies who fetched
him were late!! Tut tut for the Volunteer Car Pool. I explained
that I was seldom late—superior person! I think I know what it is
just now. Very few of us can get off before 10 a.m. We all have
jobs to do and 10 a.m. is the earliest we can leave our homes,
having done those daily jobs of dusting and tidying which must be
done. Only three of my four got done by 9.45 a.m., so that at 6.15
p.m. when I went upstairs I found the dusters and the sweeper
standing waiting for me! I thought of what Joyce would say: 'It
will be *worth* dusting tomorrow.' However I flicked the duster
round so that we could see ourselves in the mirrors!

Mr. Churchill now talks of 'summer', leaving out the 'early', as
the possible end of the war, and stresses the need for sticking it
now and not letting ourselves be satiated. Goodness knows we *are*,
but it won't do to let it be apparent outside.

Thursday 30th November
An eventful day, with visitors to lunch. This was the day
arranged for Mrs Greenslade and Edward to come and see us, and
so it was interesting to lay the table for four and to use the best
glass again. It is so long since we used wineglasses on the table that
I did not know in which box to look. However they were found
and polished up, as well as the table. It all looked very nice, with

254

the yellow mats and the jasmine and cassinea in a cut-glass vase. Our guests arrived just before 1 p.m., Edward walking slowly with his two sticks, and soon we were toasting him, Alan and each other in a good glass of sherry. Then we did full justice to the Greenslade duck and the Milburn wartime trifle and apple tart.

Edward says the mud colour of everything and the khaki is dreadfully monotonous in prison camp and how he enjoys the colour he finds everywhere here. That is just as I thought. Behind everything there is always the monotony of prison life. The lack of privacy, never, never to be alone, is also very wearing, he says. We spent the afternoon talking and hearing things. No knives and forks for prisoners of war—a bowl and spoon—and no tablecloths, of course. How deadly sick of it all they must be!

It is Mr Churchill's 70th birthday.

Sunday 3rd December

The news was preceded by His Most Gracious Majesty's broadcast to the Home Guard, who are 'standing down' from today. He spoke very well and his impediment was only apparent two or three times. There is progress at Venlo on the Western Front and at Julich and elsewhere progress is maintained, but is slow, with every house and garden wall reinforced and villages linked up, tank traps 25 ft wide and masses of mines.

Wednesday 6th December

There is civil war in Greece—and most uncivil it sounds! Too bad that we have liberated them and now they can't agree among themselves and we have to take a hand and have our people sacrificed again for such a rotten nation. I should think King George of the Hellenes hopes they won't want his services again. It can't be much of a country to live in. The Third Army is pushing on and getting nearer Saarbrücken. In the Vosges progress has been made. All around Arnhem has been flooded by the enemy breaking the dykes. R.A.F. fighter command has attacked V2 sites. There are still attacks most days and casualties and damage continue on the south coast.

An article in *The Times* tells of the Coventry Cathedral Christian Service Centre (I want to add 'and Manufacturing Co., Ltd'). What an unpleasant title! I can't think of it as a Cathedral—a brick building with stone facings, part-Anglican, part-Free Church. No, I can't take to this mix-up. Have a Christian Service Centre if it is really needed, but don't mix it up with the dignity of a Cathedral. I feel sure this is not right. When one thinks of St Michael's Church—the Coventry Cathedral of our day—one is very sad.

Monday 11th December

Not so cold today and Jack went with me and sat outside the grocer's while I collected the most marvellous things like dates, sultanas, extra sugar and margarine, another 2 lb of treacle and 1 lb suet. Well, well. Kate *was* pleased! So I came home and made the land-girls rock cakes—quite nice, too, though I says so!

Casualties due to enemy air attacks last month were 700 killed and 1,500 injured and detained in hospital. Beastly flying-bombs are responsible for these rather appalling figures. However today 1,600 American bombers, escorted by 800 R.A.F. fighters manned by 16,000 airmen and making a procession 300 miles long, went to Germany to bomb marshalling yards, etc. If they can bomb these V1s and V2s on railway trucks it is the best way of destroying their power. The time and manpower has then been used to no purpose.

The Labour Conference, with Harold Laski (ye gods!) as Chairman, have decided to stick to Mr Churchill (so kind of them—Mr Churchill *will* be pleased) 'until victory in Europe is both overwhelming and complete'. He spoke of Mr Churchill as 'that gallant and romantic relic of eighteenth-century Imperialism'. Such impertinence!

Rather more than a week ago I forgot to record that Princess Elizabeth launched a new battleship, but the name was not given to the world at large and was cut out of the recording of her high, clear voice: 'I name this ship —— ' and then the following sentence of good wishes for the safety of 'all who sail in her'.

Friday 15th December

Mr Churchill has been speaking in the House on Poland, the Lublin government versus the London leaders. It is a pity they cannot agree among themselves. There were varied opinions in the House on what ought to be done. Mr Churchill advocates transferring East Prussia to the Poles when the war with Germany is over. This is agreeable to the Russians, but one can see the Polish point of view. They find it difficult to give up territory to the Russians, who began by fighting *them* early in the war. It is sure to be a mighty problem to satisfy everyone.

Saturday 16th December

This not-so-cold day was started *with a very cheerful letter from Alan dated 31.10.44.* He says he is 'well and not bored and I have a good

256

appetite'. I hope there will be enough food to satisfy the latter, because I am sure he is working hard at gardening and taking it out of himself, from what he says. The car took me to the butcher's and Twink afterwards took me to the grocer's! At the latter a mysterious small bag was put into my basket with the words 'twopence ha'penny'. I did not know what this under-the-counter treasure was until I got home and found *two lemons*! Great excitement!

Thursday 21st December

Methinks this is the shortest day! Getting up is more and more of an effort on these pitch-black mornings. I found I had forgotten to go to the butcher's yesterday, so had to go quite early this morning. The shop was closed, but the butcher opened it and, oh my goodness, what an array! A few turkeys in feather strung up on one side, several geese plucked and more dressed, as well as a row of hens and chickens. Legs of pork hung up in rows on the high rails, and carcases of mutton on the other side of the small shop. And this on top of the lack of food in Holland, as told on the wireless last night. I came away with a bit of lamb, which we afterwards enjoyed very much. It was so tender.

Later a farmer came to see me about the non-appearance of his land-girl, who went home for the evening and had not turned up by 12 o'clock next day. These young women are a case, and the farmer said: 'My wife did not sleep a wink last night—not a wink.' I rang up the Land Army while he was here and promised to call tomorrow morning to see if she has arrived by then.

We now hear of a 30-mile penetration by the Germans into the American positions. This is very disquieting. The Germans say they will be in Paris by Christmas!! Runstedt is taking the same road he took in 1940, through Luxembourg. Paratroops are trying to cause confusion where they are dropped behind the lines. I hope we can soon call a halt to the enemy, but there is not much being told us at present. One feels it delays the end of the European war and that is a most depressing thought, though one really doesn't reckon on anything these days—least of all the end of the war! Though one does *hope*.

Friday 22nd December

Not so cold today and the fog had cleared. The farmer rang up about his naughty land-girl and asked me if I would go and 'interview' her. She had been in the Dutch barn as she returned to the farm very late the first night and dare not come out the next day! I went to the farm and saw her, took her in the car to Meriden, leaving her to catch the bus to Birmingham, where she lives. Oh dear, I do wonder what was at the bottom of the story?

I very nearly forgot to make the paste for the land-girls' party sandwiches, but put on an extra spurt and got it done. Kate was busy making cakes, including the ones I promised for the party. At 8 p.m. I went to the party along with five girls in the Crowhurst taxi 'Queen Mary' and heard Mr Crowhurst deploring once more the lack of proper headlamps—or rather the lighting of the same. He switches on his fog lamps to see the cyclists who ride without rear lamps in these narrow lanes.

It *was* a good party! The girls invited old and young—in fact, all the people who had been good to them at different times, as well as the Berkswell Guild and their own friends. I had my usual one dance, a waltz, and 'Mother' had to pay the band and the caretaker and generally keep an eye on things.

Saturday 23rd December

The situation on the Western Front is supposed to be better, but it still looks very bad to me. The Germans have penetrated 40 miles and are not far from the city of Luxembourg. The Americans are holding the enemy in the north, it is said. Enemy paratroops are coming down behind the lines to cause confusion. They dress in American uniform and sometimes drive American tanks and, of course, speak English! There is still lots of fighting in Greece and many warring parties, yet they feel there is ground for hope of settlement.

Great excitement today when the wireless told us the ban was off motor-car headlamps and we could now unmask them. This is good news and Jack was thrilled.

Sunday 24th December

Rather foggy and cold early this morning and not suitable for an old party to cycle to church, so I had one of those nice messy mornings, turning out one or two things, finding things I had forgotten and locating a few I had missed lately. The hens had a little attention and some purple sprouting was gathered for dinner. Afterwards I decided to get a few evergreens to go with my branch of holly and then I cut them up into suitable pieces and 'decorated'. A sprig of holly for Alan's photograph and a vase of red polyantha roses and two red buds for him, too. Two or three vases of jasmine and cassinea—and who'd buy chrysanthemums at heaven knows what a bloom: 1s 6d. each when I last heard!

The news is better. The Germans are being held at several points in the Ardennes battle and reinforcements are pouring in along the roads. The Belgians, at first overwhelmed by the turn of events, are now cheering the reinforcements going along through the villages.

Monday 25th December

Another Christmas Day—still at war and no Alan with us! It was very cold and we found the porch thermometer showed seven degrees of frost. It has been very foggy all day, too, and quite thick in the dip by Lavender Hall as we came back from church. Later, as we went out for our walk, I thought there was a pig squealing across at the cottages, but when we got outside I found it was only little Donald Pring with some kind of 'musical' squeaker to which he was giving his fullest attention, blowing out his thin little cheeks as he ran along the footpath.

And then the Christmas Dinner—yes, it was worthy of a capital D, the cockerel was tender, the sausages were real sausages with eatable skins, and the whole things perfectly cooked and seasoned. I felt a real pig, for I was hungry, having had an early plain breakfast. Another half-bottle of Graves was a pleasing accompaniment. Actually Kate accepted a glass and thought it marvellous. No plum pudding today, but some hefty mince pies—yes, like that, not much mince but plenty of pie—and the other sweet we left untouched.

We had a real rest all afternoon, listening to the wireless, and were glad that His Majesty was on good form at 3 p.m. and that he mentioned prisoners of war and their relatives. He said that the separation of families was one of the great trials of war. It is indeed. No-one can imagine what it means until they have experienced it.

Tuesday 26th December

The 8 a.m. news gave the news that Mr Churchill went to Athens yesterday! He was accompanied by Mr Eden and they are to have a conference with the Greeks in an effort to end the conflict in Greece. Field-Marshal Alexander and Mr Macmillan are also there. It is to be hoped that some good will come of Mr Churchill's self-sacrifice.

Wednesday 27th December

The conference in Athens took place in secret in a room dimly lighted by hurricane lamps. Mr Churchill drove there in an armoured vehicle. The streets had been cleared and armoured cars were stationed at every corner. A plot to blow up the Grand Bretagne Hotel in Athens, H.Q. of the Allied Command and Greek Government, was discovered on Christmas morning when three-quarters of a ton of dynamite was found in a sewer eight feet under the front door. This sewer, guarded by wire barricades, was inspected every night. Early in the morning a further inspection was made, and the wire was found to be cut and the explosive was discovered.

The German thrust into Belgium has now reached Dinant. The Germans are using American vehicles which they have captured, and dress in American uniforms which they took from American prisoners before shooting them. This makes it difficult for our Allies and the Air Forces, which deal out damage and destruction whenever the weather is suitable.

Thursday 28th December

Yet another lovely day, still with hoar frost, though less of it, and at midday the sun melting the beauty away from tree tops and wherever its warm rays reached. Walking down to the grocer's was perilous in parts—even the four-legged one skidded once or twice—and coming back with 11 lb of grocery in the basket was rather tiring. Cold weather takes the energy out of one—and this is, of course, just an excuse for this afternoon's laziness.

Mr Churchill and Mr Eden are on their way home. There was an 'overwhelming desire of those present at the Conference that a Regency should be established immediately'. Mr Churchill had a narrow escape from a sniper's bullet when a machine-gun opened fire across the entry of the Embassy building. His comment was: 'What cheek.' A Greek woman 200 yards away was wounded.

There are Allied counter-blows in the Ardennes and the Americans have re-captured two towns.

Saturday 30th December

And so we begin the sixth year without Alan. Today has been much warmer. Just below freezing at 9 a.m. and later rising well above. This morning I took the car to fetch a gallon of paraffin and picked up a few oddments at the ironmonger's which will do for 'useful' prizes at the British Legion Party—a dish mop, a baking tin, a colander, a saucepan brush and some packages of brown paper! Many jobs after lunch and then I joined Jack taking his rest, and simply couldn't make an effort to get going till after three. Didn't 'wanner' clean out the hen pen. It went very much against

260

the grain, but it had to be done, and I earned my tea and enjoyed it.
This evening we read more of Alan's wonderful letters and
enjoyed getting near to his present life in that way. I am afraid
food is a bit short now, and little pleasures like going to the cinema
and for walks are cut off.

King George of Greece has appointed the Archbishop of
Athens to be Regent during this period of emergency. The
Americans have recovered about a third of the ground of the
enemy's forward thrust. The most forward part now is at
Rochefort. The northern flank of the salient, where the British 1st
Army is situated, is firm. Small German raiding parties have tried
to cross the Maas. Where they were successful, they were then
disposed of. Our Allied Air Forces have been busy day and night
pounding the enemy link with their army. V bomb sites and stores
have also been bombed. V bombs have been over southern England
and caused casualties and damage.

Budapest is being squeezed by the Russians who encircle it. The
Germans are busy destroying the big buildings there and making
every house into a strongpoint.

Monday 1st January

And a Happy New Year to us all! The Allies still hold the
initiative in the Ardennes and our aircraft is keeping the Germans
on the *qui vive*. There are heavy counter-attacks of local
importance which have been beaten off. Thirty-three out of fifty
German aircraft which attacked a Belgium airfield were
destroyed yesterday. The Regent of Greece has now taken the first
step to form a government and implores the 'rebels' to lay down
their arms, telling them nothing can be done till they stop fighting.

In Budapest the grim battle goes on and two million people and
the German garrison who are supposed to defend them are
encircled and short of food and other supplies.

Tuesday 2nd January

Warmer today, with a little frost early. After shopping in
Leamington I got home to find two bicycles by the front
door—ladies' bikes! Who could have come? When I got in I found
the telephone handy men had arrived to instal a telephone
extension up into Alan's room—and they were two girls! They did
the job very well, too. Later I busied myself with fancy dress for
the two parties tomorrow, and thought later what a silly old party
I am. And next: how can we waste even a few hours on these
childish things: And then: how little relaxation one gets on the

whole, so perhaps it is a good thing.

We were thrilled to get *a letter from Alan, dated 30.11.44*. It was addressed to Jack and talks of 'after the war, and if we are retained in the Army, Dick and I (Dick is also an engineer) would like to be transferred to the R.E.M.E.s'.

'After the war' seems to have receded lately in one's mind. There is still hard work to be done.

Wednesday 3rd January

Not cold today. Kate called up the stairs this morning 'Letters!' and our mouths curled up at the corners. I was just drying my foot in the bathroom, and Jack got his glasses and soon we were reading *a letter from Alan*, dated 10.11.44, and a postcard. They are all pleased to know Edward is so near home and were all very interested to hear of my visit to him. He is in good form, he says. The coal ration has been drastically cut, so they 'will have to depend largely on the wood which the working party who go out every day can produce'.

I seem to have been trying to catch up all day. All morning I hoped to give a little attention to my fancy dress for the afternoon's party at the W.I., but with one thing and another and the telephone nothing could be done till after lunch. I spent a long time trying to put on a pointed hat and flowing veil, but it was impossible to keep on and the idea had to be given up. Jack lent a hand and I got him to cut some heavy picture chain to make a chaplet for my head. Finally I got over to the Institute about 3.30 p.m. We had a very jolly time with our games and a rattling good tea with a cake which had come from Australia (Kenilworth) to Kenilworth (England). As there wasn't a Kenilworth Institute, our W.I. had it—a lovely fruity, spicy cake. We were lucky.

Afterwards I came home for a breather and found Jack enjoying Arthur Bryant's '*Years of Victory*', which I had brought him from Leamington yesterday, so I was able to leave him happily while I got ready for the next festivity. The Lady-in-Waiting (Richard III period) disappeared and in her place a Regency lady in high-waisted frock, velvet cloak and poke bonnet appeared! A land-girl arrived and then the Crowhurst taxi, and off we went to the Berkswell Reading Room to the Girls' Club Party. Such a spread to begin with and, not having had my usual supper, I did full justice to the good food. Many land-girls were there and we judged the fancy dress, watched exhibition dancing, joined in the games and generally enjoyed things till, at 10 p.m., the taxi came to take us home.

Wednesday 10th January

Up betimes this morning so as to be ready for a Voluntary Car Pool journey at 10. Jack decided to come with me and we made our way to Coleshill and straight along the new road. One way is closed and crowded with tanks—a mile-and-a-half of them—and then a second row of armoured cars and Bren carriers. All were neatly covered with tarpaulins—standing by!

We found our patient and he came out on two sticks to go to the hospital to learn to use his artificial limb. In civilian life he was a blacksmith and, after joining the Army and going to France in 1940, managed to wade out to a ship at Dunkirk and got home. He then became a paratrooper, was injured in jumping and had to give up the Army. Next he was a Sergeant-Major in the Home Guard, and one day he was riding on the back of a motor-bike when they came into collision with an Army lorry and his leg was so badly damaged it had to be amputated. Now he is learning to walk again, and as he weighs 15 stone it is not too easy. This morning he had to walk on a board six inches from the floor. 'It don't 'arf make yer sweat!' he said feelingly as he came back to the car afterwards, still panting from the exertion.

Home in time for the news: the Germans are falling back from the western end of the salient, but not very fast in this appalling weather, which is also hindering the Allies. The enemy launched a new attack in Alsace yesterday, but this was smashed and the Germans are today 'licking their wounds'. The Russians have thrown back all the German counter-attacks at Budapest and half the city is now in Russian hands.

Wednesday 17th January

The great news is that Warsaw has fallen to the Russians and they are going forward on the Eastern Front by leaps and bounds. Tremendous advances they have made, and are now only 30 miles from the German border. They have announced what they are going to do when they get there! And no-one is going to stop them, they say in effect.

In Italy the weather is awful. In Luzon the Japanese are now attacking the Army which landed recently and is now 36 miles inland. In Burma our forces are nearing Mandalay. The 6 p.m. and 9 p.m. news gave us the Polish and Russian national anthems. Since 1939 Warsaw has been occupied by the Nazis and it is impossible to say what has happened to her million-and-a-quarter people. The city has been badly knocked about.

Hitler's communication acknowledges that on the Eastern Front 'the situation has become more acute'. He also talks of German troops 'fighting with great determination'. The tide has turned, Hitler! What will 'Schickelgrüber' do now?

Thursday 18th January

The news was tremendously interesting, with Mr Churchill reviewing the war situation and giving the Labourites a good trouncing in his firm but well-bred way, while Aneurin Bevan and Gallacher rudely interrupted in their ill-bred way. The Greek situation was well shown and some of the atrocities detailed. Immediately this truth was challenged by Gallacher. 'Tell us the old, old story,' he interjected. These people will never believe anything that does not suit them—or will pretend not to do so.

The latest Order of the Day came in at the end of the news. The Russians are 50 miles *west* of Warsaw! They are making a great sweep over Poland and on a 60-mile front their armies are advancing. Germany has been broadcasting all day—broadcasting to her armies to hold on, to her people of the gravity of the moment, and promising to do many things *soon*.

In Burma, Mr Churchill said, the Fourteenth Army—the 'Not-forgotten' Army—has advanced at some points almost 200 miles and they may well be described as 'on the road to Mandalay'. And then, characteristically: 'though I think from a different direction'.

The renewed U-boat menace, V rockets and jet-propelled fighter aircraft were referred to and we were warned to 'keep our eye on these'. The proposed meeting of Marshal Stalin, President Roosevelt and himself was mentioned towards the end of his speech, and he said: 'The Foreign Secretary and I will not fail to be present at the rendezvous' and quoted 'When the roll is called up yonder we'll be there'.

He ended: 'Whatever happens, the British Nation and Commonwealth may rest assured that the Union Jack of freedom will forever fly from the white cliffs of Dover.'

Friday 19th January

Aneurin Bevan and Co. are very annoyed with the Prime Minister and let off a lot of bad temper in the House today. In the end a division was taken and there were 340 for the Government—and 7 against! So that's that. The Russians surge forward and are nearing Silesia. Cracow is captured, they are close to Lodz and have the larger part of Budapest in their hands. The German radio has been telling the bad news all day to its people, but ends with:

'We shall emerge in victory.' All I can say is that *would* be a blow to us!

More good news from Russia on the 9 p.m. news. Nearly 400 miles of the eastern front has flamed up in white-hot activity. Lodz is captured. They have hastened up from Warsaw, too, 100 miles from Danzig! The Germans are nearly expelled from Poland, and this is grand news. At this rate they will soon be at Thorn, where Alan was sent with his fellows in 1941 as a 'reprisal'. It is still one of the main prison camps, Stalag XXA, where he was supposed to be and *was not* all those weary months in 1940 when we were without news of him.

Volume fourteen ends on a note of great hope for the next few months.

VOLUME 15

January 1945 – May 1945

Saturday 20th January

And real wintry weather, too! Snow has fallen at intervals—regular blizzards in fact—and when it wasn't falling it blew in clouds from ground and roofs. The lazy one stayed in bed—but she did get her bath before breakfast—till 10.30 a.m. and then did the daily round with only one pause: I wrote quite a lot of a proposed talk for Berkswell Girls' Club on the life of Louisa M. Alcott, did a second roughing-out and read it over, so now I can write it in a book all ready for use.

Last night at 11. 45 p.m. I finished re-reading *Little Women* and laid it down reluctantly. It must be 20 years since I last re-read it and more than 50 since my first precious copy was given to me as a Christmas present from my Father. I have always loved it and found new meanings in the old words, even though I remembered every event perfectly and many of the sayings by heart. It will be quite interesting to talk on Louisa M. Alcott with her most famous book freshly in my mind. Now I am re-reading her 'Life'.

Sunday 21st January

Outside it was lovely, but *my*, how cold! So this morning, with the fire in the living-room at last getting on, I sat in front of it and wrote to Alan. The matter of our having had 21 cars I thought would interest him, but could only count 20. Then we thought of 'Little Bert', the Austin 7 which Jack had for his job in 1940, and how the little fellow (Bert) was afterwards sold and, in the blitz, was blown up Harry's Spencer's works' stairs and pinned down with a girder. How, when the girder was removed, he was driven away gaily under his own power! I told him of Edward's recovery from his operation, which I know he will be glad to hear, and also hoped the parcels were coming in again. All day we have been making up our own fire and wondering whether Alan is keeping warm. We read the Diary after supper before the news.

Friday 26th January

Nineteen degrees at 9 a.m.! Getting colder and colder. With the plea for economy with electricity, we do not put on the hall radiator and, my goo'ness me, it *is* cold. Jack got the car out for me to take Mrs Bushill to her war job and I found it not too bad driving, if one drove slower than usual. Next Jack and I went to Leamington, also driving slowly, did a few jobs, collected a bit of Land Army uniform and a bit of this, that and the other. Having had complaints today about the lack of amenities at the Hostel, I had also to go to the Land Army Office and make a strong protest about this. Home a little late for lunch and then, about 3 p.m., I set off to visit farms, getting home about 5 p.m., *quite ready* for tea.

In East Prussia the Russians have reached the Baltic and cut off from Germany this province which has been the home of so much that is arrogant and Nazi-minded. The nearest the Russians are to Germany is less than 150 miles now. In this Diary it is recorded that certain towns have been taken, only to find later that they have not been captured. These mistakes are due to the B.B.C., which is a little previous in its statements at times.

Old William Hitchcock, our Berkswell verger, died this morning at the age of 87—a good old chap.

Saturday 27th January

Temperature 16° at 9 a.m. Wuss and wuss! And many wails about burst pipes and general winter troubles. Poor Joan Curtis had a burst somewhere up above and water poured through her bedroom ceiling in the night. Poor girl, she *is* having a trying time, getting water from next door and having to boil it all before use. Oh, these badly-planned English houses—so cold, so liable to burst pipes and the consequent damage to property in severe winters. It is high time we thought a bit and planned a lot better.

Monday 29th January

A postcard from Alan today dated 10.12.44. He says: 'Parcels seem to have stopped, but we can keep going at half per head per week until 6th January, so Christmas will be all right with this, our tin store reserve, onions from store and leeks from the garden. We are managing to keep the room nice and warm on wood issues and cones collected, and digging keeps us very fit.' The food situation does not sound very good, and I do hope they have received some food parcels by now. The thermometer today was the lowest this winter—15° at 9 a.m. I feel thoroughly 'grewsy' this evening. A little temperature was indicated and later confirmed. *Blow!*

The Russians continue to go forward towards Berlin and the Germans, still sending out frantic messages to their people, today asked the women and children to join in clearing the roads of snow. A ghost voice said: 'Don't do it—you will be killed by the advancing Russians.'

Tuesday 30th January

In bed once more! A bit of 'flu this time and a day or two in bed prophesied. I slept well, though conscious of very queer dreams. I had *three* feet with large crosses on them, and it was only towards morning that they resolved themselves into two ordinary feet, pressed firmly down at the bottom of the bed. I read a bit and dozed a bit all morning, and late in the afternoon the doctor came, wondering why I got everything as it began to go round the district. Goodness only knows! Certainly not because I want it—or them!

The great Russian advance goes on relentlessly. The Germans say they are within *50 miles* of Berlin, but the Russians say 95 at present. The people are tumbling out of Berlin, the Government is moved to Munich and there is a report of a German convoy going to Sweden to meet an Allied representative. All this is simply thrilling! *Fifty miles*—about as far from Oxford to London!

A report from one of the papers I read today talks of hanging all the Gestapo. Hurrah. I feel quite bloodthirsty about that—such a despicable job for a so-called man! I remember long ago writing what I thought of Hitler and thinking, if the Germans do get here, I should have to burn these Diaries. Now the tables are turned, thank God, and this reign of terror and bloodshed and misery should soon be over. Food is a difficulty in Europe now, and I suppose we shall soon have to provide food for the detestable Germans—after they have robbed, ravaged and plundered the Continent. If we do not, disease will be rife. Then there is also common humanity, which will not allow one's enemies to starve. I'd put the Gestapo into the gas chambers, having made them dig their own graves first, though they'd be best burnt and done with, not fouling the land.

Thursday 1st February

A warm night it was, with myself flinging off the blankets and not sleeping much until nearly time to waken. Jack is now well away with a heavy fluezy cold, but about 11 a.m. I began to get up and it was good to come downstairs to lunch, even if the bit of mutton was too tough to get one's teeth into. This morning our favourite little hen was killed, and if food for them were not so scarce I believe I would have kept her as a pet. She was such a nice, neat little hen, very talkative and known as Chatterbox, but she was three years old. When the milkman had done the horrid deed, he told Kate they had a pet hen who was *nine* years old. I didn't think they would be sentimental about a hen. I wish now we had kept Chatterbox—too late, too late!

The enemy says the Russians are only 40 miles from Berlin and they can already hear the thunder of their guns. Hastily they are making tank traps and barricades at the edges of the city, and the Volksstürm were exercising hurriedly last night. On General Zhukov's front 5,000 Germans were killed and 17,000 taken prisoner. In East Prussia only one-sixth of the province is still free, and in Silesia Koniev's forces still press forward. The roads are full of refugees and the Red Army has moved so swiftly that people are awakened at night by knocking on the doors and windows: 'Get up and harness the horses and go away as quickly as you can—the Russian tanks are coming.' Where are they going, I wonder? One remembers the pathetic streams of refugees in France in May 1940, bombed and machine-gunned by German planes. And now? . . .

The Americans are doing well in Luzon and the Burma campaign moves forward, too, under Admiral Louis Mountbatten. Try as one will, one's main focus at the moment is Europe. Things are so intense that one's mind goes to it again and again.

Monday 5th February

With what impatience I sewed brass hooks on blackout curtains in the first weeks of the war. So firmly they were sewn with strong black thread that none had moved a fraction of an inch. Tonight I removed about 40 hooks—very gleefully—with a razor blade. I thought when I put them on what a happy moment this would be—and so it is, though the war isn't ended yet.

Manila has been captured by the Americans. The other day they made a commando raid and freed a lot of prisoners on Luzon. The poor things were very emaciated and many had died of undernourishment. In the seizure of this concentration camp at Santa Tomas there were 3,700 internees, 700 of whom were British, 100 Australians and 60 Canadians. The Americans knifed their way through Japanese resistance to reach the camp.

Tuesday 6th February

To hospital to see Edward Greenslade. He was a bit surprised to have a visitor and we were soon talking of Alan and he was reading *the two letters and postcard* which came from him today. They were good letters, too. The Germans insisted that all reserve stocks of food be used up by 4th January before any more parcels were allowed in the camp. So they had a marvellous Christmas Dinner, and the menu—very decorative—was sent inside one of the letters. A five-course dinner, followed by coffee and cigars(!!). The card, dated 26th December, says: 'We had a grand Christmas, easily my best in Germany. ...'

Wednesday 7th February

Jack very kindly listened to my Louisa M. Alcott talk this afternoon and pronounced it 'Very good, my Dear', so I thought it must sound all right. A change and a little meal and then I went to deliver it. It was a brilliant night, with the brightest of stars in a dull blue sky—just lovely. And, best of all, one could use headlights instead of creeping about in a state of strain, and everywhere see the lights of home in little glowing squares of all sizes as one drove past. It was most cheering. I drove down to Berkswell and parked my car in the Rectory drive, then walked up to the Reading Room. Only about 20 'girls'—aged from 12 to 55!—were there, and it's a lot of work for 20 girls for half an hour, but I hope to be able to give the talk elsewhere later on. I think it took from four to six hours to look up and put together.

Monday 12th February

A cold night presently resolved into quite a warm day, with that feeling of spring round the corner. I had to go to the sweep's, for our living-room is always full of smoke and we cannot get a fire without smoke. So he is to come tomorrow afternoon. With the turning-out of the living-room in view, I have turned out my own desk, hoping to come across the lost 'personal points', but no luck.

After the 9 p.m. news a special broadcast was given disclosing that the Conference of the heads of the Allies—Britain, America and Russia—met at Yalta on the Crimea and several of the decisions arrived at were outlined. All kinds of people have given their views—at meetings in Parliament and in the newspapers—from the Bishop of Birmingham to the T.U.C., who want to arrange and manage the world after the war. Now the decisions, crisp and clear cut, have been made and published to the world by those best qualified to do it.

The Greek Civil War is over and agreement has been reached. This, however, is but the first step. The carrying out of the agreement will show how things are.

Tuesday 13th February

The rain was pouring over the gutters when I woke just before 8 a.m. and the paths were flooded. By the time we were ready to go to Leamington it had ceased, and when we got there it wasn't very long before the sun came out and the temperature was decidedly up. Such a lot of kit-bags and gumboots and things to take to the Uniform Department of the Land Army and, later, many things to bring back. A lot of little jobs were cleared up at Olave Roy's—shortenings and tightenings and general tidying-up, and sadly I poured out 18 coupons for my new suit-to-be.

Budapest is now in Russian hands, with 110,000 prisoners taken. Over 300 guns have fired 24 salvos each to celebrate this in Moscow tonight. So Hitler has lost an army in this battle for the capital of Hungary. General Koniev is still dashing forward in Silesia and taking town after town on the way to Dresden. Several prisoner of war (German) camps have already been over-run by the Russian Armies and eight have been mentioned in tonight's news. On the other hand the men from many camps have been moved westward, going on foot 16 or 18 miles a day. It sounds a chancy business to me.

Saturday 17th February

One thousand, five hundred aircraft have attacked Japan. They were launched mostly from aircraft-carriers and kept the attack up for nine hours—wave after wave going over Tokio and Yokohama and bombing their industrial districts and works. And there was more bombing of Tokyo today.

My odd jobs done this morning, I soon went across to the Institute, for this was the day for the British Legion Wounded Soldiers' Party. I was first, so I got the keys, then took over evergreens, my cakes and pickles, Mrs Whitaker's cakes, too. Then, of course, they wanted a tin opener, a knife, a fork, tablecloths, drawing-pins, pins, etc., etc. At 11.30 I came home to cut the promised sandwiches and managed to get over again once before lunch, and finally arrived clean and tidy at 2.30 ready for the fray. When the soldiers arrived we greeted them at the door. Many crutches came along with them, and sticks, too, but they were an exceptionally nice lot of men. They are volunteers of Canada, not the conscripts, and I remarked on this to Mrs Wheatley, who goes to the Canadian Hospital at Marston Green three times a week. 'Yes,' she said, 'aren't they *pets*?' Two or three of the officers came to shake hands and say thank you, and we had a little talk. One of them was very pleased with the way they were looked after and treated and entertained in England—and rather surprised, too! They don't know how much we like them and how proud we are of their voluntary help for the Mother Country.

Friday 23rd February

The 9 p.m. news is on and says the Germans report a new attack this morning on the Western Front. An aircraft Armada of Fortresses and Liberators, with their escort of fighters, numbered over 2,000. Poznan has been captured and 23,000 prisoners taken. The Soviet advance flooded over Poland and onwards, leaving Poznan an encircled island of resistance. The Germans have ruined the city in their occupation of it, made the cathedral and churches into dumps, butchered the intellectuals and important people, and reduced the population by half. The news now says that 25,000 Germans have been killed at Poznan. Turkey has now declared war on Germany and Japan, and so just qualified for entry into the Peace Conference.

Temporary houses have gone out of favour with the Government and, though we are to have pre-fabricated bungalows from America later in the year, it is not now intended to put up many temporary dwellings. The difficulty of sites, roads and drainage seems just to have been realized.

Thursday 1st March

Taking a patient from Curdworth to Birmingham hospital today, we met dozens of little red-brown armoured cars. No-one could be seen driving them, even through the slit where each driver must have been watching the long ribbons of road winding along in front of him. At Coleshill I cast my eyes right at the double road and observed the many tanks and smaller vehicles with caterpillar tracks, still in store for some future date.

München-Gladbach has been captured by the U.S. 9th Army. The silence which was imposed on this front has been lifted for this news. American troops are just outside Treves, the oldest town in Germany, and aircraft have been harassing the oilplants and railway yards today. The Germans have just told their people of the loss of Poznan—accompanied, as usual, by lying statements. American ships are now using the port of Manila for the first time for three years.

The House of Commons approved by an overwhelming vote of 413 to nil the decisions of the Yalta Conference. This is excellent. Such a united front is a grand thing to show to the world at this time. President Roosevelt spoke in the House of Representatives and said if the U.S.A. refused to collaborate with the rest of the world 'we shall have to bear the responsibility for another world conflict'.

Friday 2nd March

Beautifully sunny all day, but there has been a rather piercing north wind. Everybody in the village stops me to ask if I have heard from Alan, and the people in the shops do so too. It is very, very kind of them all. Alas that we have to say: 'No, not for the last month.'

The war news is very good: F.-M. Montgomery's blackout curtain is lifted and we hear that the Allies are fighting a great battle west of the Rhine. Venlo is captured and Straelen, north of it. Krefeld also has been taken, and Neuss, beyond München-Gladbach, which is very near Düsseldorf. Also we are very close to Cologne and this town is being heavily bombed. The Germans lost 92 planes in severe attacks today. Dresden and Chemnitz were bombed. In fact, a very good day for the Allies.

The Red Army also is pushing on and looks like leaving Danzig in a pocket. In the Far East the Americans are landing at fresh places on the various islands and establishing themselves. It has been said that the Japs can replace the losses of aeroplanes as fast as they lose them and, though they have four million men under arms, they still have three million available.

Sunday 4th March

Cologne is nearly wiped out. The Germans won't surrender, they say. They would apparently rather have their cities destroyed one by one as the Allies advance. They must know that they cannot win now. General Eisenhower broadcast 'instructions' from the Luxembourg Radio calling on the German civilians west of the Rhine to 'stay put' and not to evacuate their towns and villages, to keep off the roads and not to become 'victims of a senseless blood bath'. Some German soldiers were found in an air raid shelter getting into civilian clothing! There are lots of bowler-hatted, correctly-attired civilians in the captured territory in the East. Decidedly suspicious! Some civilians asked the Russians what they were going to do with them. The Russians replied: 'Exactly what you did with our civilians.' The Germans turned pale!

The 6 p.m. news says the enemy is trying hard to get the remnants of his two shattered armies across the Rhine. He has five bridges for this purpose between Wesel and Hamburg. The R.A.F. was busy strafing the retreating enemy. At Krefeld 3,000 British

and other Allied prisoners were freed—mostly Air Force men—
and how delighted they would be.

Tuesday 6th March

A grey, coolish day, and Kate and I have been hard at it spring-
cleaning Jack's bedroom, and myself finishing off the bathroom.
We slogged along till teatime and, when I came down to make tea,
I took a cup to Kate and she was so revived she finished the job
while I had tea! After that a little walk round the garden in the
gathering dusk, a little mending and supper. From 8 to 9 seems the
only time for writing, and I must do this Diary every day.

The war news is good: General Patton's Army has made a
sensational advance today—I think his Army is on the way to
Bonn—and the Americans are now in Cologne. A splendid
advance has been made by the Red Army in Pomerania, reaching
the coast north of Stettin and taking 500 towns and cities! The
bombing of the German oil reserves is bring their store to a very
low state and they are feeling this very badly. Hurrah! Mr
Churchill has been to see General Eisenhower and Field-Marshal
Montgomery and has also been to Jülich in Germany, where he
fired a shell on which he chalked 'Hitler—personally'. He is a lad!

Yesterday we heard that Princess Elizabeth had joined the
A.T.S.! We did *not* approve. Not that it mattered what *we* thought
about it, but it is surprising for the Heir Apparent. Jack said: 'I
shall write to George and tell him we don't like it at all—and is it
necessary?' I think the Princess wants to see what an ordinary girl's
life of today is like. The Royal Family is far from conventional as
Royal Families go. Not at all like Queen Mary, that rigid
conventionalist and stickler for etiquette and ceremony.

Wednesday 7th March

More spring-cleaning for Kate today and the guest room
(known as the spare room) is nice and fresh-smelling and bright
again. It was a pleasant morning for the V.C.P. journey to the
Meriden Hostel, where a little boy who was going to have his
tooth out was ready. The girl who came with him appeared soon
after. While I waited for them at the dentist's I saw a row of five
American girls in uniform, arm-in-arm, all solidly chewing gum.
They went to the policeman on point duty and asked the way, and
seemed to be giving him the glad eye. I could see his row of teeth as
he smiled at their sallies. In half an hour they were back again,
evidently having filled in a bit of time between trains in seeing
bombed Coventry. They ogled the policeman again as they went

by and one of them smiled so massively at me that I said 'Good morning'—and she to me.

At 12 o'clock all the sirens sounded. I heard them unmoved—only a trial trip to see if they were still working well. After an hour's wait the little boy came out, glad to be rid of an aching tooth. But as it was a front one, it was rather disastrous. He told me about his daily life and his food and the books he read. 'I've read so many fairy stories I almost believe there are fairies,' he said. And: 'I'm glad I had my tooth out today, because we're going to see Peter Pan tomorrow.' They seem to do them very well in these hostels. An evacuated child from Croydon he was, and I wondered whether he had parents or didn't know he had lost them. He *said* he had parents, but had been away five years. These little homeless ones do make one's heart ache. They miss so much.

Thursday 8th March

A bridgehead has been established *across the Rhine* between Coblenz and Bonn! Isn't that marvellous! The security blackout imposed on this section has been (this is today's phraseology!) lifted to tell this good news. Marshall Zhukov's forces have cut off Stettin from the sea and it is reported from Stockholm that the Germans are evacuating the two experimental V bomb stations on the Baltic island of Usedom because of Marshal Zhukov's forces being within 40 miles. The Allies' Rhineland offensive has brought 68,000 prisoners into the bag. The Burma offensive is going well. Our Army has arrived at Mandalay!

Friday 9th March

We are told today that the crossing of the Rhine took place at Remagen, where our men found the bridge intact with everything fixed ready for blowing it up. Our sappers got to work and removed the explosives and our troops streamed across and established a good bridgehead. They have been streaming across ever since!! So far there has not been any violent opposition and no counter-attack has developed. Since D. Day one million prisoners have been taken and 54 generals. In Burma we have now captured Mandalay—we're getting on.

Later: The Remagen bridgehead is now nine miles long and three miles wide. Linz and other towns and villages have been captured and this evening the Allied Army is fighting 4½ miles north from the bridgehead. Up till now 123,000 prisoners have been taken in the west of the Rhine battle, and we shall be sure to hear of more. Twenty-three thousand were taken in the Wesel pocket, now closed—or were these annihilated? Four hundred and fifty square miles of the Ruhr valley are devastated. Not a town or industrial works remain standing. How terrible it all is! They say there is no reply on the German side to the dreadful 4,000 lb bomb with showers of incendiaries which our aeroplanes drop. The Germans were told we would devastate their war industries, and we are doing this very thoroughly. What hatred all this will cause, alas! But they have only themselves to thank.

This is Germany's 'heroes' day', and Hitler has been speaking to the people and lying indiscriminately. Goebbels' speech is a travesty of Churchill's famous 'We will fight them on the beaches'. How my heart sank when I heard that speech! Could the Germans really be coming *here*? And then one had a glow of patriotic determination and felt that if such a time did come, one's chin must be up and we would do whatever had to be done. Thank God it didn't happen!

Monday 12th March

The great news this morning was that, according to the *Daily Telegraph*'s special correspondent in Stockholm, negotiations are actually taking place between the British and the Germans about an exchange of able-bodied, long-term prisoners. *ALAN*!!!! Of course, there are the usual 'ifs' and 'highly probables' and the matter 'is still in its preliminary stage', and so on, but *there* was the hope. Nuff sed! Of course we also began to think of one thing and another. I went to the grocer's on my way to Berkswell and scrounged a pound of Atora suet to make some mincemeat, just in case—and all day things have been turning over in my mind. If he came . . .

As soon as I read the article in the *Telegraph* I rang up Joan Spencer. 'Engaged.' 'Yes,' I said, 'she has read it and is ringing up Ethel to talk about it.' Later the telephone rang—Joan. So we chatted away and wondered and hoped, and Joan said she felt 'all of a jelly' at the thought of it. Marvellous, brave little Joan!

Thursday 15th March

A very pleasant, though somewhat colder day. Jack and I went early to Kenilworth and he brought a toothless hag back with him. At 5. 30 p.m. he took the toothless hag and brought back a respectable elderly woman! In between there were all the daily jobs, a bit of stitching on the machine and gardening. It is DOG'S birthday and he is 9!! He had a sweetie today all to himself—and swallowed it whole! Such waste.

The Remagen bridgehead is being strengthened and is now 10 miles long and five miles wide. General Patton's troops are over the Moselle and have linked up several bridgeheads. The dragon's teeth and the pill-boxes of the Siegfried Line have been ploughed up by bulldozers before we made a further attack. 'Hanging up the washing.' There have been great attacks on Germany with the new 10-ton bombs. Railway yards and oil refineries have been hit, and 46,000 tons have been dropped on Germany in March.

Friday 16th March
To a Land Army meeting in Leamington this morning. Business went quite briskly and I ended up with my Berkswell Hostel woes. We went into the 'Golden Butterfly' for lunch, where many other W.L.A. people were already gathered. There we feasted on salad and a cup of tea, with bread and butter as a foundation, and I learnt what the District Reps. are known as in office circles—but it cannot be written!! Like all women today, we talked of our houses and gardens, our help—if we had any—and our work. We all planned to give much of it up when the War ends. Some land-girls are on strike since they are not to have a War gratuity. At one hostel the warden said if they struck she would strike, too. So she refused to cook their breakfast and they had no food cooked for them for a day-and-a-half!

The Duke of Windsor has had enough of his job as Governor of the Bahamas for nearly five years and is giving it up. When France is more settled he hopes to live there.

The autobahn to the east of the Remagen bridgehead has been cut in two places by our Forces. The American Seventh Army is pushing north on a 50-mile front from Saarbrücken to the Rhine. The fall of Coblenz is imminent. General Patton is over the Moselle and six miles beyond it the bridgehead is 19 miles wide. Ribbentrop sent an emissary to get in touch with the British Legation in Stockholm a few days ago to make a Nazi peace offer. One cannot make peace with Nazis, so it was completely ignored. In Burma, Mandalay is being captured gradually.

Sunday 18th March
The bridgehead at Remagen is now 16 miles wide. The middle span of the bridge has collapsed, and this sounded bad. But we are told it does not matter as for a week a pontoon bridge has been supplying the bridgehead and the bridge was used only for foot traffic. Coblenz has fallen to the Americans and the enemy crossing the Rhine in steamboats and barges was utterly destroyed

by Allied aircraft. General Patton's troops are over the Saar and pushing north with tanks and making corridors through the German troops. British destroyers have been active in the Gulf of Genoa, sinking German ships. The Brenner Pass is bombed regularly, and this must make the difficulties of supplying the German troops extremely awkward.

British food reserves are to be sent to Europe to feed the liberated people suffering great hardship. Americans are to have their meat ration cut and, as the President has told them, will need 'to tighten their belts' to help the undernourished people of Europe. The clothes' rationing period is to be extended owing to shortage of supplies. There may be a reduction in the next period—certainly no increase.

Last night piloted enemy planes were over northern England and damage and casualties also occurred from V bombs in the south.

Wednesday 21st March

And what a lovely first day of spring! It was mostly spent out of doors for us, though Kate had a big job on spring-cleaning the larder. There is so much extra china there, innumerable bottles and jars, a good deal of bottled fruit and still a few tins of things. On my trip to the butcher's and grocer's I met several people with whom I was obliged to have lengthy conversations. Then I had a word or two with Mrs Parsons, asking so kindly and sympathetically for Alan and giving words of hope and cheer. All these stops by the way take time, but perhaps they are part of one's work for the day. It was 12.30 p.m. when at last I got home, bringing ½ lb of cooking chocolate which the kind lady at the grocer's had scrounged for me to make a cake for Alan!

The Remagen bridge is down! It collapsed (and killed some American soldiers who were crossing), but we are told this makes no difference to our bridgehead as a pontoon bridge was already established and had been used for heavy traffic for some time. I hope we have more than this one. General Eisenhower has broadcast to the foreign workers to leave the Ruhr towns and go into the country as the Ruhr industries will be destroyed and the whole Ruhr area become a death-trap. Civilians, too, were told: 'Your life depends upon the immediate execution of these orders.' The enemy has lost 45,000 men killed, wounded and prisoners between Mainz and Ludwigshaven. The roads and lanes are choked with traffic as they try desperately to extricate themselves from the catastrophe that has overtaken them.

The 9 p.m. news says it has been a day of colossal air attacks. The 1st and 7th German Armies have been put out of action and our forces have taken Ludwigshaven. All the industrial Saar basin is now in our hands. The Russians have captured Altdamm, the German fortress at the mouth of the Oder. There was heavy resistance. Near Königsberg, 9,000 Germans were killed in one day. More ground has been gained in Upper Silesia. There has been a Naval battle off Japan, where the Americans wrought great destruction in a harbour full of ships thought by the Japanese to be 'safe'. The Japanese also lost 475 aircraft.

Mandalay was definitely captured yesterday.

Thursday 22nd March

I rang up Ethel Spencer today and she told me a postcard had arrived for Peggy from Alan. It said the Germans had taken away their furniture and palliases by way of reprisals, but they were going to make the best of it. Oh, these damnable, mean Germans! Taking reprisals on poor helpless prisoners! The wretches! It made me feel very distressed. It was cold then and the poor things would be miserable. They really deserve all they are getting, these Germans—and they are getting it pretty badly now.

Mainz has been cleared and 50,000 prisoners captured in the last 48 hours. The Remagen bridgehead has been widened and is now 29 miles long and nine wide. Field-Marshal Montgomery has a smoke-screen 60 miles long, concealing his preparations from the enemy.

Berlin is attacked nightly by Mosquitoes.

Friday 23rd March

At last a letter from Alan, dated 10.1.45. Evidently the condition described on Peggy Spencer's postcard did not prevail on 10th January. Alan thinks he is one of the few lucky ones there, since there are now neither cinemas nor walks for them. He is a gardener and gets out on a working party in the town all day. They had been having real wintry weather with 20° of frost and 'the old ears and fingers get nipped a bit first thing. Of the eight men of the 7th Battalion, R.W.R. Mess who were captured, only three now remain—Nevill, Philip and I'. A dearth of letters since Christmas, he said.

The devastating air attacks on the Ruhr continue and Berlin expects an attack 'in the grand style', as the German military spokesman puts it. Stettin is burning after heavy shelling by the Russians.

Saturday 24th March

The biggest Armada of the War flew from England over the Reich this morning and at dawn today Field-Marshal Montgomery's attack, so long awaited, began. But more of this after the 9 p.m. news. It has been another good day with lots of sunshine, though with the wind in the east and a steady barometer after a fall yesterday.

At lunchtime the Robinsons rang up to know if they could come out and see us, and read us letters from their son, Captain Nevill Robinson, in Oflag VIIB. They had received three letters today. One repeated Alan's news to Peggy Spencer of the dismantling of their rooms 'as a reprisal for the treatment of German prisoners in Egypt'!! The Germans said that was how their prisoners were treated. Any lie will do for Germans. The other two letters were quite cheerful and the dates were sometime in February, I think. Mrs Robinson had heard definitely from someone that prisoners hear the B.B.C. news every day, at least in Oflag VIIB. This is marvellous and must keep their spirits up. Alan's letter yesterday ended 'Looking forward to the summer'. It is grand to think they know what is going on. The Robinsons' visit was much enjoyed and they seemed reluctant to go. They enjoyed coming into the country after being in their blitzed Coventry house.

Later: Montgomery's Armies have crossed the Lower Rhine and have established bridgeheads. This is the biggest combined operation since D. Day. So far all is going well. Huge boats of a new type, 80 ft long and for carrying bulldozers and troops across the river, were taken through narrow streets and over long roads—a curious way for the Navy to begin an operation. 'Buffaloes' carried the troops down to the water's edge, guided by tracers. Over went the airborne troops, with Dakotas and gliders, landing on the east of the river. Now that Armies are safely across, the great need is for bridges, and bridges over the Rhine are not easy to establish. However—we shall see.

Sunday 25th March

Mr Churchill has been across the Rhine, says the news, and for a short cruise on the river itself! What a man! Field-Marshal Montgomery, Sir Alan Brooke and the American General Simpson were with him. The airborne troops have joined up with the other forces on the east side and two or three other bridges have been made and crossed and bridgeheads established. Never before in this War, said correspondents, have the Allies had such favourable weather for a major operation. All these great doings were preceded by shattering aerial and artillery bombardment of record proportions. As the land forces stormed across the Rhine in assault craft there was a dense cover of artificial smoke and swarms of bombers and fighters thundered ahead, blasting and rocket-shelling German strongpoints. The vast fleet of assault boats and amphibious craft included a number of a nature still secret. Two hundred and forty Liberators dropped supplies and altogether nearly 6,000 aircraft were engaged in the bridgehead operations. In a message to his troops on the eve of the great assault, Montgomery said: 'The 21st Army Group will now cross the Rhine'!! It did!

Wednesday 28th March

We are thrilled to the core with the war news. The Allied Armies are pushing east from the Rhine and there is no very strong resistance except in the north. Even there it has lessened. General Patton, U.S. 3rd Army, is our hope for the liberation of Oflag VIIB. He is pushing on from Frankfurt, Offenbach and further still today. Joan Spencer rang up, full of excitement and counting the possible miles between the latest place mentioned and Eichstatt. All day long I, at least, consider the possibilities of release for Alan and wonder how the journey home would be affected. And then off one goes into dreamings and imaginings till one finds oneself doing the same thing twice, or going upstairs when one meant to go in the garden—even picking up the kettle to go and feed the hens! They wouldn't care much for hot water!

Thursday 29th March

A pleasant morning, except for a strong wind and, having at last made my silver fit for a decent house, I went off with Twink to get Good Friday buns (a questionable custom for such a day!). However the baker (who is also the grocer) had so much bread to bake, as they are closing tomorrow, that he could not be bothered with buns. We picked up some scones and soup elsewhere and got back with a few minutes to spare before 1 p.m.

The news tells of the Allied Armies sweeping forward on the Western Front, but there is a blackout on the news from parts of this Front so as to confuse the Germans. It is probable that we are much further into Germany than expected. General Patton's Army interests *us*, of course. All kinds of vehicles in enormous quantities have crossed the Rhine—bulldozers, tanks, self-propelled guns, Bren carriers, lorries, etc. There seems no organized resistance and in the villages and little towns the people hang out white flags of surrender. The Russians announce that they have reached the Austrian border and are only 45 miles from Vienna. Near Königsberg they have killed and captured thousands of the enemy, and 600 tanks have either been captured or destroyed. Enormous quantities of booty have been taken.

This is an amazing time to us, after so many dark years. May we soon be able to liberate Northern Holland, where the Dutch are being slowly starved by the Germans.

Monday 2nd April

As we sat at breakfast this morning Kate came in to say a man named Robbins was at the back door and wanted to see me. I found an elderly man who wanted to come and do some gardening for us! It is a wonder I didn't *swoon*! I seemed to know his face, and found he lived at the little house in Green Lane, where I always look and admire the garden. Long ago I asked him if he would come and do a bit of digging for us, but he said he went to work daily and his time was full up. We walked round the garden and he was interested. Then Jack came out and we fixed up with him for two days a week, winter and summer. He said: 'I wish I had come when you first asked me.' I wish he had, too. Later in the day we thought we would have him for three days a week, if he hadn't fixed up with anyone else, so when Twink and I walked up Green Lane after tea we saw him and made arrangements for three days weekly. Grand! I can scarcely believe it.

The morning slipped away with daily jobs a bit late owing to interviewing the gardener, and then I dyed several pairs of stockings and hung them in the yard in a fluttering row, for it has been rather windy all day. Jack, having removed the white paint from the front bumper of the car—another sign of the improved times—then washed it.

Montgomery's Army is 100 miles from the Rhine. We have now 5,000 square miles of Germany east of the Rhine, have crossed the Dortmund-Ems canal and reach Munster. The Germans are coming out of Holland and our aircraft could find no enemy activity in the V-rocket area. There has been no aircraft activity over England since Thursday. The Ruhr is encircled by the linking up of two Allied Armies and it is believed 100,000 Germans are trapped there.

Paris has had a moving Eastertime. There was a huge military parade in which thousands of men took part. Colours were brought out from places where they had been hidden during the occupation and the flame of the lamp was re-kindled on the

Unknown Warrior's Tomb. Mrs Churchill has arrived in Moscow to inspect Red Cross hospitals, particularly at Rostov-on-Don, where the amount of Mrs Churchill's Fund—£40,000—is to be used to build and equip two hospitals.

A weather forecast has been made this evening. The last one was given in the regional bulletin of 31st August 1939! The weather report was 'Rather unsettled'!

Tuesday 3rd April

German transport was pulling out of Northern Holland all night—attended to by our aircraft! Eisenhower speaks of 'the magnificent feat of arms—the battle of the Ruhr'. Here a great German force is encircled and is endeavouring to find a way out, but the flanks have been widened and now there is activity from the east trying to force an opening from outside to let the enemy force out. Wiener Neustadt, captured by the Russians, is an important stronghold on the way to Vienna less than a dozen miles away. The intention is to make a stand at Vienna, and so this beautiful and interesting city will suffer the devastation which has attended on all those defended by the enemy.

Thursday 5th April

General Bradley has over a million men under his command now and Field-Marshal Montgomery is now leaving the Ruhr to him, while Monty concentrates on Holland. Minden-on-the-Weser has now been reached, the British are 40 miles south of Bremen, Osnabruck has been in our hands for a few days and Hamelin—Pied Piper town—has been reached. General Eisenhower does not think Germany will make a national surrender, so that victory can only be proclaimed by us, when we feel the time has come to declare it.

The Germans have offered a large reward for information concerning an incident a few days ago when a car with a chauffeur and two or three passengers was driving away from Berlin: The chauffeur and two passengers were shot and killed. A correspondent in Stockholm thinks that Goering was one of the passengers, but whether he was one of the two killed, or the third who escaped, does not seem to be known. It is suggested all this may have been staged by Himmler, who may want to clear the way for himself.

Russia has now denounced her neutrality pact with Japan, and Japan's government has resigned.

Saturday 7th April

Things are progressing quite quickly in the European war, with Hanover only 10 miles away and Nuremberg about 40. The Russians are at the outskirts of Vienna and soon, I suppose, it will be all smashed up—the beautiful city of which we have heard so much. How it has figured in novels and crime stories of the past!

The battle for Mandalay is finished and Lord Louis is made a K.C.B. Now a new battle is beginning for Rangoon. A Naval action has taken place and Japan has lost her 15th Army, 150 planes and a further 116 later, the battleship *Yamato*, three destroyers and two cruisers. There has recently been a change of Government and a 77-year-old Admiral has formed a Cabinet.

Sunday 8th April

A cold morning turned into a lovely day with a grand blue sky and consequent bright sunshine. We snoozed a bit after lunch and, when three o'clock struck, we rose and went forth to our work and to our labour till teatime. I forked and weeded the polyantha rosebed while Jack had the M.G. outside the shed doing little bits of tidying and painting. After tea we went out again. Jack finished his work on the little car and we *shoved* it in and put the dust-sheet over it again, as we have done many times in the last five years.

Allied Forces have reached Creilsheim. This is 50 miles from Eichstatt, and now we wonder whether Oflag VIIB has been transferred elsewhere.

Monday 9th April

Bremen and Hanover are burning, but whether from a scorched-earth policy of the Germans or slave labour setting fire to the town is not known. The 12th Army Group is thrusting beyond Cassel towards Leipzig and the 6th Army Group further south is making for Nuremberg. (Oh, be quick, be quick!) The Russians are entering Vienna so quickly that the enemy has been unable to destroy some parts of it by fortifying it house by house and street by street, as in other large cities. It is to be hoped it will not be ruined as they are.

In Holland 10 Dutchmen were found dead. Some had been tortured to death, others shot. The bodies were shown to a captured German. He protested that they had not done it—they were soldiers. It was the Gestapo, he said. He was asked if he could understand now why the Germans were the most hated race. 'Yes, oh yes,' he replied.

More rockets and rocket trains have been captured—and so many British civilian lives saved. Hamm is ours—that great marshalling yard which we bombed so hard and so often. 'Dropping eggs on Hamm,' as we called it.

Tuesday 10th April

Hanover has been entered by the American Army today and the motor division has cut the road to Hamburg. In Holland the German forces have been cut up in corridors and Canadians are only 25 miles from Emden. The enemy in the Ruhr is being gradually squeezed and it is thought he is trying to get some of his troops out by plane by night. Every day and night the Allied bombers go forth and bomb in German and occupied territory. Mosquitoes pound Berlin night by night. Konigsberg has fallen at last and the survivors surrendered yesterday. The Russians are in the centre of Vienna. Troops of the 8th Army have launched an attack in Italy, preceded by a great air assault. We hear stories from and about the liberated prisoners and their privations and sufferings have been great, especially those who marched 500 miles almost starving. We do so wonder whether Alan has been moved from Eichstatt.

Wednesday 11th April

The morning flew by. Such a lovely morning, too—warm and sunny, like early summer. The birches are shaking out their dainty little leaves, the orchard apple trees are in bud, the damsons in full bloom, or even shedding their petals, and pears are also full of blossom. Jack says: 'I'm rather interested in my fruit.' And I must say the trees look very promising. Both Early Victorias and Bramleys Seedlings are full of buds.

The Canadian First Army launched an attack to release Rotterdam and Amsterdam today. With Hanover captured, our forces have by-passed Brunswick and are now only 100 miles from Berlin. Bremen is encircled, Essen has been taken and the Ruhr is being pressed still more. The pocket battleship *Scheer*, sister ship to the *Graf Spee*, has been sunk by our aircraft, and in the last six days 1,700 German aeroplanes have been shot down, or shot up on airfields, by our aircraft.

Friday 13th April

At 8 o'clock we heard the tragic news of the death of President Roosevelt. An artist had been painting his portrait at Warm Springs, the country house where he was taking a restful holiday.

He complained of a headache and shortly afterwards became unconscious and died in a few hours of a cerebral haemorrhage. This is a great loss to everyone, just now particularly. We thought he looked rather a sick man in the pictures of the Yalta Conference in early February. Many tributes have been paid to his memory.

Essen has been captured and the Ruhr pocket is being reduced. The American 9th Army has entered Brunswick. Coburg and Erfurt have also been taken and the French 1st Army has entered the northern spurs of the Black Forest south of Karlsruhe. Here they have met fanatical German resistance. There has been stiff fighting at Creilsheim and the Germans claimed to have surrounded a battle group and say they now hold Creilsheim.

Sunday 15th April

There was a description of the concentration camp at Buchenwald after the news tonight—a heart-rending account of what Edward Morrow, the American war correspondent, had seen when the place was liberated. Oh, these evil Germans! And those poor, poor souls. There were starved and emaciated bodies of those still in the land of the living, and dead bodies piled in a yard—250 of them—like cordwood. Thousands of people have been starved to death in this camp, and others have died of diseases caused by under-nourishment, while outside the wire were fields and farms and well-fed Germans. How can one forgive such horrible deeds—or even forget them! We must *not* forget. This would have been happening here if the Germans had invaded and conquered England.

Monday 16th April

This morning I did rise from my bed betimes, so as to be downstairs to greet the gardener. I went out as the clock struck eight and found Robbins at the shed waiting for instructions. I soon started him on sowing peas and spinach and then he suggested manuring a trench ready for the runner beans. All this he did in a workmanlike manner by lunchtime, or just after, and later suggested digging and manuring a piece of ground for main crop potatoes. This was a good suggestion and so he got going on this. The weather has been simply glorious and very warm all day. This afternoon there were one or two little jobs to do in the garden, only it was too hot to do much. After supper I went over to Wilkes and told him we now had a regular gardener and thanked him for tiding us over the worst.

There are 75 square miles burnt out in Japan and two P.O.W.

Camps have been liberated. Some of the prisoners have been marched hundreds of miles and are half-starved. Most are under-nourished and many have been very unkindly treated. It makes one cold with righteous anger.

President Roosevelt was buried yesterday in the garden of his home. The new President, Mr H. Truman, gave his first Presidential speech this evening.

Tuesday 17th April

Tonight's news tells of the American Army conducting local Germans round Buchenwald camp. Some were stolid, some fainted, and some women wept and wrung their hands, and some said they did not know these things were going on so near to their homes. *They know now* and cannot pretend in the future, as they did after the last war. The inmates of Buchenwald have been moved—those who could be moved—to German barracks and are being fed from the prosperous farms around. Excellent!

Progress is being made on the Western and Eastern Fronts. Many aircraft lying on German airfields, probably grounded for lack of petrol, are being shot up, and 1,451 are mentioned today. In Holland there is further progress. In Italy it is a stiff job against a strongly resisting enemy. Both the 5th and 8th Armies are now on the offensive.

In Leamington today I wanted a bottle of sherry in case Alan John should come home soon. I know it is like asking for gold, but eventually a bottle, duly concealed in a wrapping of newspaper, was obtained.

Wednesday 18th April

There have been steady, if not spectacular, advances on the Western Front today. Magdeburg has fallen, though a few snipers remain. The stubborn defence of the old city of Halle has now been overcome. Having said yesterday that Nuremberg was captured, the early news today said it was encircled. Now, at 9 a.m., it had been entered at four points. Allied forces are now only 20 miles from Bremen.

Still lovely warm weather and summer frocks are being worn and old straw hats come out once more. I dashed off to the butcher's to see much fat pork lying around, but a very nice bit of best end of neck of mutton came out of the refrigerator for me. I was thankful. Pork in this weather makes one feel a bit queer.

Friday 20th April

All organized resistance has ceased at Nuremberg and the Americans are pushing on to Munich. This is indeed thrilling—20 or 30 more miles to Eichstatt!! Everybody is asking: 'Have you any news?' I have to say no, but explain that we are hopeful, if only prisoners of war have not been moved from Oflag VIIB.

A party of M.P.s is going to Germany by invitation of General Eisenhower to see something of German atrocities at Buchenwald. Elsewhere still more dreadful things have been perpetrated.

It is good to hear Edward Ward broadcasting again. Speaking tonight from Leipzig, he tells of going into a house where the Burgomaster, his wife and daughter had poisoned themselves. He described them as they sat in their chairs round the table; and again another house and room where more people had done the same. Dreadful!

Kate has been spring-cleaning. I can't think how she does it—hall, landing and stairs, carpets up, beaten and down again, all herself! As Alan's university friend would have said: 'Mar-r-vellous woman!'

Saturday 21st April

This morning two kind people rushed across the road to inquire about Alan, but I have to say: 'No news yet.' Was ever any time as long as this!

Nuremberg is properly occupied now, so we hope they are getting on to Eichstatt. We also heard that prisoners had been escorted by German guards to the Swiss border and that, having delivered up the prisoners, the guards then surrendered. If this is the case, Alan might be among these. The Germans say the Russians are shelling Berlin from 14 miles away and that the Americans are only 40 miles from the Russians! The Russians say little at present, but it is thought they are sweeping round the south of Berlin 'sickle fashion'. Good simile!

Bologna has fallen. This is the culmination of the advances of the last few days and 'the best news since Cassino and Rome', says a war correspondent. Escape routes from Bologna are being cut. In Burma the 14th Army has made a drive which has carried them a quarter of the way to Rangoon. There has been security silence on this front just lately.

Mr Churchill says there can be no Victory Day till the Generals tell us.

Sunday 22nd April

The Russians are battering at the suburbs of Berlin and advancing west beyond Dresden. When the Germans found the Red Army advancing, they threw in new fresh troops, but all of no avail. The scores of ring roads round Berlin were all heavily fortified, but still the Russians advanced. Prison camps are being overrun continually and some are in a pitiable state—this while German prisoners in this country are actually being better fed than the ordinary inhabitant!! Yes, they have more meat, sugar, bacon and fats than we have!! This because we are observing the Geneva Convention. So when the well-fed Nazi prisoners return home they will be well-nourished and cocky, and off will go the beginnings of a new war—if we let it. Our merchant seamen have had to go through all their dangers and sufferings to bring food for Nazi beasts.

Monday 23rd April

And what a St George's Day! It makes me think of Shakespeare's words:

> 'This England never did, nor never shall,
> Lie at the proud foot of a conqueror.'

Thank God for that. The conqueror might have been the Nazi, and what a dreadful doom would have been ours. Now it is the Nazis, and the Germans who allowed them to rise and dominate Germany, who are suffering a terrible fate. The Russians are getting further and further into Berlin and the great city is being destroyed. If the prisoners are still at Eichstatt—or were still there—the Americans may have got there, too, for the 9 p.m. news speaks of places round about east and west of it.

No 'dim out' tonight and we sat with all the lights on for some time and the curtains not drawn. What a relief to be free from the restraint of blackout and dimout. Yesterday and Saturday Jack removed bits and pieces of rod and fittings here and there. Last week Kate washed the kitchen curtains, which had been hanging up well over 5½ years and weren't they filthy!! We could never do without them, so they just had to stay up.

Tuesday 24th April

Our shopping day in Leamington, and I went straight down to the florist's shop and got three nice boxes of snapdragons and then picked up the amusing brown hat at Francis'. A queer contraption, but nevertheless I can wear it. And then to hairdressing and a 'reet good swill' and set while I mooned over love stories in magazines, read their recipes and tit-bits about the Royal Family. When I came out I soon saw Jack and we went into Bobby's furnishing department to hear the news, where I have often heard it. But today the wireless was *not on*! So we returned to the car and our lunch therein. Back at home, Kate was having another field day spring-cleaning the scullery. Perfectly marvellous, she is.

Fighting around Augsburg today. Ulm is captured and it looks as if the Armies were swimming all around Eichstatt. We hear from one and another how the prisoners of war come home. Some just arrive on the doorstep without any preliminaries, it seems. We are told they need feeding every two hours, as most of them are ill-nourished and underfed.

The Russians are getting right round Berlin, and nearly encircling it. Hitler is supposed to be in Berlin, and Goebbels, too. Goering seems to be missing. A Mercedes car with an escort of S.S. motor-bikes was bombed by our planes. A direct hit on the petrol tank and it burst into flames. Was it Himmler? He has been reported in that district.

Wednesday 25th April
A pleasantly warm, though somewhat hazy day, which I spent very happily at home, thankful not to have to dash off by a certain time to a certain place, as so often one has to do these days. The morning was a really useful one and, what with mending towels and all the bits and pieces which have been lying by, it soon came to 1 p.m. The afternoon sped away and, after tea, I said: 'I am going out to *look* at the garden.' 'I'll come, too,' said Jack. But I went first and couldn't resist getting the hoe and a basket.

Presently I looked up and saw a thin young man in a new-looking suit with a trilby hat, carrying gloves! The gloves rather frightened me and I though he wanted to sell me something. He raised his hat and said: 'Mrs Milburn? I'm Jack Mercer, and I was in the same camp as Alan in Germany. I got home five days ago.' Well, that was grand. Down went the hoe and soon Jack was in and we all sat down to drink a glass of sherry and have a long talk.

He hadn't seen Alan for 18 months, when he was moved away to Oflag 1XA. The Americans liberated them after their German guards had tried to march them away. They refused to go, so the guards went away and left them. Soon the Americans came and they were freed. Jack Mercer left us just before seven, after having a look at Alan's car, and we saw him off at the gate with his bicycle. He found it quite hard work cycling here from Stoke.

I thought I really would sow a few seeds then, and had just

spread a few quaint marigold seeds on the finely-raked soil when I heard the telephone and went in. At long last I heard a very faint voice say 'Anne Stapleton'. She was ringing up from Chester to say that a friend of hers, whose husband was in Oflag VIIB, had heard from someone who is at the Red Cross in London that Oflag VIIB is liberated. This message came by telegram today. She promised to ring up again if she heard any more news. It sounds absolutely true, and don't we feel excited! So, of course, I rang up Joan and she was thrilled to the marrow and was going to ring up Harry and Ethel and suggested I should tell the Varleys. So after supper I got Mrs Varley. Goodness, this has been an exciting day!

Berlin is now encircled by the Russians. There is a tough fight going on for Bremen and a great drive forward in Bavaria. Munich is the next town to be bombarded and, one supposes, laid in ruins. Berchtesgaden has been bombed and Hitler's chalet got a hit.

In spite of Hitler's threats to the people of Berlin, white flags of surrender are being put out of windows, but Russia says it is the worst street fighting of the War.

Thursday 26th April

The telephone rang many times during the day with people ringing up for news of Alan. The news I gave to Joan Spencer from Anne Stapleton came back to me as 'news' in a very roundabout way. Joan Spencer rang up, rather depressed by reading in an evening paper that a camp containing British, Canadians and Americans had been rushed away from the Lower Danube just before General Patton's troops arrived. Was it *our* camp? And so we go on, up one day, down the next, but never losing hope.

Stettin has fallen. The Burgomaster, or Mayor, of Bremen has surrendered the city, but there is still fighting in the streets. The Red Army is getting near the centre of Berlin. Hitler is still said to be there. There is splendid progress in Italy and our Army is near Verona. In the north, the Italian partisans are rising and the enemy is retreating in disorder.

Friday 27th April

This has been another thrilling day for War news. Americans and Russians have linked up at Torgau near the Elbe and there was great joy over this. Russian guns have barked out salvos from 324 guns in Moscow. Bremen has fallen. The Red Army is 40 miles west of Stettin. Patton's troops are advancing in Bavaria and Ingolstadt (south of Eichstatt) has been cleared. The bombing of Berchtesgaden a day or so ago did much damage to Hitler's chalet.

Mussolini (that fat pomposity), yellow with fear and fury, has been captured trying to cross the Swiss border!

In Italy there has been marvellous work. More towns have fallen than one can remember north of the Po—Milan, Verona, Turin, etc., etc., and the German Army is retreating in disorder. Italian partisans have greatly helped the Allies and are now giving up their arms in a ceremonial parade and receiving a certificate signed by General Alexander showing what they have done in a good cause.

Saturday 28th April

Such a cold day, with an icy wind, and actually there were two or three mild snowstorms during the day. I wore my fur coat—and on 18th April we were wearing summer frocks!

There is a rumour that Himmler has asked for peace and would surrender unconditionally to the Western Allies. It is said this has been conveyed to the British and U.S. Governments and that they have informed those who delivered Himmler's message that unconditional surrender can only be accepted on behalf of *all* the Allies. The Russians are capturing Berlin suburbs one after another and more link-ups will be taking place between them and the other Allies.

Many Stalag P.O.W. camps have been relieved and some numbers were given. There was 'Stalag' VIIB, not 'Oflag' unfortunately. Things in Italy are good and there is good progress in Burma. In fact everything is moving fast now and it is difficult to keep track of it all. There has been a revolt in Munich, but now it is said it has been quelled and the Nazis are in power again.

Sunday 29th April

Another bitterly cold day with an icy wind, and it was mostly spent before the fire. Mrs Greenslade rang up early to say: 'Aren't you excited?', thinking that Oflag VIIB (and not Stalag VIIB) was liberated. Joan rang up to say there was a War Office message in the London *Telegraph* of yesterday saying Oflag VIIB had been marched to Munich. Kate's paper told of 30,000 prisoners in the Alps, and so we don't know where we are. Never mind, May will soon be here and Alan will come.

The truth about the proposed surrender of the Germans is that it came through a private individual from Himmler and was immediately turned down by the British and Americans and an answer sent from 10 Downing Street. The Allies stand together— no splitting up as the Germans hope—and they have been given till

Tuesday to make up their minds. In the meantime Berlin is being hammered street by street and house by house. The 'rats' that have gone into the sewers and tubes are being got out by one devilish device after another. The flame-thrower sounds a terrible thing, but these enemies must be brought to bay. Thousands of Germans are killed each day and their sufferings must be ghastly, but how unnecessarily they have made others suffer—and are not sorry.

Goering is supposed to have died. Hitler is supposed to have had a cerebral haemorrhage and may die in a few days. Maybe he has already been shot or committed suicide. It is a monstrous thing that one cannot believe anything the Germans say. Italian patriots say they have executed Mussolini and most of his Fascist Cabinet. There are stories of the hanging of Mussolini's body in a square in an Italian town and that his mistress' body lies near, with others who were of his regime. It is said that people pass by and spit on his body and that one woman took out a revolver and shot five times at the corpse, for the assassination of her five sons.

On the kinder side, we hear of food being dropped in Holland. Weeks of preparation had gone into these doings and the food 'bombs' were duly dropped in the appointed places today. Delighted Dutch people waved frantically as they stood in crowds along the roads or on the roofs of houses. Orange flags were also spread for the planes to see. How good all this is. To be able to feed our starving Allies is great.

In Italy the Italian Army has surrendered and the 5th and 8th Armies are going strong. City after city falls into our hands. Milan is captured, and Spezzia and Vincenza.

Monday 30th April

War news is grand. The 27,000 Allied prisoners of war liberated at Moosburg now are found to number 100,000! Surely Oflag VIIB must be amongst these. Joan rang up this morning to say a London newspaper had said that Oflag VIIB was definitely among the liberated camps. It surely cannot be long now.

The wireless mentions over and over again the business of Himmler and unconditional surrender to the Western Allies. In Paris they rejoiced for an hour or two, thinking the War was ended, and in America they got quite excited. In England the old sobersides have been had once too often and took things in their usual phlegmatic manner—waiting to be quite sure first. It will be deep thankfulness and not so much 'mafficking' with many of us.

Italy has removed Mussolini's and all the other bodies to the mortuary now—a sorry spectacle, I think, and one hopes there will not be too much of this kind of thing. At Dachau, a concentration camp just freed, the same terrible things have gone on as at Belsen, Weimar and Buchenwald. In a letter today in the *Telegraph* it is suggested that if Hitler dies his body should be buried at Buchenwald with his victims—nasty for them—so as to prevent making a hero of him and his grave a place of pilgrimage.

It seems as if the fighting is nearly over in Italy. What is left of the German army there is disorganized and many prisoners are being taken. Things go well in Burma, too, but we seem so occupied with events in Europe that our minds cannot take in all the happenings there too. Progress is good on the Elbe section, but not much is said of Holland except about the dropping of more food containers today.

May tomorrow—the month of Alan!

Wednesday 2nd May
The 8 o'clock news says Hitler is pronounced dead by the Germans!

There was a great to-do about the announcement on the German radio—solemn music, the leading up to a great item of news, people told to stand by, roll of drums and then the announcement that the Fuehrer had died for the Fatherland, killed in Berlin! One villain the less, if one can believe it. Anyway, he is dead officially. So Mussolini, Hitler and Goering are now wiped out. Admiral Doenitz is appointed Fuehrer in his place. Such a staging of facts for the last week or two that one quite expected the news of Hitler's death in *action* in Berlin. But one does wonder whether he has flown to South America or whether he is now lodged in Hades? And who bumped him off in the end?

Joan Spencer rang up to say she had persuaded her mother to ring up the Red Cross for any information they could give about Oflag VIIB and our prisoners of war. They had definite news that our men were marched away from there on 15th April, but no other news of their arrival elsewhere. However we still hope they are among the 110,000 at Moosberg, now liberated. I came back from the butcher's with a bit of 'black market' bacon and a dozen eggs—the former 'ready for your son when he comes home'. Good business! Kate was pleased.

Later: The story of Hitler's 'heroic' death is discredited already and Himmler's statement about his having cerebral haemorrhage is thought much more likely. I wonder whether we shall ever know? Von Runstedt has been captured in a hospital in the south and the bag of German prisoners mounts daily. In Burma there has been an amphibious landing which will make a great deal of difference to our advance on Rangoon.

9 p.m.: Great news! The enemy's sea, land and air forces in Italy have surrendered to Field-Marshal Alexander. Cessation of hostilities at 12 noon today. This was signed last Sunday. Nearly a million troops will now surrender to the Allies—a record for this war. General Alexander, giving a message to the sailors, soldiers and airmen under his command, says: 'You stand today as victors of the Italian Campaign.' Not only is this the surrender of Northern Italy, but it also includes parts of Austria and is a tremendous victory.

Schleswig-Holstein has been cut off and, of course, Denmark farther north. Hamburg and Kiel are also cut off. Rostock has been seized by the Russians and 120,000 prisoners have been taken in Berlin. More food has been sent to the Dutch and 400 Flying Fortresses and our Lancasters have dropped the 'bombs'. Lorries have also been allowed, under a truce, to take in loads of food up till 3 p.m. today.

What a DAY!

Thursday 3rd May

Another DAY! Berlin has fallen!

The Red Army captured the city yesterday afternoon and 70,000 prisoners were taken. Hitler and Goebbels are now said to have committed suicide. Hamburg has surrendered. In Burma, Rangoon has fallen—two capitals, Berlin and Rangoon. The flag was soon hoisted this morning! Prague has been declared a hospital city, whatever that may mean! So many prisoners have been taken that generals are 'ten a penny'.

All that was at eight o'clock, and now we are all looking for some news of Alan. Many people, having seen the Union Jack flying today, think that he has come home.

The surrender of the German armed forces in Italy is proceeding smoothly. It is three years and two months since Rangoon was evacuated by our Armies, and now they are back again. A grand advance of 300 miles and an amphibious landing contributed to this victory. Trieste, which was not part of the Italian surrender by the Germans, has now surrendered. Two German divisions gave themselves up—intact—and there are more armies anxious to surrender to the Western Allies, rather than the Russians. They know the Russians will not forget what has been done to them and that they will exact justice. The Russians and the Western Allies have met on a wide front.

The food taken into Holland is terribly needed. The poor Dutch are dying wholesale of starvation—a pitiful situation.

Friday 4th May

And another thrilling day! Northern Germany, Denmark, Heligoland and the Friesian Islands are surrendered—and, Jack says, Western Holland!! Now isn't that grand!!

Joan Spencer rang up just after lunch and told me that our men left Eichstatt (Oflag VIIB) on 1st April, but that as they were lined up to be marched away American bombers came along and they were bombed. Twelve men were killed and some wounded. She said the next-of-kin had already been informed, so they were not ours. There was other information, too, but just after 2.30 p.m. Jack rang up the Red Cross and got some of this over again. The procedure was that on 14th April the camp (Oflag VIIB) Prisoners were lined up ready to march away from Eichstatt when U.S.A. planes bombed them and there were some men killed and some wounded. They were all then returned to the camp until the next day, and on 15th April they were marched away to Moosberg, where about 1,000 have been liberated. The other 600 or 800 have been marched still further to Garmisch in the Tyrol.

I rang up the War Office and asked to speak to the Under-Secretary, Mr G. W. Lambert, who wrote to me so kindly when Alan was missing and the War Office made the bad mistake of saying he was in Stalag XXA. Mr Lambert was very kind and soon told me exactly the same story—no more, no less. Joan's news of the bombing gave one a very nasty feeling and one was very sad for those whose relations were killed or wounded—100 of whom were left behind at Eichstatt.

Oh, if only we could hear of our men, it would be quite easy to wait.

Saturday 5th May

The unconditional surrender of Western Holland, Denmark, Northern Germany and the adjacent islands, with a certain amount of shipping, has been spoken of all day in the various broadcasts. This morning we heard Field-Marshal Montgomery's clear, incisive and somewhat nasal voice proclaiming his thanks to the victors of the land, sea and air forces in this great campaign.

V.E. Day seems to be much to the fore in the news. When V.E. Day ('Victory in Europe') is announced, that day and the day following are to be holidays, and many arrangements have been made by the Government for the people to take part in the rejoicing. In our villages, as well as the towns, thanksgiving services are to be held in our churches. At Berkswell there will be a service at 11 a.m. and the British Legion Men and Women's Section are to attend.

Sunday 6th May

A pleasant, warm day with a slight chill in the wind still, though a great improvement on the weather lately. Jack wasn't well—had a throat which felt very uncomfortable—so he stayed in bed all day. I went to church and had many inquiries again, all prophesying: 'He will soon be here.' I brought a few people back in the car, walked Twink and got back in time to take the loudspeaker upstairs for the news.

Yesterday there was an S.O.S. call from the Czechoslovak patriots in Prague asking the Allies to come to their help. Apparently they had risen in revolt against the Nazis and needed our assistance. Today General Patton's Army is pushing along well and is now 50 miles away. Viscount Lascelles, The Master of Elphinstone, Lieutenant Dahamel and one or two other high-ranking officers have been released from somewhere in the Alps, where the Nazis hoped to hold them as hostages.

Monday 7th May

A nice warm day and Robbins has got on well in the garden, putting out snapdragons and forking ('fa-arking' he calls it) over borders. The 1 p.m. news was thrilling, but even more thrilling later in the day when one heard that the German radio spoke of 'unconditional surrender'. So we have listened to news headlines at 4 p.m. and 5 p.m., to the 6 p.m. news and then again at 9 p.m. It was said that Mr Churchill would make an announcement at 3 p.m. tomorrow and that tomorrow is to be V.E. Day. Well, well, it's a funny business.

In Prague the Germans continue to fight and it seems to me that V.E. Day would have been better *after* Mr Churchill's announcement. Anyway, V.E. Day will be when Alan comes home.

Flags and bunting have been put here and there in the village and Jack has made me a diagram to show me how to hoist the flag. I hope I can do it tomorrow. Kate is annoyed to know that Viscount Lascelles is home before Alan!

Tuesday 8th May, V.E. Day!!

With Jack still in bed and running a little temperature, we had a day of thrilling broadcasts from 8 a.m. on and off till 10 p.m. The great day—so long awaited—arrived at last and, very soberly and with a great inward pride in the men and women of *our* nation particularly, we rejoiced at our deliverance.

My first thought was *bread*, and so I went out early and brought back two piping-hot loaves on my bicycle, and then did the daily duties. It was very sultry then and the sky was dark. I had only just got back when rain began to fall, and then there was a terrific thunderstorm. One crack of thunder seemed just overhead and was almost simultaneous with the lightning. Even the invalid came downstairs in a hurry, wondering whether the chimney pot had perhaps been struck. Then down came heavy rain until, this afternoon, the sun came out and we had a few hours of bright weather till evening, when it clouded over. The weather report, which we haven't heard on the wireless for over 5½ years, was given out again today. It may be much the same weather tomorrow.

Mr Churchill broadcast at 3 p.m. And what a historic announcement: 'The unconditional surrender' of the German forces, the Channel Islands freed ('our dear Channel Islands', as he said) and Norway liberated at last. He ended: 'Advance Britannia. . . . God save the King.' At 8 p.m. there was a short thanksgiving service, with the Archbishop of Canterbury speaking in a clear, dignified manner. He always seems so unselfconscious—no pomposity nor undue humility—just himself doing his job. After the service came a sort of world-salute to the King. Men and women from the Services in our Empire, men and women who have done civil war work, all paying their tribute to the King as the Head of our great Family. Then His Majesty spoke to all of us at 9 o'clock.

Next the news, and then we were 'taken over' to London, where we heard the cheering crowd outside Buckingham Palace and the voices of the Heads of the Services, beginning with General Eisenhower. At 10 p.m. we closed down, and when we came to bed fireworks began banging off—as if there hadn't been enough bangs in this War. Useless things, like salvoes of guns. I opened my bedroom door and a very frightened little Twink rushed in. He remembers the awful bombing nights.

This morning's weather seemed symbolic. It was as if in the thunder one heard Nature's roll of drums for the fallen, then the one loud salvo of salute over our heads and the tears of the rain pouring for the sorrow and suffering of the War. And then the end of the orgy of killing and victory symbolized as the sun came out and shed its brightness and warmth on the earth.

The flag was well and truly hoisted after careful reading of Jack's instructions, but as there was not much breeze it mostly hung limply against the pole. Alan's room was vacated by me today and made entirely ready for him, and here am I writing in the spare room. The time is 11.20 p.m., the fireworks seem to have finished and the dancers gone from the room across the way.

I hope the noise is ended and we can get a peaceful sleep.

Wednesday 9th May

A Day of Days!

This morning at 9.15 the telephone rang and a voice said: 'I've got a very nice telegram for you. You are Milburn, Burleigh, Balsall Common 29?'

'Yes,' I said.

The voice said: 'This is the telegram. "Arrived safely. Coming soon. Alan".'

I nearly leapt to the ceiling and rushed to the bottom of the stairs. 'We've got the right telegram at last!' I cried.

And then all three of us, Jack in bed, Kate nearby and myself all choky, shed a tear or two. We were living again, after five-and-a-half years!

At 11.15 a.m. the telephone rang again and it was a long-distance call. 'Is that Burleigh, Balsall Common?'

'Yes! Is that Alan?' I said.

'Yes.'

And then I said: 'Oh, bless you, my darling.' And off went Alan into a description of his leaving Germany and arriving here, ending by saying he might arrive late tonight or early tomorrow and would ring up again later, and so we said 'Goodbye'.

I wrote 19 postcards and one letter, had three or four long-distance telephone calls and about two dozen others during the day. I made two long-distance calls, and when I asked for a third the operator said: 'You're keeping me busy.'

'Yes,' I said, 'this is a thrilling day.'

'Something special?'

'Yes, my son has arrived in England after five years as a prisoner of war.'

'Exeter,' said the operator's voice, and then to me: 'Was he in Germany?'

'Yes.'

'He'll be glad to get home—there you are, call out, please. They're waiting.'

Such mateyness, it is amusing.

And here we are at 7.15 p.m., and so far no other word from Alan.

Thursday 10th May, He came!

All evening we waited and hoped, myself scarcely daring to move from the house, though I did take Twink to post. Biggs, who saw me on the way back, said the last train from London came in at 9.20 p.m., so we hoped and waited. I hung out of the window looking, looking . . . and then, tired with the day's exertions and happenings, I went to bed and presently to sleep.

The next thing I knew Jack was saying: 'Can't you hear the telephone? It's ringing . . .' I shook myself into wakefulness and went into Alan's room, picked up the receiver, declared myself and heard: 'This is Alan.' He was at Leamington station and it was getting on for 12 p.m.

I soon dressed, went down, got out the car and drove off into the warm, clear night—meeting few people or vehicles until I got into Leamington. There crowds thronged the Parade and I blew the horn at intervals to clear a passage for the car. At the station I saw the trellised metal gates closed at the entrance and in front of them were two figures, one in khaki in a beret and a figure in blue.

The khaki beret wouldn't be Alan, I thought, but it detached itself, came to the car and said: 'Is it Ma?', and so out I flung myself and, as the blue figure drew discreetly away, we had a good hug and a kiss and then soon were speeding home, talking hard. At home we found Jack up and dressed, and Kate, too. Soon Alan was disposing of two boiled eggs with bread and butter, and we all drank chocolate while we talked and talked. At last we got to bed at 2.30 a.m. and today have not felt quite as energetic as usual, as may be imagined.

It was good to hear the old familiar noises about the house again. Jack, a bit tired after so much excitement on top of a temperature, stayed in bed for a few hours and Alan and I soon went down to the grocer's to get the double rations, making a sort of triumphal procession, shaking hands with people we met, from the farmer to the window-cleaner, everybody smiling and looking pleased. At the grocer's we got the extras and came home laden with groceries and oranges.

The telephone has been ringing when we haven't been ringing up from this end, and I had a special message from Berkswell W.I. Committee expressing their delight at Alan's return. This afternoon Alan drove the car to Berkswell and went into the Whitaker's, where I picked him up ten minutes later, and so back to tea. Next he went walking to Cooper's house and saw the little family of five, and then through the fields to 'Willo's' in Needler's End.

The feeling of being able to walk in green fields and gardens is grand to him after the drab and dusty prison camp.

Friday 11th May

A lovely warm day and Alan and I went to Leamington. Much handshaking in shops, and dewy eyes and good wishes. He went to the hospital and saw Edward Greenslade and we met his mother later in the Stores. We got home a bit late for lunch and, as Kate went out, Alan gave a hand with the washing-up. He began to look at the M.G. and at last we heard it started up and away it went.

Everything is *very* good. All the old familiar noises about the house, the same cough, the same bangs here and there. The doctor came after lunch and stayed a long time, and just as we were finishing tea out of doors the Clay family came. As they didn't go till after seven, it was a bit late when we had supper, and then Alan walked Twink to fetch medicine from the doctor's. And so ends another good day.

Nevill Spencer got home today. Joan and the children met him at the station and then all went to Spinney Croft, where Peggy just happened to be at home, too.

Saturday 12th May

Still warm and sunny and the M.G. went roaring out, taking one to the butcher's and grocer's. I managed to thread myself in and out of the weird little seat and enjoyed being driven. We met quite a lot of people and Alan was shaking hands here and there, 'telling the tale' at the baker's while a crowd stood around. All Balsall Common knows that I drove to Leamington at midnight to fetch him home! I find there is a bit of mending to be done for Alan (and how I have longed to have the little toffee tin of grey trouser buttons out again all these long five years) and a few things to store and put away.

Alan, still enjoying the garden, sat in a deckchair for a time after lunch and then did a bit of work on his car. Jack got into his overall coat and there they were just as they were six years ago, working together in the garage. A rest for Jack after tea—and we had Joan Curtis in just before and so she stayed for tea in the Corner—and Alan and I did a bit of gardening. They were all 'bits' today, nothing serious. It was too hot. The telephone rang at intervals all day with messages, all full of kindness and congratulations. Many letters arrived too—I shall be busy tomorrow.

I walk about in a half-dream and the long, bad years of war begin to fade a little as Alan's voice is heard, the M.G.'s 'voice', too, and the house is once more a real home.

The intense relief at the ending of the European war is felt everywhere. No longer do we live under the strain of it, though we shall have it at the back of our mind, and its scars before our eyes, all our lives.

And here the 'Burleigh in War Time' Diary ends with Victory bells for

'O with hope and patience we have awaited for the day
When the tank is filled with petrol and the dust-sheet stowed
    away.
The engine's running smoothly—the M.G. free to roam
For Oflag's gates have opened wide and . . .
Alan John is home!'

FAREWELLS

By Judy Milburn

MRS MILBURN sensed somehow that Alan would come home that month. She wrote 'May—the month of Alan!' in the last volume of her Diaries, and happily that forecast was true. But he still had six months to serve in the Army before being demobbed, and he was posted to a mixed battalion in Leamington. He and other officers were billeted at The Oaks, the hotel my mother owned in Leamington, and that was where we met. It was summertime, and I remember we had the most glorious weather and Alan was very tanned from his outdoor work at the prison camp. We met in the August and became engaged in December. In the following September, of 1946, we were married.

I got on very well with my mother-in-law. She was, as can be seen from her Diaries, a very practical and always-busy woman, and if she wasn't *actively* busy, she'd be reading, writing, painting. She was unique in many ways. She could be firm, and even difficult, too. When I was expecting our first child she drummed it into me that I just *must* have a boy, another Milburn boy. It must have been a disappointment when Sarah was born, but I had a letter saying she wasn't *really* upset that I'd had a girl. Even so, I'm sure she was doubly delighted when our next baby, Robert, was born. She loved the children, and was a most thoughtful grandmother to them. Everything a grandmother should be.

But as our family life was beginning, hers was ending. Jack died in January 1955, and Kate, who had gone to live with a sister in Rugby, died there a month before her 75th birthday, in July 1955. My mother-in-law had never lived in a house on her own, and the thought of doing so did not appeal to her at all. When a house near us became vacant, she announced that she would live there. She organized the move, in the summer of 1955, in her usual practical fashion, and I think the move from Burleigh was not too much of a wrench.

Burleigh was, after all, far too big for just one person. She had many friends in Kenilworth, she would be near us and, as she was not too well, it was good for us, too, to know that she was very close, just over the road. She called her new home 'a doll's house' compared to the one she'd left, but although it was much smaller, she made it look very similar to the way she had Burleigh. There was a large enough garden, too, and she was, of course, kept very busy in that.

Alan had gone back to Alfred Herbert after the war, but was later offered and accepted a job at the Rover company in Solihull. He eventually sold his beloved M.G. and he and a friend built a Trials Special, with which they had a lot of fun. But this was replaced by a more conventional car when Sarah was born. On occasions, so that I could have the car for shopping and other trips, Alan would get a lift to Solihull—and on one such morning, in November, 1959, he was seriously hurt in an accident, caused when an L-driver overtook a lorry on a greasy road. Alan died two days later.

I remember a friend from his university days writing to me to say what many people felt: what a tragic waste it was after he had come through the war and all that time in prison camp. His mother felt that deeply and, a year later, became seriously ill.

She died, just 18 months after Alan, on 29th May, 1961, at the age of 77.

Kenilworth, August 1989.